EXPLORING LITERARY AMERICA

ALSO BY MARCELLA THUM

Exploring Black America:
A History and Guide

BY GLADYS AND MARCELLA THUM

The Persuaders:
Propaganda in War and Peace

EXPLORING LITERARY AMERICA

by Marcella Thum

Atheneum 1979 *New York*

Library of Congress Cataloging in Publication Data

Thum, Marcella. Exploring literary America.

Includes index.

SUMMARY: A travel and reference guide to
literary landmarks, sites, and settings associated
with American authors from the 18th through
the early 20th centuries.

1. Literary landmarks—United States—Juvenile
literature. 2. Authors, American—Homes and haunts
—Juvenile literature. 3. United States—
Description and travel—Juvenile literature.
[1. Literary landmarks. 2. Authors, American—
Homes and haunts. 3. United States—Description
and travel] I. Title.
PS141.T5   917.3′04′92   78–13297
ISBN 0–689–30668–7

FOR
Dr. Harry Cargas

CONTENTS

vii

CONTENTS

ix

EXPLORING
LITERARY
AMERICA

INTRODUCTION

Readers interested in America's literary history are supposed to be a vanishing species. Yet each year thousands of tourists, young and old, descend upon Hannibal, Missouri, to visit the boyhood home of Mark Twain. Thousands more are welcomed at Louisa May Alcott's Orchard House in Concord, Massachusetts, where *Little Women* was born, and at Washington Irving's home, Sunnyside, in the Hudson River Valley, haunt of Ichabod Crane and Rip Van Winkle.

Unfortunately, over the years, many historical literary sites have disappeared, destroyed by urban sprawl or indifference, so that not all sites, and thus not all of America's literary greats, can be included in this book.

Nevertheless, there are more than sixty authors—who lived from the seventeenth through the mid-twentieth century—who have homes or sites connected with their lives or writings still in existence. Not all the authors in this book have written great literature. Yet even those who did not write masterpieces were, for a span of time, the "best-selling" authors of their day.

In many cases, a hometown or geographical area was a major influence on an author's writing. Can one imagine a John Steinbeck developing anywhere but in Salinas Valley, California, or a Willa Cather emerging from any place other than Red Cloud, Nebraska, or a William Faulkner from somewhere besides Oxford, Mississippi? Visiting the scenes amid which an author lived or worked, therefore, helps bring us closer to that writer and his or her works.

The biographical information included for each author is necessarily brief, intended simply to provide background material about the author for tourists visiting or planning to visit the literary sites described in this book. Since some of the sites are maintained only by the dogged determination of a faithful few, the hours—and months of the year—during which the site is open to the public may fluctuate. It is usually best before visiting any of the sites to phone or write ahead and make sure of opening and closing hours. In addition, special tours are often provided for small groups if arrangements are made in advance.

CAPTAIN JOHN SMITH
1580–1631

Within Jamestown Festival Park in Virginia stands the three-cornered, wooden-palisaded James Fort. It is within the original site of this fort that the first book in the English language was written in America in 1608—not by a scholar but by a daredevil soldier of fortune named John Smith.

Born in Lincolnshire, England, young Smith ran away from home when he was fifteen years old. From that day on, his life story reads like an exciting adventure novel. For ten years he fought as a mercenary soldier in Europe, Turkey and the Near East. Then, in 1607, under the sponsorship of the Virginia Company of London, John Smith sailed with one hundred and four men and boys for the New World.

Unlike the more practical, industrious men and women who settled Plymouth Colony, Massachusetts, some thirteen years later, the colonists who settled Jamestown were, as

Smith wryly described them, "poor gentlemen, tradesmen, serving-men, libertines and such like." Their only ambition was to discover gold and return to England as wealthy men. Instead of gold, they found starvation and illness and the constant threat of death at the hands of unfriendly Indians led by the great Chief Powhatan. Within the first seven months of their arrival in Virginia, two-thirds of the company died and were secretly buried at night so the Indians wouldn't suspect how feeble the colony had become. Laziness, greed and bickering among the colonists as to who would be their leader added to their hardships.

During the terrible winter of 1608–09, the company owed its survival to Captain John Smith who took command of the colony and enforced a stern rule: "He who would not work, would not eat." The Captain also bartered, stole or forced the Indians to provide the small James Fort with much-needed food. It was on one of these bartering expeditions that Captain Smith was captured by the Indians. His life traditionally, though perhaps not completely accurately, was saved by Pocahontas, favorite daughter of Powhatan. Whether or not, in fact, the Indian girl did save Smith's life, it was certainly true that later she married one of the gentlemen of Jamestown, John Rolfe, went to England to live, and charmed London society with her wit and grace.

Despite the obstacles the captain faced, he not only somehow kept the remnants of the Jamestown colony alive, but also found time to write a brief history of the colony. His manuscript, which he called *A True Relation of Such Occurrences and Accidents of Note as Hath Happened at Virginia,* was sent back to England and published in London in 1608. Although other books had been written about the New World, John Smith's history became the first book in English actually written in America.

Captain Smith, himself, returned to England in 1609, but not before he had explored and mapped the New England coast north of Virginia. These maps later proved extremely valuable to the Puritan settlers. Although the Puritans turned down Smith's offer to join them on their expedition to Plymouth in 1620, they were quite happy to have Captain Smith's maps along.

Captain Smith did not return to Virginia once he left it. However, he did make two more exploring trips to New England and wrote several more books, including a history of Virginia and New England, and his own autobiography, published the year before he died. Years later historians pointed out that the captain was inclined to exaggeration in his writings, especially when it came to describing his own deeds of valor. If so, Captain Smith was not too different from other author-explorers of his time who didn't believe in letting the literal truth spoil a good story.

And if John Smith was, in fact, the "first teller of tall tales" in America's literary history, he was also America's earliest and most enthusiastic promoter, luring settlers to the New World with his writings. His descriptions of the plant and animal life in America, the climate and soil, and particularly his descriptions of Indian life, were amazingly accurate and have provided an invaluable record for historians.

Today, little remains of the seventeenth century Jamestown colony, except the ruins of a church tower and foundations of buildings that have been exposed by archaeologists. A visitors center, just across the footbridge at Jamestown Island, has films and a museum that displays the early tools unearthed in the ruins. A walking tour is also arranged to show the visitor the original layout of the colony.

About a mile away from Jamestown is the Jamestown

Festival Park, with a replica of the fort Captain Smith helped build, including within the fort eighteen reconstructed wattle and daub buildings and a guardhouse. Guides in the costumes of soldiers and settlers man the fort and take visitors through the exhibits. Full-scale reproductions of the three ships that brought Smith and the colonists to Jamestown are docked in the James River.

An Old World and New World Pavilion are also a part of the Festival Park. The Old World Pavilion has costumed wax figures, guns, armors, coats of arms and Captain John Smith's huge sea chest. Also on exhibit is a portrait of Princess Pocahontas and one of her cameo brooches. The original of the painting hangs in the National Gallery in Washington, D.C.

Location: JAMESTOWN ISLAND is located a half-hour drive west on Interstate 64 from Newport News, Virginia, to the Colonial Parkway that connects the information centers at Jamestown, Williamsburg and Yorktown. Admission charge.

Location: JAMESTOWN FESTIVAL PARK is a mile from the historic settlement of Jamestown, Virginia, and adjoins the Colonial Parkway and Route 31. Admission charge.

WILLIAM BRADFORD
1590–1657

Thousands of tourists flock each year to view Plymouth Rock in Massachusetts, although there is some question as to whether or not the Pilgrims ever actually set foot on Plymouth Rock when they arrived in the New World. In any case, the true rock upon which the fledgling Plymouth Colony was founded was not a granite boulder, but a remarkable man, William Bradford. Without Bradford's leadership, the tiny colony would almost surely have perished. Equally important, without William Bradford's journal, much of what we know today of the life of the early Pilgrims would have been lost forever.

William Bradford started life as a prosperous farmer in Yorkshire, England. In 1620 he sailed on the now-famous *Mayflower* with a group of men and women who for the most part, like himself, wanted to leave the state-run Church of England and worship in another way. The group on the *Mayflower* called themselves Separatists, or Saints. It wasn't until many years later that the name Pilgrims was tagged to them.

The *Mayflower* landed at Plymouth in December, 1620, and although Bradford never mentions Plymouth Rock in his journal, he did report that the wind was so icy off Cape Cod Bay when the settlers landed that the coats of the sailors were glazed by the frozen sea spray. He also described the area where the Separatists put down their first settlement as a "hideous and desolate wilderness full of wild beasts and wild men."

A desolate wilderness, indeed. Within six months of their arrival at Plymouth, over half of the colonists were dead from starvation, disease or Indian attacks. One of the first to die, while still aboard the *Mayflower*, was William Bradford's young wife, Dorothy.

After the death of John Carver, first Governor of Plymouth Colony, William Bradford, despite his youth, was elected to the post of Governor, and re-elected thirty times. It was a job that brought with it no salary, little glory and a great many problems. Not only did Bradford have to act as military commander, defending the colony from the Indians without, but he also acted as ruling magistrate, protecting the colony from the dissenters within. Bradford also had to use all his diplomacy against the greed of the merchants in London who had financed the colony and were more interested in turning a quick profit than in the spiritual salvation of the colonists.

Under Governor Bradford's leadership, Plymouth Plantation, as the colony was called, grew and prospered and influenced the future of America far beyond the colony's modest beginning or small size. It was at Plymouth that the first attempt at a classless society was begun, and the Plymouth town meetings were the start of the democratic system of government that gradually evolved in America.

Finally, William Bradford performed another valuable service for the Plymouth Colony. At age forty he began writing a journal, called *Of Plymouth Plantation,* a history of the Plymouth Colony. The book, which Governor Bradford intended for his grandchildren, is written in a plain, direct style, describing the daily life and the struggles of those early colonists to survive in an unknown wilderness. Many romantic legends surround the valiant Pilgrim fathers (although very little has been written about the equally valiant Pilgrim mothers!) , but through Bradford's history one learns that not all the members of the Plymouth Colony were "saints." Bradford writes disapprovingly, for example, of roguish Thomas Morton who traded guns and powder with the Indians, and set up a Maypole in a neighboring area, inviting the Indian women to join him in "drinking and dancing about it many days together."

Bradford's journal was never published in his lifetime. During the Revolutionary War the manuscript disappeared, only to mysteriously reappear in London in 1855, where it was finally published in 1856. Bradford's original manuscript was returned to America and is now one of the most valuable treasures of the Library in the State House at Boston.

The original Plymouth Plantation fell into ruins after the colony moved north to the present location of the town of Plymouth. When the state of Massachusetts decided to reconstruct the original settlement, Governor Bradford's journal was one of the books consulted to determine just how Plymouth looked in 1627. Today, thanks to Bradford's journal, visitors are not only able to visit an exact replica of the early village but may watch authentically costumed men and women perform the daily tasks about which Bradford wrote.

An Indian Summer Camp has also been constructed to show how Native Americans of the time lived and worked.

At Burial Hill, where Governor Bradford and other early Pilgrims are buried, each Friday in August at 5 p.m., local citizens, dressed in Pilgrim clothes, reenact the thanksgiving church service of the fifty survivors of that first terrible winter of the Plymouth colony.

The *Mayflower II* may also be visited, docked near Plymouth Rock in the town of Plymouth. Aboard the ship can be seen the cramped quarters and primitive accomodations of the first *Mayflower*.

Pilgrim Hall, the oldest public museum in the country, contains the most complete collection of Pilgrim possessions in the country, including their weapons and household objects, as well as a library housing some of Governor Bradford's books and manuscripts.

Location: PLYMOUTH PLANTATION is located 3 miles south of the town of Plymouth, Massachusetts, off SR 3A. Plymouth, itself, is less than one hour from Boston on Rte 3 expressway to Cape Cod. Closed winters. Admission charge.

Location: MAYFLOWER II is moored at Frazier State Pier on Water Street, Plymouth, Massachusetts. Closed winters. Admission charge.

Location: PILGRIM HALL MUSEUM, 75 Court Street, Plymouth, Massachusetts. Admission charge.

COLONIAL LITERATURE

AN AMAZING NUMBER OF COLONISTS TO THE NEW WORLD KEPT
A DAILY RECORD OR JOURNAL OF THEIR EXPERIENCES. THESE
DIARIES, HISTORIES, AND AUTOBIOGRAPHIES, WRITTEN BY EX-
PLORERS, POLITICAL AND RELIGIOUS LEADERS—AND ORDINARY
MEN AND WOMEN—BECAME AMERICA'S FIRST LITERATURE.

Captain John Smith was not only a daredevil soldier of fortune and
explorer, but America's first author. His brief account of the settlement of Jamestown, Virginia, written and published in 1608,
became the first piece of literature written in America, in English.
Captain Smith's statue is on Jamestown Island, not far from the
reconstructed James Fort in Jamestown Festival Park. COURTESY
JAMESTOWN FOUNDATION

Visitors to Plymouth Plantation, Massachusetts, today see Pilgrim life as it was actually lived during the early years of America. A great deal of painstaking research had to be done by historians in order that Plymouth Colony, settled in 1620, could be accurately reconstructed. Much of this research could not have been accomplished without William Bradford's journal, *The History of Plymouth Plantation*, which he began writing in 1630 while he was Governor of Plymouth Colony. PHOTO BY DANIEL GILMORE

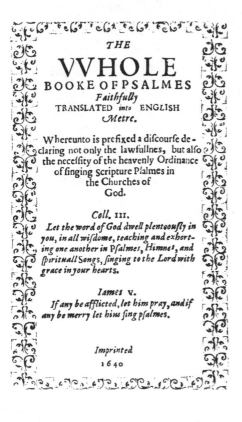

THE
VVHOLE
BOOKE OF PSALMES
Faithfully
TRANSLATED *into* ENGLISH
Metre.

Whereunto is prefixed a difcourfe declaring not only the lawfullnes, but alfo the neceffity of the heavenly Ordinance of finging Scripture Pfalmes in the Churches of God.

Coll. III.
Let the word of God dwell plenteoufly in you, in all wifdome, teaching and exhorting one another in Pfalmes, Himnes, and fpirituall Songs, finging to the Lord with grace in your hearts.

Iames V.
If any be afflicted, let him pray, and if any be merry let him fing pfalmes.

Imprinted
1640

The first printing press in America was located in Cambridge, Massachusetts. The first book to be published on this press in 1640 was a collection of hymns called the *Bay Psalm Book*. Copies of the book are now extremely rare —only eleven copies are still in existence. The *Bay Psalm Book*, which originally sold for little more than one shilling, now sells for a quarter of a million dollars! The frontispiece is from a facsimile edition.

Some of the earliest literature in America were personal journals and collections of sermons written by religious leaders in the colonies such as Jonathan Edwards. The church where Edwards preached, the First Church of Christ, Congregational, still stands in Northampton, Massachusetts. Other religious leaders who wrote and published in colonial America were Cotton Mather, who was involved in the Salem Witch Trials, John Woolman, a Quaker minister, and Roger Williams of Rhode Island. COURTESY YALE UNIVERSITY ART GALLERY

Many diaries and journals written during colonial times were personal and not meant for publication. Sarah Kemble Knight kept a journal of a trip she took through Rhode Island and Connecticut in 1704–05. Her journal, its frontispiece shown right, is filled with amusing descriptions and sharp observations of life in colonial America.

Among other well-known personal diaries was Samuel Sewall's *Diary,* which paints an unforgettable picture of life in colonial Boston from 1674–1729, including his bumbling courtship of a rich widow. Another inveterate diary keeper was Virginia plantation owner, William Byrd II, whose diaries are filled with such intimate details that he wrote them in code. The Byrd diaries weren't completely published until 1941.

THE

JOURNAL

OF

Madam *KNIGHT.*

❖❖❖❖❖❖❖❖❖❖❖❖❖❖❖❖❖❖

*Monday, Octb'r. y*e* second,*
1704.

ABOUT three o'clock afternoon, I begun my Journey from Boston to New-Haven; being about two Hundred Mile. My Kinsman, Capt. Robert Luist, waited on me as farr as Dedham, where I was to meet y*e* Western post.

PENNSYLVANIA, DELAWARE, MARY-
LAND, AND VIRGINIA
ALMANAC,
FOR THE
YEAR of our LORD 1795;
Being the Third after Leap-Year.

BANNAKER.

One of the most popular books in early America was the almanac, found in almost every colonial household. Although Benjamin Franklin's *Poor Richard's Almanack* is the best known, Franklin was not the only writer and printer to publish almanacs. A black man, Benjamin Banneker (also spelled Bannaker), wrote and published a successful almanac in 1795, frontispiece shown above. In addition, like Franklin, Benjamin Banneker was a scientist and inventor. COURTESY MARYLAND HISTORICAL SOCIETY, BALTIMORE

The first two published women writers in America were Anne Bradstreet (right) and Phillis Wheatley (below). The backgrounds of the two women could not have been more dissimilar. Anne Bradstreet (1612–1672) was the wife of the Governor of the Massachusetts Bay Colony; Phillis Wheatley (1753–1784) at the age of eight was sold as a slave to the Wheatley family in Boston. Both women wrote poetry, mostly with religious themes, but Bradstreet also protested women's plight, and Wheatley, slavery. Anne Bradstreet's book of poetry, *The Tenth Muse,* was published in England in 1650, while Phillis Wheatley's *Poems on Various Subjects* was published in 1773.

The Anne Bradstreet photograph is from a detail from a window in St. Botolph's Church, Boston, Lincolnshire, England.

WHEATLEY PICTURE, COURTESY LIBRARY OF CONGRESS

ANNE BRADSTREET

Published according to Act of Parliament, Sept. i. 1773 by Arch.d Bell.

Bookseller N.º 8 near the Saracens Head Aldgate.

BENJAMIN FRANKLIN
1706–1790

What has been called America's first best-selling book was published in 1732 at a printshop located between Third and Fourth Street in Philadelphia, Pennsylvania. The book, *Poor Richard's Almanack,* was written by Benjamin Franklin, who was also the publisher of the book and owner of the printshop.

Benjamin Franklin's literary and publishing career, however, did not begin in Philadelphia. It started in Boston, where at the age of twelve he was apprenticed to his older brother, James, who was also a printer and publisher. The two brothers did not get along very well. The only way Benjamin could get anything into his brother's newspaper was to write essays under a pen name—Silence Dogood, supposedly an old widow—and slip them under the door of the newspaper office at night. James published the widow's humorous essays for several months with great success before discovering that "Silence Dogood" was, in fact, his own sixteen-year-old brother.

A year later the young apprentice had a final quarrel with his brother and ran away to Philadelphia. He arrived in that city on a Sunday morning with only a few pennies in his pocket, which he promptly spent on "three great puffy rolls." He ate the rolls walking up Market Street, past a doorway where a young woman, Deborah Read, who was later to become his wife, watched him, amused.

Benjamin Franklin decided to make his fortune in the printing business and set about it in the same determined, practical fashion with which he had written the Silence Dogood essays. Within seven years, and with the help of the frugal, industrious Deborah, whom he married in 1730, he had his own printing business and was the publisher of the newspaper, *The Pennsylvania Gazette*.

It was Benjamin Franklin's writing ability, though, that brought him his greatest success in the printing business. Books were an expensive, seldom-bought luxury in colonial America, but Franklin noticed that the two books that could be found in almost every eighteenth century home were the Bible and an almanac. In 1732 Franklin published *Poor Richard's Almanack* for the first time. Other publishers printed almanacs, too, but Franklin's was different. In between the forecasts for weather, tides, sunrises and sunsets, and other necessary items, he inserted wise and humorous sayings, supposedly written by the editor of the almanac, a man named Richard Saunders, or Poor Richard, as he called himself.

"Poor Richard" was, of course, Benjamin Franklin. Not

all the proverbs and sayings that Franklin wrote for his almanac were original—he borrowed widely from other languages and other literatures—but he skillfully rewrote the proverbs to make them more interesting. For example, the English proverb "Three may keep counsel if two be away" became under Franklin's pen, "Three may keep a secret if two of them are dead." The Scottish proverb, "Fresh fish and new guests smell by they are three days old," in Franklin's hands became short and to the point: "Fish and visitors smell in three days."

Poor Richard's Almanack was so successful that Poor Richard's sayings were quoted in homes all through the New England colonies. Then in 1757 Benjamin Franklin gathered a group of the proverbs from the almanacs into another book, which he called *The Way to Wealth,* a sort of how-to-become-successful book. *The Way to Wealth* was printed and reprinted widely in the colonies and is still being published and read today.

Benjamin Franklin was certainly qualified to write such a book. By age forty-two he was wealthy enough to retire from the printing business and turn his attention to another great interest in his life—science. The pamphlet he wrote about his experiments with electricity was the first important scientific writing published in America and, published abroad, made Benjamin Franklin internationally famous.

Benjamin Franklin, however, was too busy to devote all his time to either science or writing. The young American colonies were involved in a growing political controversy with England. Benjamin Franklin was sent to England to try to secure a peaceful settlement of the difficulties between the colonies and England. When his efforts failed, he returned to America and helped draft the Declaration of Independence, which proclaimed American independence from England. Although Thomas Jefferson actually wrote that famous document, he always said the only reason Franklin had not been entrusted with it was the fear that Franklin might conceal a joke in the middle!

When war started with England, Franklin was sent as a minister to France and successfully arranged a much-needed alliance with that country. At the end of the Revolutionary War he helped negotiate the peace treaty.

In all, Franklin spent almost thirty years abroad in the service of his country. It was while he was living in England in 1771 that he began writing his most notable book, the story of his life, beginning with his childhood experiences in Boston. Through the years he added to his *Autobiography,* (although he never completed it), writing the last section only weeks before he died.

Benjamin Franklin's *Autobiography,* the classic story of the poor but struggling, industrious young man who makes a fortune through hard work and his own wits, was America's first "rags to riches" success story. But Franklin's *Autobiography* is much more than that. It is America's first literary classic, the story of a remarkable, many-talented man— printer, editor, inventor, statesman, diplomat, philanthropist and scientist. In addition, Franklin possessed the one talent that made all the others possible, the ability to write in a deceptively simple style, concealing the art behind the simplicity. Benjamin Franklin always believed that good writing ought to be "smooth, clear and short."

Franklin's *Autobiography* was first published in Paris in 1791 and has never been out of print since. It is as difficult to imagine American history without Benjamin Franklin as it is to imagine America's literary history without

Franklin's *Autobiography*.

Despite all the honors heaped upon during during his lifetime, when Benjamin Franklin died at the age of 81 and was buried at Christ Church Burial Ground in Philadelphia, he requested that the inscription on his gravestone read simply: Benjamin and Deborah Franklin.

Very little of the Philadelphia that Benjamin Franklin knew exists today, although Elfreth's Alley, a street of carefully remodeled eighteenth century homes and narrow cobblestone pavements, is a reminder of how Philadelphia looked when Franklin first arrived there.

Recently, however, the National Park Service has restored the Philadelphia site of Benjamin Franklin's home and printshop where *Poor Richard's Almanack* was first published. Steel-framed structures within Franklin Court outline the sites with interpretive exhibits about Benjamin Franklin's life as printer, writer and member of the Philadelphia community. On the west side of the Court is an Underground Museum, which, through exhibits, films and sound and light presentations, tells the story of "Franklin—the Man of Many Ideas."

Near Franklin Court at 320 Market Street is a working printing press and bindery, the sort of printshop operation that was a vital part of America's early literary history.

The National Memorial to Benjamin Franklin also in Philadelphia, is owned and operated by the Franklin Institute. A fascinating museum complex, the Institute includes numerous mementos from Franklin's life, such as his mystery clock, the bifocal spectacles and lightning rod Franklin invented, his lap desk, printing tools and illustrations from *Poor Richard's Almanack,* among many other items of interest. In the National Memorial may also be seen an exciting multi-media production covering the many facets of Benjamin Franklin's life.

Location: FRANKLIN COURT, site of Franklin's print-shop and home, is located in Philadelphia, Pennsylvania, in the city block bounded by Market Street, Third Street, Chestnut Street and Fourth Street. The working printshop is located at 320 Market Street. No admission charge.

Location: THE BENJAMIN FRANKLIN NATIONAL MEMORIAL is in the Franklin Institute, Benjamin Franklin Parkway at 20th Street, Philadelphia, Pennsylvania. Admission charge.

JOHN DICKINSON
1732–1808

Most of the writing done in America just before and during the Revolutionary War was political writing, arguing for or against rebellion against England. Radical writers like Thomas Paine, Samuel Adams and James Otis wanted an immediate and, if necessary, violent end to British rule. John Dickinson, a conservative lawyer and farmer, took the unpopular stand of opposing violence, observing that "The cause of liberty is a cause of too much dignity to be sullied by turbulence and tumult."

Called the "Penman of the Revolution" because he was responsible for many of the important American "protest documents," John Dickinson's most famous protest pamphlet actually argued against revolution. In his "Letters from a Farmer in Pennsylvania to the Inhabitants of the British Colonies," published in 1768, Dickinson clearly and concisely pointed out British injustices, but urged the colonists to "be upon your guard against those who may at any time endeavor to stir you up, under pretense of patriotism."

Dickinson's "Letters" were reprinted in almost every newspaper in the colonies, as well as abroad and, because of their polished prose and keen logic, have been called "the most brilliant event in the literary history of the Revolution." However, Dickinson's moderate, non-violent beliefs made him very unpopular, especially in New England.

Nevertheless, when war was declared upon England, John Dickinson was one of the only two members of the Continental Congress who actually joined the Continental Army and fought for the American cause. Later, he is credited with having helped write other important political documents, including the Articles of Confederation in 1777 and the Constitution of the United States in 1787.

Although John Dickinson was popularly known as the "Pennsylvania Farmer," he spent his early years in Delaware in a five-bay brick house that was built by his father at St. Jones Neck near Dover. When a fire destroyed the third floor of the house in 1804, Dickinson restored the home in a much simpler manner than his father had originally built it. Nevertheless, the house is still a good example of the moderately wealthy landowning class that existed in America during colonial days, just as John Dickinson's writings represented the more moderate approach in the "protest literature" written in America before the Revolutionary War.

The John Dickinson home was acquired by the State of Delaware in 1952 and many Dickinson family furnishings are on display in the mansion.

Location: JOHN DICKINSON MANSION, 6 miles south of Dover, Delaware, on US 113, then ½ mile east on Kitts Hummock Road. No admission charge.

THOMAS PAINE
1737–1809

The Revolutionary War was a war of words as well as bullets. The most effective literary ammunition in this war was not the book or the newspaper but the pamphlet, which could be quickly printed, cheaply sold and easily distributed. Between 1763 and 1783 it is estimated that some two thousand pamphlets on the political issues of the day were written in the colonies. The most pressing issue was, of course, should the colonies break free of British rule? A great many people in the colonies did not think so. Although they might resent British restraints on their trade, the thought of openly rebelling against England, one of the great military powers in the world, was too radical and far-fetched for most colonists.

Then in January, 1776, a small pamphlet, which sold for two shillings, entitled simply *Common Sense*, was published in Philadelphia. The pamphlet fairly "burst from the press," and as one historian said, "revolutionized the thinking and the future of America more than any battle ever fought, or any book ever written." Within three months, more than 120,000 copies of the pamphlet had been sold.

Surprisingly, the author of the pamphlet, Thomas Paine, was not an American colonist but an Englishman, almost completely self-educated, who had tried and failed at numerous occupations in England. He arrived in America at age 37, only six months before the Revolutionary War began. He had no money and little prospects for the future except an enormous talent for words and a burning hatred of the English government. Most important, Thomas Paine was a born propagandist.

Other pamphlets had been written in America before Paine's, urging independence for the colonies, but, like John Dickinson's *Letters from a Pennsylvania Farmer*, such pamphlets were written for the educated reader. Thomas Paine wrote for the common man. He used simple, emotion-filled words and dramatic, singing phrases that aroused passions to a fever pitch and united the colonists against England as nothing else had managed to do. Although Paine knew he was writing treason, he took the startling and radical ideas of liberty and independence and made them seem inevitable. "A continent," he insisted in his pamphlet, "could not remain tied to an island. Everything that is right or reasonable pleads for separation. The blood of the slain, the weeping voice of nature cries, *'Tis time to part.'* "

After the publication of *Common Sense,* Thomas Paine joined General Washington's army in its agonizing retreat across New Jersey. With the army's morale at its lowest ebb, Paine sat down by the light of a campfire in the winter of 1776 and wrote the first of a series of sixteen broadsides called *The American Crisis.* In the first *Crisis,* published in pamphlet form on December 23, 1776, Paine blasted the "summer soldier and sunshine patriot" who deserted the Army and duty when the going became difficult—"the times that try men's souls."

So compelling were Paine's words that General Washington had *The Crisis* read to his troops before the Continental Army's victorious surprise attack on Trenton and during the terrible months at Valley Forge. General Washington had wisely learned that Thomas Paine's words were capable of "working a powerful change in the minds of many men."

After the Revolutionary War was won, Thomas Paine was hailed as a hero and awarded a farm in New Rochelle, New York, by a grateful government. Yet, ironically, twenty years later, when Paine returned to America after living abroad for fifteen years, he had become an outcast, an object of virulent hatred in his own country.

Now, instead of remembering the important role Thomas Paine had played in securing American independence, he was remembered as the radical who had been outlawed from England for writing a controversial book in 1791 called *The Rights of Man.* The book called upon the English people to overthrow the monarchy and set up a republic as America had done. Paine had also spent some time in a French prison during the French Revolution. In prison he had written an even more controversial book called *The Age of Reason,* which had been called by those who had not bothered to read it, "the atheist's bible."

After his return to America, Paine discovered that a more conservative America was no longer interested in reading the words of a rabble-rouser and radical thinker, as he was now considered. Paine was a revolutionary who had lived past his time. Stubbornly uncompromising, though, he never stopped fighting for the rights of the common man—and woman—for Paine was one of the first to write in favor of civil rights for women.

Paine divided his last years between his farm in New Rochelle and New York City. The man about whom John Adams once said, "Without the pen of Paine, the sword of Washington would have been wielded in vain," died all but forgotten in Greenwich Village in New York. Even after his death, however, Paine was not allowed to rest in peace. Buried on his farm at New Rochelle, his bones were later dug up and taken to England, where after a series of misadventures, they finally disappeared forever.

Today, the small cottage that was Thomas Paine's last home has been made a National Historic Site. When Thomas Paine lived there, a friend, visiting, said, "We found the old gentleman living in a small room like a hermit, and I believe the whole of the furniture in the room, including a cot-bed, was not worth $5.00."

Paine was not popular with the people of New Rochelle because of his religious beliefs. On Christmas Eve, 1805, a gun was fired into his house in an attempt on Paine's life. And the man who had helped secure independence for America was refused the right to vote by the citizens of New Rochelle. It is interesting to note in the reception room of the cottage there hangs a letter that several years ago posthumously restored Paine's voting rights!

In 1908 the Huguenot Association of New Rochelle moved the Paine cottage to another section of the farm and turned the Paine home into a museum. Thomas Paine left few physical possessions, but the rear room on the first floor of the house, known as the Paine Room, contains several mementos of the author's life.

A short distance from the Paine cottage is the Thomas Paine National Historical Association Museum. In the museum may be seen Thomas Paine's wallet, gloves, spectacles, watch and other small personal possessions, including something of special interest as a literary memento—Thomas Paine's small portable writing desk. Of humorous interest is a ceramic jug made in Paine's likeness in England during Paine's lifetime. On the jug are the lines: "Observe the wicked and malicious man, projecting all the mischief that he can."

Location: THOMAS PAINE COTTAGE, North and Paine Avenues, New Rochelle, New York. No admission charge.

Location: PAINE MEMORIAL BUILDING is located north of the Paine cottage at the corner of North Avenue and Valley Road, New Rochelle, New York. No admission charge.

THOMAS JEFFERSON
1743–1826

In a modest two story house on the corner of Seventh and Market Streets in Philadelphia, Pennsylvania, was written one of America's most important political and, because of the eloquence of its prose, literary documents—the Declaration of Independence.

The author of the document was Thomas Jefferson. By profession a lawyer (although he would have preferred to become a scientist), Jefferson entered the political world at an early age. He served as a member of the Virginia House of Burgesses, was a representative to the Continental Congress, Governor of Virginia, American diplomat to France, Secretary of State under George Washington, Vice-President under John Adams, and twice elected President of the United States, 1801–1809.

But Thomas Jefferson was much more than a statesman

and diplomat. He was a man of many interests and talents, ranging from science and architecture to philosophy, music and agriculture.

Thomas Jefferson was only thirty-three years old when he was chosen by the Continental Congress in June, 1776, to write America's Declaration of Independence from England. Jefferson was selected for the task because he was already noted for his "master pen" and "peculiar felicity of expression." He wrote the Declaration in two weeks, in the second floor parlor of a young German bricklayer, named Graff.

Although the other delegates to the convention made some changes in the document—one drastic change was removing Jefferson's attack on the slave trade—the Declaration was adopted very much as Jefferson wrote it. The document bears the unmistakable stamp of Jefferson's talent for writing simply, but boldly and eloquently. The words, "We hold these truths to be self-evident: that all men are created equal; that they are endowed by their creator with certain unalienable rights; that among these are life, liberty and the pursuit of happiness," have probably been quoted and re-quoted more often than any words ever written in a political document.

In 1782 Jefferson temporarily retired from public life to his plantation at Monticello, Virginia, and began writing a book, *Notes on the State of Virginia*. This was the only book written by Jefferson that was published during his lifetime. The book—a collection of informal, and at times outspoken, essays—was first printed and circulated in France in 1785, for Jefferson wasn't sure how well the book would be received in America. Since that time, however, the book has been often reprinted in America and became one of the most popular books of the late eighteenth century.

All his life Thomas Jefferson was a man of great contradictions. Although born into an aristocratic Virginia family, he was opposed to the idea of a man's position in life being determined by his family and wealth. A large slaveowner, himself, who maintained his luxurious life at Monticello with slave labor, Jefferson detested the institution of slavery and was instrumental in outlawing the importing of slaves to Virginia in 1778. And although he was a passionate advocate of human rights, he did not include women and black Americans as having those inalienable rights to "life, liberty and the pursuit of happiness."

When Thomas Jefferson died at his beloved Monticello on July 4, 1826, despite his many accomplishments it was as an author he most wanted to be remembered. He requested the following words to be put on his tombstone, "and not a word more." "Here was buried Thomas Jefferson, Author, of the Declaration of American Independence, of the Statue of Virginia for religious freedom, and Father of the University of Virginia."

Monticello, which Thomas Jefferson designed himself, is a National Shrine. The house and grounds today look as they did when Jefferson lived at Monticello. Many of the ingenious contraptions in the house Jefferson devised himself, for he was a skilled inventor as well as a compulsive gadgeteer. Some of the "gadgets" he invented are a revolving chair, a walking stick that turns into a chair, a revolving music stand, a writing box that serves also as a reading stand and a seven day clock that also tells the day of the week. Two of the most interesting items in this fascinating home is a polygraph, or copying machine, which Jefferson used in conducting his voluminous correspondence, and a replica of the portable writing desk upon which the Declaration of Independence was written.

The actual house in which Jefferson wrote the Declaration of Independence, the Graff house in Philadelphia, has been reconstructed and may now be visited by the public.

The Jefferson Memorial in Washington, D.C., has a central memorial room containing a large bronze statue of Jefferson. The panels of the room contain inscriptions from the most significant of Jefferson's writings.

Location: MONTICELLO, Jefferson's home, is located on SR 53, 3 miles southeast of Charlottesville, Virginia. Admission charge.

Location: GRAFF HOUSE, southwest corner of Seventh and Market Streets, Philadelphia, Pennsylvania. No admission charge.

Location: JEFFERSON MEMORIAL is on the southeast side of the Tidal Basin, Washington, D.C.

REVOLUTIONARY WAR PERIOD

THE REVOLUTIONARY WAR WAS THE MOST HIGHLY PROPAGAN-
DIZED WAR IN AMERICAN HISTORY UNTIL WORLD WAR I. IN THIS
"WAR OF WORDS" THE MOST EFFECTIVE LITERARY AMMUNITION
WAS THE PAMPHLET. OVER TWO THOUSAND PAMPHLETS WERE
WRITTEN BEFORE AND DURING THE REVOLUTIONARY WAR, TRY-
ING TO SWAY THE OPINIONS AND EMOTIONS OF THE COLONISTS
FOR OR AGAINST THE REBELLION.

The winter camp of General Washington's Army in Pennsylvania
has become Valley Forge National Historical Park, shown above.
It was at army camps like Valley Forge, during the Revolutionary
War, that Thomas Paine's pamphlet *The Crisis* was read aloud to
the starving, freezing soldiers. Paine's stirring words were thought
by John Adams to be as important as Washington's sword in holding the ragtag Continental Army together. COURTESY UNITED STATES
NATIONAL PARKS SERVICE

After the Revolutionary War,
a small farm cottage in New
Rochelle, New York, was given
to Thomas Paine in recognition
of his services in the cause of
independence. The rear room
of the house is where Paine
lived very simply in his last
years. Both the cottage and the
nearby Thomas Paine Museum
contain mementos from his
life. PHOTO BY AUTHOR

Not all writers in the American Revolution were radicals, like Thomas Paine. John Dickinson, called the "Penman of the Revolution," urged a more conservative approach toward the colonies' problems with England in his *Letters from a Farmer in Pennsylvania.* The Dickinson family home near Dover, Delaware, has been restored as an example of a moderately wealthy colonial home before the Revolutionary War. COURTESY DICTIONARY OF AMERICAN PORTRAITS

The home and possessions of Philip Freneau (1752–1832), called the "Poet of the American Revolution," have not fared well. There is no literary site connected with America's first war poet that may be visited today. It was Freneau's "The British Prison Ship" and his poem to the American dead at the Battle of Eutaw Springs that made him an important propagandic poet for the American cause. After the war, Freneau settled near Freehold, New Jersey, where he tried his hand at journalism and farming as well as writing lyrical poetry. Called by some, the "Father of American Poetry," Freneau died in poverty, almost forgotten. COURTESY DICTIONARY OF AMERICAN PORTRAITS

Women, too, used their literary talents to further the American cause of independence. Mercy Otis Warren (1728–1814), an advocate of colonial women's rights, was also a popular playwright and poet. She wrote *The Adulateur* (1773) and *The Group* (1775), political satires directed against the British and the American Tories who sided with the British. After the war, she wrote a three-volume history of the Revolution that has not been surpassed for its insight into the causes of the war and the leading figures on both sides of the conflict. COURTESY DICTIONARY OF AMERICAN PORTRAITS

Thomas Jefferson was one of the few American presidents who was a notable author as well. An eloquent writer and author of America's Declaration of Independence, Jefferson also collected America's first important library in his home at Monticello, Virginia (shown above). The books in Jefferson's library later became the start of the Library of Congress. In the rear of the library may be seen a polygraph—one of the gadgets Jefferson dearly loved. With the polygraph, the thousands of letters that Jefferson wrote with one pen were duplicated by the other, automatically making a copy of every letter he wrote. COURTESY THOMAS JEFFERSON MEMORIAL FOUNDATION

Although Benjamin Franklin is best known as a writer for his *Poor Richard's Almanack* and his *Autobiography*, he also wrote political pamphlets before and during the Revolutionary War. A highly successful man of the world, Franklin often deliberately gave the appearance of being homespun and provincial, such as when he arrived as American Minister to France wearing the fur hat on the right. COURTESY YALE UNIVERSITY ART GALLERY

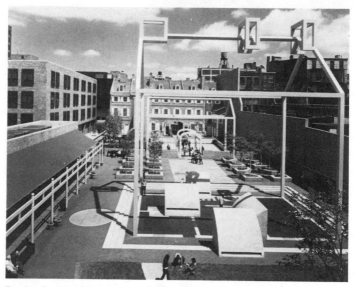

Benjamin Franklin made a fortune through his writing and his printing business. The site of the original Benjamin Franklin Printshop (shown above) can be seen in Franklin Court, Philadelphia. Near Franklin Court on Market Street is a reconstructed working printing press and bindery, reminiscent of the early printshop operations that were an important part of America's Revolutionary War and literary history. COURTESY INDEPENDENCE NATIONAL HISTORICAL PARK COLLECTION

NOAH WEBSTER
1758-1843

A small farmhouse in Connecticut was the boyhood home of Noah Webster, who wrote the book that has outsold every book in the English language, except the Bible. Properly speaking, Webster was not an author but a lexicographer—a compiler of words or dictionaries. Nevertheless every American author owes him a great debt of gratitude. For Noah Webster literally helped invent the American language as we know it today.

After the Revolutionary War, America was politically independent from England, but American schoolchildren still learned to spell from English textbooks and dictionaries. Young Noah Webster, who had become a schoolteacher after graduating from college, saw no reason why Americans should copy the English language as it was spoken and written in England. After all, over the years the colonists had developed their own way of speaking and spelling. Why shouldn't America be as independent in literature as she was in politics?

In 1782 he wrote the first of his many famous "blue-backed spellers." Spelling in America in the eighteenth century was apt to be a hit or miss affair, with the correct spelling of a word varying from state to state. In his spelling books, Webster standardized the spelling of words and stressed American spellings; for example, *honor,* instead of the British way of spelling it, *honour, jail* instead of the British *gaol.*

And where British spelling books glorified the great deeds and events in British history, Noah Webster in his spelling books wrote about American history and American heroes and heroines, so that students would become familiar with their own country's heritage.

In time, Webster's spellers became almost the only spelling books used in American schoolrooms. Over fifty million copies were sold in Webster's lifetime alone. Unfortunately, because authors in nineteenth century America did not have copyright protection for their books, Webster received only a small portion of the profits. Unscrupulous printers and booksellers pirated his spellers and pocketed the profits that should have been Webster's.

Nevertheless Noah Webster traveled extensively around the country, lecturing and publicizing his spelling books. During his travels, he discovered that the American language was splitting more and more into regional dialects. Southerners pronounced and spelled words in one fashion, New Englanders in another. Just in New England, people in Connecticut spoke differently from people in Massachusetts. Webster was afraid that eventually each part of the country would be speaking a separate language. He decided what America needs was a national language as well as a national government.

To accomplish this end, Noah Webster set about writing, alone and by hand, a dictionary of the American language. Each morning he would go to his study and sit at a large semi-circular table on a chair mounted on casters. He would start at the right end of the table and go through stacks of grammars and dictionaries, tracing a particular word through as many as twenty languages as he rolled from one end of the table to the other.

The task of compiling the dictionary took Webster twenty years and used up most of the money he had received from his spellers. By 1828, though, he had finished the greatest and most complete of the five dictionaries he was to compile and publish in his lifetime. The book was called *The American Dictionary of 1828*. Noah Webster wrote the history, definition and pronunciation of each of the 70,000 words in the dictionary.

Webster not only standardized the spelling and pronunciation of the American language, but he was the first lexicographer in the world to include scientific and technical terms in his dictionary. He also included strictly American words, such as "tomahawk," "skunk," "dime," and "dollar," and his definitions were so exact that many are still in use today. The Webster Dictionaries found in many homes and classrooms in our day are based, to a large degree, upon Noah Webster's original *The American Dictionary of 1828*.

By the time of Webster's death, he had become the acknowledged "father of his country's language," as important, in his own way, as any great literary figure, military hero or captain of industry.

Noah Webster's boyhood home stands on a ridge and commands a fine view of Hartford, Connecticut, where he first taught school. A typical eighteenth century farmhouse, seven members of the Webster family crowded into the four small rooms, built around a central fireplace. Noah was born in the chamber directly behind the parlor. Later, the house was enlarged to its present size. Noah's father, recognizing his son's ability, mortgaged the farm to get the money to send him to college. Authentic furnishings in the home recreate a sense of the past and the growing years of the boy, Noah.

Noah Webster's later home in New Haven, Connecticut, where he compiled his first dictionaries, was dismantled in 1938 and moved to Greenfield Village in Dearborn, Michigan. When the house was moved, it was discovered that the second floor study where Noah did his work, had double walls so the lexicographer would not hear his seven children as he worked.

Location: NOAH WEBSTER BOYHOOD HOME is located at 227 South Main Street, West Hartford, Connecticut, north of Route 84, Exit 41. Admission charge.

Location: NOAH WEBSTER HOME, Greenfield Village, Village Road and Oakwood Boulevard, Dearborn, Michigan (adjacent to Detroit, Michigan.) Admission charge.

WASHINGTON IRVING
1783-1859

The lower Hudson River Valley of New York state, with its "wild, woody and rugged" Catskill Mountains, is one of America's most famous literary regions. For this is Washington Irving's Sleepy Hollow country, the setting for many of his most popular short stories. It was in the Catskills that Rip Van Winkle slept away twenty years of his life. And if one follows the Post Road north from Tarrytown, one comes across the very bridge over which Ichabod Crane of the "Legend of Sleepy Hollow" fled on his horse, Gunpowder, with the Headless Horseman in fast pursuit.

When Washington Irving was a young man in the late eighteenth century, sleepy Dutch villages like Tarrytown could be found all along the Hudson River Valley, and ghostly legends about the valley were still being told around firesides at night. Although Irving was born into a wealthy

New York family, he enjoyed the rural life of the Catskills as much as he enjoyed the theaters and pleasures of city life. As a young man, he often roamed the Hudson River Valley and later said that he knew every spot in the Catskills "where a murder or robbery had been committed or a ghost seen."

Because writing for a living was not considered a respectable occupation for a gentleman, Washington Irving went to work in his family business. Nevertheless, he did occasionally try his hand at writing, although he always used a pen name. In 1809 he wrote a humorous *History of New York* using as a pen name one that was supposed to belong to an elderly gentleman, Diedrich Knickerbocker. In his history, Knickerbocker poked gentle fun at the early Dutch burgers and their wives who had settled New York. One early Dutch governor was described by Knickerbocker as "exactly five feet six inches in height and six feet five inches in circumference . . . very averse to the idle habit of walking."

The descendants of the early Dutch settlers still living in New York were not too happy with the history, but it was very popular with the rest of the New Yorkers. When it was discovered that the mysterious Knickerbocker was really Washington Irving, popular young man about town, Irving became the literary celebrity of his day.

In 1815 Irving traveled to England to work in the family business, but the War of 1812 had driven the company into bankruptcy. Irving was left penniless. With that he turned to writing, not for his own amusement, but to support himself. Using his memories of the ghostly legends he had heard years before in the Catskills, and combining them with the folk stories he had heard while traveling around Europe, Irving wrote a collection of short stories, called *The Sketch Book*.

This time he used the pen name Geoffrey Crayon.

The Sketch Book, published in 1820, was a great success both in America and Europe. Irving from then on was able to live on the money he made from his writing and became America's first professional man of letters. Most important, *The Sketch Book* introduced three unforgettable characters to the literary world: Rip Van Winkle, Ichabod Crane and the Headless Horseman.

Irving remained in Europe for seventeen years, writing and traveling, and because he was so well-liked, acting as an unofficial American ambassador. He wrote several more books during this time, perhaps the most enduring being a biography of Christopher Columbus, and the *Alhambra* (1832), romantic sketches of Moorish Spain.

When Irving finally returned to New York in 1832, he was greeted as a conquering hero. Before Washington Irving, American authors were so little regarded in Europe that a critic could write contemptuously in 1820, "In the four quarters of the globe, who reads an American book?" *The Sketchbook* changed all that. It was translated into seventeen languages. No longer could it be said that American books were not read abroad, and that America didn't have a literature and an author of its own.

After returning to America, Irving took a trip west to the Shawnee and Osage Indian country. He used this experience in a book called *A Tour of the Prairie,* then went on to write *Astoria,* a story of John Jacob Astor's fur empire. With these books, Irving became the first American author to use the American Indian and the West—although highly romanticized—as a subject for popular American literature.

No matter where he traveled, Irving always returned to the Hudson River Valley that he loved. In 1835 he bought an old stone Dutch-gabled farmhouse on the banks of the Hudson River. He completely remodeled the farm cottage, studded its roof with weather vanes, and turned the simple cottage into what he called "an elegant little snuggery . . . as full of angles and corners as an old cocked hat."

Washington Irving never married, but his home was always filled with relatives and friends, so many that a three-story tower with a pagoda roof was added to the house to handle the overflow. Irving never stopped remodeling the house, which, with its whimsical charm, perfectly reflected the character of its owner, just as Irving's short stories and sketches, like fine paintings, reflected the beautiful, legend-haunted Hudson River Valley.

It was at Sunnyside that Washington Irving died, having completed his last work, a biography of George Washington. The popular author was buried in Sleepy Hollow Cemetery and the day of his funeral was declared a day of mourning in the city of New York.

Although Washington Irving has been called the Father of American literature, he, himself, considered his work "light and trifling," appealing "to the feelings and fancy of the reader." His prose style may have been overly senti-mental, yet he added his own quiet charm and dry wit to his writing, making Knickerbocker's *History of New York* the first great book of comic literature produced by an American. And because of Irving's knowledge of local color and history, his writings were always peculiarly American in style and uniquely his own in spirit.

In 1945 Washington Irving's Sunnyside was bought and restored by John D. Rockefeller to look as it had when the famous English author, Thackeray, visited Sunnyside in the nineteenth century and described it as "a funny little in and out cottage, little bits of small parlours, a little study, old dogs trotting about the premises, flocks of ducks sailing on the pond."

Everything in the house is placed just as it was when Irving was alive. One room in the house has been turned into a picture gallery containing original illustrations from Irving's books. The house is surrounded by beautiful grounds, and a nearby reception center provides visitors with information and tours of the house.

In North Tarrytown, New York, is the seventeenth century Dutch church where Ichabod Crane gave Katrina Van Tassel singing lessons, and it was from this churchyard that the Headless Horseman made his nightly trips. It was when they passed the church that the Headless Horseman rose in his stirrups and flung the pumpkin at the fleeing schoolmaster. The nearby ruins of a haunted mill is mentioned in Geoffrey Crayon's *Chronicles*.

The Van Alen homestead at Kinderhook, New York, built in 1737, is furnished in the fashion of an eighteenth century Dutch farm. Washington Irving was for a short time a tutor for a family who lived near the Van Alens, and local tradition has it that Irving used the Van Alen home for the scene of his famous party in "The Legend of Sleepy Hollow." The character, Katrina Van Tassel, is supposed to have been based upon a member of the Van Alen family.

Not far from the town of Kinderhook is a small, one-room schoolhouse that has become known as the "Ichabod Crane Schoolhouse" because its schoolmaster in the eighteenth century, one Jesse Merwin, is supposed to have been the character, Ichabod Crane, in Irving's short story.

Location: THE TOWNS OF TARRYTOWN, IRVING-

47

TON AND NORTH TARRYTOWN, New York, on the east bank of the Hudson, where the river widens to become the Tappan Zee, are all part of Sleepy Hollow Country. Washington Irving's home, SUNNYSIDE, is located one mile south of Tappan Zee Bridge on West Sunnyside Lane, just off Route 9.

A Washington Irving memorial bust with a background of characters from his stories is located at West Sunnyside Lane at Broadway, Tarrytown, New York.

During the summer months a production of Rip Van Winkle is staged at Sunnyside under a tent, with a candlelit tour of Irving's home as part of the evening's entertainment. Admission charge to Sunnyside and theater production.

Location: VAN ALEN HOME is located 1 mile east and south of Kinderhook, New York, on SR 9H. Admission charge.

Location: ICHABOD CRANE SCHOOLHOUSE is located on SR 9H, a short distance from the Van Alen House. No admission charge.

Location: HEADLESS HORSEMAN BRIDGE carries US 9 across the Pocantico River, North Tarrytown, New York.

Location: OLD DUTCH CHURCH is on the Albany Post Road, US 9, North Tarrytown, New York.

JAMES FENIMORE COOPER
1789-1851

In a gemlike setting of hills and forests in central New York State lies shimmering Otsego Lake. Noted for its natural, scenic beauty, the lake is also the famous "Glimmerglass Lake" of James Fenimore Cooper's popular Leatherstocking Tales. It was in the forests around this lake that America's first fictional frontier hero, Natty Bumppo, known in the first novel of the series as the Deerslayer, roamed with his Iroquois Indian friends. So exactly did Cooper describe the site of the frontier scout's adventures in his novels that some of the localities may be identified today. There is Council Rock "still showing its chin above the water" where the Deerslayer met with the Delaware Indians before they went on the war path; the cave in the hillside overlooking the eastern shore of the lake where the wilderness scout barricaded himself against the officers of the law, and Five-Mile Point where he was taken prisoner by the Indians.

Cooper knew the countryside around Otsego Lake from having fished and hunted through the hills and woodland as a boy. The town of Cooperstown, which sits at the foot of the lake, was named after the author's father, who owned enormous tracts of land in the area. When Cooper's father settled the area in 1790, the Indians still inhabited the primitive wilderness. When young Cooper was growing up, however, the wilderness was already in retreat. The tales of Indians and Indian uprisings, which the author was to use later in his novels, he heard from his father and from the old frontier scouts who still passed through the town.

A high-spirited young man, James Fenimore Cooper was expelled from Yale University and joined the U.S. Navy, where he was a midshipman for several years. He left the Navy when he married a wealthy landowner's daughter and began leading the quiet, rather dull life of a country gentleman in Westchester County, New York. One evening as he read aloud to his wife from the latest English romantic novel, he remarked, disgusted, that he could write a better book himself. His wife immediately challenged him to try.

Cooper's first book was not a success, but encouraged by the popularity of Sir Walter Scott's historical novels, he decided to try again. His second novel, *The Spy,* set in West-chester County, used actual historical events from the American Revolutionary War as a background, with Cooper's fictional hero, Harvey Birch, acting as a secret double agent.

The Spy, published in 1821, was a huge success, not just because Americans liked to read romantic tales about their past, but because the novel was a fast-moving tale of adventure and intrigue.

Cooper immediately began to produce other novels,

thirty-three in all. He also wrote books of history and social criticism, but it is as America's first important novelist that he is best known. One of the most interesting of his novels was *The Pilot,* published in 1824. In writing *The Pilot,* Cooper drew upon the knowledge of ships he had gained while he was in the Navy. No other author had used the sailor's life aboard ship as a background for a novel, and it has been said that with *The Pilot,* Cooper invented the sea story.

But Cooper's first love was the wilderness, and it is undoubtedly for his wilderness novels that he will be the longest remembered. Using as a setting the central New York region stretching from the Mohawk Valley north to Lake George, and remembering the stories of frontier life he had heard as a boy, Cooper created a series of five novels, called The Leatherstocking Tales, which have become literary classics.

The Leatherstocking Tales follow the life of Natty Bumppo, wilderness scout, from his young manhood into old age. The five novels, published over a period of twenty years, were not written in chronological order. The scout's early adventures in the New York wilderness are described in *The Deerslayer,* published in 1841. Deerslayer's adventures are continued in *The Last of the Mohicans* (1826); *The Pathfinder* (1840); *The Pioneers* (1823) and ends with *The Prairie,* published in 1827, with civilization in the form of a wagon train moving in upon the wilderness.

Single-handedly, with these five novels, Cooper created a mythology of American wilderness life—the legendary, heroic frontiersman and noble Indian—that has lasted to this day.

A portion of The Leatherstocking Tales was actually

written while Cooper lived abroad. Like another American author, Washington Irving, who was his contemporary, James Fenimore Cooper lived in Europe for several years. However, unlike the genial and beloved Washington Irving, when Cooper returned to America, he was not greeted as a returning hero. Although his novels still sold very well, the author, himself, had become one of the most detested men in America.

An aristocrat by temperament, Cooper did not approve of the America that had come into being with President Andrew Jackson. He was suspicious of the common man that was now running the government. Although Cooper liked to praise the noble, natural man in his novels, in real life he found the common man to be vulgar and boorish. He wrote several books that vigorously criticized America, thereby antagonizing his countrymen.

During his last years, Cooper lived part of the year in New York City, but also maintained a home in Cooperstown. Unhappily, he became engaged in endless lawsuits over property rights in his hometown, so infuriating the townspeople that it was suggested that Cooper's books be banned from the Cooperstown Public Library. Nevertheless, at his death Cooper was buried at Lakewood Cemetery at Cooperstown, and the town today still holds many memories of Cooper's life there.

Cooper's novels, particularly his Leatherstocking Tales, have remained popular, not just in America but abroad. Europeans, as well as Americans, are fascinated by his tales of frontier heroes, larger than life. Cooper's prose was often awkward, and he never bothered to revise his writing, but he created memorable characters in his men of the woods. With his brisk, narrative style and lively plots, his novels are filled with adventure and action from start to finish. And, of course, with his creation of the courageous frontier hero and his use of the wilderness as a setting for his novels, Cooper started a trend in American literature that continues to this day.

Otsego Hall, the Cooper family home in Cooperstown, which is described in detail in *The Pioneers,* has long since been torn down. Upon the site now stands the Fenimore House Museum, which, in addition to its outstanding collection of folk art, has a special James Fenimore Cooper room, filled with paintings, manuscripts and memorabilia associated with the author.

The nearby Farmer's Museum and the recreated Village Crossroads show, through their reconstructed buildings, how life was lived in Cooperstown from 1783 to 1840, when the author was a controversial and influential member of the town.

The Cooperstown Indian Museum has dioramas and exhibits that show the everyday life of the Indians of New York State. They played a prominent, if somewhat romanticized, role in Cooper's wilderness novels.

A visit to Otsego Lake, however, and the countryside around it, is one of the best introductions to Cooper's wilderness novels. Many of the scenes from the novels are located on the west shore of the lake. A statue of the hero of the Leatherstocking Tales with his faithful dog, Hector, may be seen at the Lakefront Park, overlooking Otsego Lake.

Location: COOPERSTOWN AND OTSEGO LAKE are located 70 miles west of Albany, New York, and 30 miles south of the Thruway. From the west, use Exit 30 at

Herkimer (Route 28); from the East, use Exit 29 at Canajohaire (Routes 10, 20 and 80.)

Location: FENIMORE HOUSE MUSEUM, 1 mile north on SR 80, Cooperstown, New York. Admission charge.

Location: THE FARMERS' MUSEUM AND VILLAGE CROSSROADS, 1 mile north on SR 80, Cooperstown, New York. Admission charge.

Location: COOPERSTOWN INDIAN MUSEUM, 1 Pioneer Street at the Lakefront, Cooperstown, New York. Admission charge.

WILLIAM CULLEN BRYANT
1794-1878

The lovely Hampshire hills near Cummington, Massachusetts, inspired the first poem by an American to win international acclaim. The poem entitled "Thanatopsis," meaning view of death, was written by a sixteen-year-old poet, William Cullen Bryant.

Born in Cummington, Massachusetts, William Cullen Bryant was a sickly child, not expected to live, which may explain his youthful preoccupation with death. His doctor father, however, in addition to encouraging his son's interest in poetry, set the boy upon a sensible regime of exercise and long walks in the Berkshire foothills around Cummington. This healthy outdoor life not only increased Bryant's life span—he lived to the ripe old age of 84—but aroused in the young man a deep interest in nature, which became the central theme of most of his poems.

It was on one of those walks into the Hampshire hills near his home that the young poet received the inspiration to write "Thanatopsis." Bryant's childhood had been overshadowed by his grandfather's harsh Calvinist views of death, that man was inevitably doomed to "hell's fire." Now he brooded, as he walked, asking himself, "How shall I face death?" And finding comfort and serenity in the immortality of nature, gave his answer in "Thanatopsis."

Although Bryant had had some poetry published earlier in local newspapers, he did not attempt to publish "Thanatopsis." It was his father who, several years later, found the poem in his son's desk and sent it to the *North American Review*. The editor, at first, thought the poem too fine to have been written by an American poet. When the magazine finally published the poem in 1817, Bryant, who realized he could never make a living selling an occasional poem, was practicing law in the Berkshires. However, he continued writing poetry in his spare time.

In 1821, the year of Bryant's marriage, a small collection of his poetry was published, called simply *Poems*. The collection included the poem "Thanatopsis." Bryant's love of nature can be found in the titles of some of the other poems in this volume: "The Yellow Violet," "Green River," and "To a Waterfowl."

With the publication of this book, Bryant's fame as a poet spread in America and abroad. So admired were Bryant's poems that in his day no child graduated from school without having memorized the words to "Thanatopsis."

In 1825 Bryant put aside the practice of law and accepted an editorial position on the *New York Evening Post*. In time, he purchased the newspaper. Under his management, the *Post* became one of America's great liberal newspapers, fighting for the abolition of slavery and the right of laboring men to join unions.

With his writing, and his editorial position, Bryant became one of the leading literary figures of nineteenth century America. However, because managing the newspaper took up so much of his time, or perhaps because as he grew older Bryant became "as quiet, cool and dignified as a smooth, silent iceberg," his later poetry never reached the greatness of the poems he had written as a youth.

Bryant was a traditional poet who believed that a poem should teach "direct lessons of wisdom" and moral values. At the same time, he believed that "the·most beautiful poetry is that which takes the strongest hold on the feelings." His best poems were his nature poems, describing the American landscape with a naturalist's eye but seeing nature with the fresh imagery and sensitivity of a poet. One critic has said that in Bryant's poetry you can actually hear "the sound of the woods, the hum of bees and the chirp of the wren . . ."

Even after he became a city dweller, Bryant found his greatest happiness in the country. He bought a summer home in Roslyn, Long Island, New York, called Cedarmere, to which he was forced to add several cottages because of his many visitors. The home was recently bought by Nassau County and is in the process of restoration.

Bryant's boyhood home at Cummington is open to the public. His bedroom under the eaves looks out over the Berkshire hills. Also in this room may be seen the barbells Bryant used in his daily exercising. He continued the physical regime he had learned as a boy his whole life long. He would rise at 5:30, take an hour's exercise, chinning himself from his bedroom doorframe, and then jumping back and forth over his bed, aided by a vaulting pole!

The wild beauty of the woods and hills surrounding Cummington that inspired Bryant's early poetry can still be enjoyed today. One walking path follows the Hampshire hills from Cummington to the small village of Plainfield. It was on this pathway one December evening as the sun was sinking that Bryant saw a solitary bird outlined against the rosy evening horizon. It was the inspiration for one of his most popular poems, "To a Waterfowl."

Location: WILLIAM CULLEN BRYANT HOMESTEAD, Cummington, Massachusetts, is located 20 miles from Pittsfield, 1½ miles south of SR 9, on SR 112. Open summers only. Admission charge.

AFTER REVOLUTIONARY WAR UNTIL EARLY 1800s

IN THE YEARS AFTER THE REVOLUTIONARY WAR AND UNTIL THE EARLY 1800s, AMERICAN AUTHORS WERE LITTLE KNOWN OR RESPECTED ABROAD. THE THREE AUTHORS WHO CHANGED ALL THAT WERE WASHINGTON IRVING, JAMES FENIMORE COOPER, AND WILLIAM CULLEN BRYANT.

The major American poet after the Revolutionary War was William Cullen Bryant. He followed in the romantic, lyrical tradition made popular by English poets. COURTESY DICTIONARY OF AMERICAN PORTRAITS

Washington Irving lived in this charming house, called Sunnyside, on the banks of the Hudson River near Tarrytown, New York. The author of "Rip Van Winkle" wrote his stories in a study of this house, stories that brought American literature international acclaim for the first time. PHOTO BY AUTHOR

One of the most popular short stories ever written in America was Washington Irving's "The Legend of Sleepy Hollow," published in 1819. Shown above is a scene, drawn by Felix Darley, of the schoolteacher, Ichabod Crane, being pursued by the headless horseman. Near Sunnyside, Irving's home at Tarrytown, New York, may be seen the Old Dutch Church of Sleepy Hollow and the graveyard from which the headless horseman is supposed to emerge each night. COURTESY OF SLEEPY HOLLOW RESTORATIONS, TARRYTOWN, NEW YORK

James Fenimore Cooper is also credited with having been the author of America's first sea story. As a young man, Cooper served in the U.S. Navy and is shown in his midshipman's uniform below. It was his experience in the Navy that he used as a background for his book of sea life, *The Pilot*. COURTESY DICTIONARY OF AMERICAN PORTRAITS

A statue of America's first fictional frontier hero and his dog, Hector, from Cooper's Leatherstocking Tales, may be seen at Lake Front Park, Cooperstown, New York. The statue looks out over Lake Otsego, the Glimmerglass Lake of the novels.

JOHN GREENLEAF WHITTIER
1807–1892

The sturdy, old New England farmhouse, four miles east of Haverhill, Massachusetts, was already more than a century old when the Quaker poet, John Greenleaf Whittier, was born within its solid oak walls—walls that were still able to withstand the storms of a New England winter. Sometimes snowbound for weeks during the winter months, the Whittier family would gather around the huge brick fireplace in the kitchen, with mugs of hot cider, telling ghost stories, or tales of witchcraft and long ago Indian raids.

The young John Whittier listened, fascinated, to these legends and stories as he watched the snow fall, turning the clothesline posts "into tall and sheeted ghosts" and the hitching post into "an old man with the high cocked hat." Many years later, Whittier was to remember those cozy winter days by the fireside, and using the setting of the old farmhouse, write one of America's most popular and nostalgic narrative poems, *Snow-Bound*.

Unlike the other well-known New England writers from Concord, Cambridge and Boston, Whittier was a country boy, born and bred. His deeply religious Quaker family had little money, so the young Whittier's schooling was brief. Yet, although he spent long hours working on the farm, he managed to read every book that came into the farmhouse, particularly the poetry of the Scottish poet, Robert Burns. Secretly he dreamed of becoming a poet, too. His practical father warned him, however, that "poetry will not give you bread."

At nineteen, Whittier had his first poem accepted by William Lloyd Garrison. Garrison, who was later to edit the *Liberator*, the foremost abolitionist newspaper, encouraged young Whittier to continue writing. To support himself, Whittier accepted various editorial assignments in Boston, but more and more he found himself involved in the abolition movement, lecturing and writing anti-slavery tracts and poetry.

The early supporters of the anti-slavery movement in America faced a great deal of hostility. Many New Englanders were afraid the freeing of slaves would cause an economic hardship; others simply didn't want to become involved. Several times during his lecture tours, Whittier was attacked by mobs. Once his carriage was hit with a hail of bullets. And in 1838 a mob set fire to the newspaper office where Whittier worked.

Nevertheless, for thirty years Whittier continued to lecture and write against slavery. In 1846 he published a collection of anti-slavery poems, called *Voices of Freedom*. He did not hesitate to appeal to the emotions of his readers in his poetry. He aroused their anger against slavery with such propagandic words as "Our fellow countrymen in chains!" "No fetters in the Bay State!" His poems also had emotion-arousing titles such as "The Farewell of a Virgania Slave Mother to Her Daughter Sold into Southern Bondage." He even dared to attack in his satirical poem, "Ichabod," the popular statesman, Daniel Webster, when Webster supported the Fugitive Slave Bill.

Other New England authors of the day—men like Longfellow, Emerson, Thoreau and Lowell—also wrote of the evils of slavery, but none were as passionate or effective as Whittier. (In the South, the poet Henry Timrod was writing just as passionate poetry in support of slavery.)

By the time the Civil War finally broke out, bringing an end to slavery, Whittier had exhausted himself physically and emotionally. He retired to Amesbury, Massachusetts, where his family had moved from the farmhouse at Haverhill. The most famous poem he wrote during the war years was "Barbara Frietchie," which is still a popular poem today.

After the war, Whittier turned from writing propagandistic poetry to poems that told New England history and legend and that celebrated the simple, rural life. Among his popular poems were: "Maud Muller," "Barefoot Boy," "Skipper Ireson's Ride" and "Telling the Bees."

Then in 1866 Whittier wrote *Snow-Bound,* using himself and his family as characters in the poem. Whittier described the poem as "a winter idyl"—a picture of an old-fashioned farmer's fireside in winter. Ironically, the way of life Whittier described so vividly in his poem was already fast disappearing from the American scene. Much to Whittier's surprise, and perhaps because of the nostalgic quality of the poem, *Snow-Bound* was extremely successful, making Whittier enough money that he never needed to worry about finances again.

Whittier, like Longfellow, lived to a ripe old age, and also like Longfellow, he became one of the most popular poets of his day. A tall, handsome man with piercing dark eyes, he had several unhappy romances but never married.

Essex County, Massachusetts, with its sunny villages, shaded farms and sparkling rivers running to the sea, served as the favorite background for Whittier's poems, and it was in Essex County, in the Quaker section of the Union Cemetery in Amesbury, that Whittier was buried.

Whittier is at his best when he is describing the life and folklore of the New England country people he knew so well. Called the American Robert Burns, there is in his work flashes of greatness, and his descriptions of the landscape of New England are unsurpassed for their simple beauty and rugged strength.

John Greenleaf Whittier's birthplace in Haverhill, Massachusetts, the solid farmhouse and surrounding countryside he describes so exactly in his poems, is substantially the same as when Whittier lived there. He wrote his early poetry in the kitchen of the farmhouse at a desk that had belonged to his great-grandfather. Outside is the old barn, to which the Whittier boys had to tunnel through the snow. Fernside Brook still flows not far from the house. The stepping stones, the garden with its daffodils, the old poplars guarding the house, may still be seen. So accurately did Whittier describe scenes in his poems that one can still walk from Haverhill to specific sites mentioned in the poems "Haverhill," "Suicide Pond," "The Sycamores," and "Homecoming of the Bride." Electricity has been added to the house, and a highway runs nearby now, but visiting the Whittier homestead is like taking a step back in time to a simpler, less complicated America, where such farmhouses were the rule and not the exception.

The home in Amesbury to which Whittier and his mother, aunt and sister moved in 1836 is also open to the public. Whittier's sister, Elizabeth, was also a poet and a staunch abolitionist, and she had a great influence on his life. In the house are many furnishings from the Whittier family, as well as memorabilia from the years that Whittier was in the forefront of the fight against slavery. In the parlor is a photograph of the first Jubilee singers of Fisk University, who visited the poet at his Amesbury home after their triumphant singing tour of Europe in 1879.

Location: WHITTIER HOMESTEAD is 4 miles east on SR 110, Haverhill, Massachusetts. Small admission charge.

Location: JOHN GREENLEAF WHITTIER HOME, 86 Friend Street, Amesbury, Massachusetts. Small admission charge.

RALPH WALDO EMERSON
1803–1882

In the middle of the 1800s, a small, New England town gathered within its borders an extraordinary collection of distinguished literary figures. For a short space of time the town of Concord, Massachusetts, became the most important literary center in America. So important was its influence on American literature that Concord has been called "the intellectual seedpod of the nation." The fact that this New England village of less than 2,000 people became the focal point of so much literary talent was due, in part, to one man—Ralph Waldo Emerson.

Emerson was descended from nine successive generations of ministers and seemed inevitably headed for the quiet life of the ministry. And in 1826, he did become pastor of the Second Church of Boston. But the strict Calvinistic religion of the early New England Puritans—with its belief in man as a predestined sinner, doomed to eternal damnation—was no longer accepted by many young people. In 1832 Emerson quit the ministry, stating that "I have sometimes thought in order to be a good minister, it was necessary to leave the ministry."

After touring Europe and talking with the great philosophers and literary men of England and Germany, he returned to America and settled in Concord, which was to be his home for the rest of his life. First, he lived in his grandfather's home, The Old Manse; then, marrying for the second time in 1835 (his first wife had died, tragically young, after only two years of marriage) , he bought a home at the edge of town, a square white clapboard house surrounded by pine trees. Needing an income to support his family, Emerson took to the Lyceum or lecture circuit.

The Lyceum lecturer was a new phenomena in nineteenth century America. Men and women traveled from town to town delivering lectures to which the people flocked for education as well as entertainment. It was a hard life for the lecturers. They traveled on bad roads and uncomfortable stage coaches, often in sub-zero weather, stayed at primitive hotels, and, if their lectures were not well received, were booed or hissed from the platform by the audience. Yet this was the way Emerson managed to successfully support his wife and growing family.

When he was not on the lecture circuit, Emerson's life followed a simple pattern. Each morning he walked in the fields or woods around Concord and returned home to his study to write down his thoughts in a journal. The material he used in his lectures, on literature, biology, natural history and philosophy, was taken from these journals. Surprisingly enough, considering his success as a lyceum lecturer, Emerson was an indifferent public speaker. He often lost his place and omitted passages, yet the wisdom of his thoughts, the power of his carefully chosen words, his quiet sense of humor, dominated his audiences.

In 1836 he gathered some of his lectures into written essays, which were published in a book entitled *Nature.* In 1841 and 1844 he turned more of his lectures into books of essays. These collections of essays gradually gained Emerson a world-wide reputation, both as a writer and a philosopher.

It was in his first book, *Nature,* that Emerson presented his ideas on Transcendentalism, a new, partly religious and partly philosophical movement that was to take hold in New England and influence philosophers and authors for years to come. Transcendentalism is not easy to explain. It is not a precise system but rather a practical philosophy of how to conduct one's life. In a way, Transcendentalism was a revolt against the establishment, the old systems of religion, society and government.

Emerson believed that "who so would be a man, must be a non-conformist." That each person can learn the truth of God and Nature "not in a dead church but in a man's own soul," through his own intuition and experience without the need for formalized instruction. Many of the ideas in Transcendentalism are based upon Oriental and Greek philosophy, as well as Quaker teachings, all of which have been reworked and reformed into an almost peculiarly American approach to life.

In what is perhaps his most famous essay, "Self Reliance," Emerson stressed that each individual has the right to make his own decisions, to be self-sustaining. Part of Emerson's philosophy was that America should have done with all the dead cultures of Europe. "Americans," he said, "must walk on our own feet. We will work with our own hands, and we will speak our own minds."

Such controversial ideas, openly expressed by Emerson in lyceum lectures, as well as lectures at Harvard Divinity College, brought cries of outrage from traditional believers. The young people, however, crowded into Emerson's lectures and made pilgrimages to his home in Concord.

Other visitors to Emerson's home were authors like Bronson Alcott, Henry Thoreau, Nathaniel Hawthorne, Margaret Fuller, Louisa May Alcott, and notable people who were not authors, like John Brown, who preached the violent abolition of slavery. Great minds, as well as crackpots and visionaries, came to Concord, and Emerson listened to them all, while his wife, Lydia, patiently fed them and at times put them up as houseguests.

In his old age, Emerson continued to go out on the exhausting lecture circuit, traveling as far west as California. He also made several trips to Europe, where he was received with great honor. Yet in Concord, itself, Emerson lived the life of a plain citizen, taking part in all the town activities. Although some of the more conservative citizens did not always agree with Emerson's beliefs, when his home caught fire, it was the townspeople who volunteered their services to repair the building. And it was Emerson who was asked to write the dedication for the Minute Man monument, which commemorated one of the first battles of the Revolutionary War, fought at the North Bridge in Concord. Emerson's popular poem may be read on the base of the Minute Man monument.

Emerson died in Concord on April 27, 1882, and is buried on Author's Ridge in Concord's Sleepy Hollow Cemetery.

In his own day, Emerson was probably better known as a lecturer than as a writer. Although he also wrote excellent poetry, today it is for his essays, not his lectures or poetry, he is remembered. Emerson had a unique style of writing in which he relied not on logically constructed paragraphs, but on short, incisive sentences that "flashed like thunderbolts" across the page.

Many of these sentences, or aphorisms (short, pointed sentences that express a truth or precept), are often quoted today: "Nothing great was ever achieved without enthusiasm." "To be great is to be misunderstood." "Always do what you are afraid to do." "Hitch your wagon to a star . . ." Reading Emerson today, many of his words appear as fresh and new and sensible as they must have when they were first written.

Emerson's comfortable two-story house in Concord, where he lived from 1835–1882, still belongs to the Emerson family and remains much as it was when Emerson put down his pen for the last time. The house is open for conducted tours in the summer. Emerson's study, however, arranged exactly as Emerson left it at the time of his death, with his writing material on the round table where he worked, his favorite Boston rocker, his books along the wall, has been moved to a fireproof room in the Museum of the Concord Antiquarian Society across the road from the Emerson homestead.

There are still woods around Concord, Emerson's "study under the pines," where he walked and did his best thinking. The white pine was the writer's favorite tree, and many that the author planted still stand near his home. Although the town of Concord has grown since Emerson's day, it is still a charming place to visit, with over a half-dozen famous literary sites open to the public. Emerson always thought that "Concord was sufficient universe in itself." He saw all of life he needed to know within the confines of this small town, enough to fill his journal with more ideas and thoughts than he could use in his lifetime.

The Old Manse in Concord, the home of Emerson's grandfather, where Emerson wrote the first draft of his book, *Nature,* is also open to the public. Emerson did his writing in the study of the house, looking out upon meadowlands stretching down to the Concord River. Another noted author, Nathaniel Hawthorne, was to live and write in this house, using the same study as Emerson, but he found the view too distracting and faced the wall instead.

Location: RALPH WALDO EMERSON HOME, Cambridge Turnpike and SR 2A. Concord, Massachusetts. Open summers only. Small admission charge.

Location: MUSEUM OF THE CONCORD ANTIQUARIAN SOCIETY, ½ mile southeast on SR 2A, 200 Lexington Road, Concord, Massachusetts. Open daily, summers; weekends only during winter months. Guided tours. Admission charge.

Location: OLD MANSE, Monument Street, Concord, Massachusetts. Open summers only. Admission charge.

HENRY DAVID THOREAU
1817-1862

If there is any one literary site in America that is treasured above all others, that site may be a patch of land in a pine grove near a lake in Massachusetts. Within a small cleared area, cement posts have been carefully placed, outlining where the walls of a tiny cabin once stood.

The lake is, of course, Walden Pond. And the grove of pine trees is where Henry Thoreau came in July, 1845, at age 28, and built his now world-renowned cabin in the woods. For twenty-six months, Thoreau lived alone at Walden Pond because, as he wrote, "I wished to live deliberately, to front only the essential facts of life. . . . and not, when I came to die, discover that I had not lived."

Thoreau kept a journal of his thoughts and experiences while living by the lake. These notes were later gathered into a book that has been called "one of the few great and truly original books in American literature." Titled simply *Walden, or Life in the Woods,* the book has been read and reread with delight by generation after generation.

Yet to the citizens of Concord, where Henry David Thoreau was born and lived all his life, with only brief excursions away, young Henry was simply the town's ne'er-do-well, the eccentric character who refused to hold a steady job.

Thoreau attended Harvard College but early showed his independent streak by attending chapel in a green coat because college rules insisted that students must wear black. After college, he taught school. He got along famously with his students but when ordered to cane an unruly student by the school board, he lined up his students, caned them all, and promptly quit.

In the years that followed, Thoreau tried lecturing, but he was never the successful lecturer that his friend Ralph Waldo Emerson was. He became instead the town handyman. Despite the accusation of laziness, Thoreau was, in fact, a competent and hard worker, skilled at gardening, house-painting, surveying and carpentry. While working for a time at his family's pencil making business, he devised a new and better technique for producing pencils.

Work, however, for Thoreau was never an end in itself. Living, Thoreau believed, was the object of life, living in harmony with nature and as simply as possible, with as few possessions as possible. In Thoreau's opinion, a person's wealth was really determined by the number of things he could do without!

In July of 1845 Thoreau decided to test his theory of living simply, deliberately in harmony with nature, and built his small hut by Walden Pond. Here he spent a short time each day tilling his bean field and potatoes. The rest of the day he studied the nature of the woods and water surrounding him, kept his journal, and wrote *A Week on the Concord and Merrimack Rivers.* The book, which Thoreau paid to have published in 1849, told of a boat trip he and his brother John had taken in 1839.

It was while he was living at Walden Pond in 1846 that Thoreau refused to pay his poll tax and spent a night in the Concord jail. He refused to pay the tax because he did not wish his money to support a government that approved of slavery and was fighting what Thoreau considered an unjust war—the Mexican War of 1845.

Thoreau's night in jail did little to change or influence the course of government. However, a lecture he gave in 1848, later published as an essay called "Civil Disobedience," was to have a tremendous impact on the lives of men and women all over the world. In his essay, Thoreau insisted on the individual's right to be responsible only to his own conscience and not the state. The philosophy of "passive resistance" to unjust government presented in "Civil Disobedience" was little noted during Thoreau's time. It did not die, however, but eventually spread as far as India, where it helped Mahatma Ghandi overthrow the British government, and to Dr. Martin Luther King who displayed passive resistance to racial injustice from a Birmingham jail.

Thoreau, himself, was not a leader of crusades. He would help a slave escape to Canada or deliver a eulogy for the unpopular militant abolitionist, John Brown, but he did not preach that other men should live as he did. He went his own way. He occasionally attended the Transcendentalist group that met in Concord, but he was not a joiner. Described as "prickly as a hedgehog and touchy as a snapping turtle," he had few close friends in Concord.

Within his lifetime Thoreau published only a few articles and two books, the most important being *Walden* in 1854. *Walden* caused little stir in the literary world when it was first published, receiving better reviews in England than in America.

In his last years Thoreau returned to his father's house to live. He continued taking daily walks into the woods around Concord, studying and collecting nature specimens (although he was by no means a trained naturalist) and writing in his journals. He had no desire to leave Concord, which he considered to be "the most estimable place in all the world."

In his last illness, he was able to say, despite constant pain, "I am enjoying existence as much as ever, and regret nothing." When an aunt asked him if he had made his peace with God, he replied calmly, "I did not know that we had ever quarreled."

Thoreau died on a May morning in 1862. Four-hundred schoolchildren followed his wild-flower-covered casket to the graveyard. Louisa May Alcott later described the scene, "with the birds singing, early violets blooming and pines singing the soft lullaby as if Nature were welcoming her loving son . . ."

For many years after his death, Thoreau's writings were known to only a faithful few. Several books were made from his journals and published posthumously: *The Maine Woods* in 1864, *Cape Cod* in 1865 and *A Yankee in Canada,* 1866. Little by little over the years, Thoreau's reputation grew, finally reaching far beyond the borders of quiet Concord.

Critics began to appreciate Thoreau's vigorous, terse

prose style. Like Emerson, Thoreau was the master of the sentence wrapped around an idea. He cut at each sentence like a sculptor to get the exact form and meaning he wanted from each word. Today Thoreau is considered to be not only one of the best prose writers of all time but also one of America's most original thinkers.

All of Concord, as well as Walden Pond, was the background for Thoreau's writings, but it is the cabin site at Walden Pond that is most visited by Thoreau enthusiasts today. Visitors are often surprised to discover that the pond is not far from Concord, less than a mile away. Thoreau, however, never claimed to live the life of a complete hermit at Walden. He often walked into town from Walden Pond and visited friends.

Today, although a swimming beach and picnic tables have been added, Walden Pond is much as it was when Thoreau knew it, with an Indian path still ringing it. The one-room cabin that Thoreau built about two hundred feet from a cove on the pond's northern shore is long since gone, but the site of the cabin is well-marked.

A replica of the cabin, complete in every detail, may be seen behind Thoreau's Lyceum in Concord, along with reproductions of objects Thoreau made for the hut, including the cane bed and desk at which he wrote. Within the Lyceum, there is a museum area displaying Thoreau memorabilia.

Thoreau left few possessions when he died. What possessions he did have—his bed, desk, snowshoes, surveying equipment, books, his beloved flute—were donated by his sister to the Museum of the Concord Antiquarian Society. They have been placed in a small, simple, slant-ceilinged room on the second floor of the museum.

Thoreau's grave may be visited on the east ridge in Sleepy Hollow Cemetery (off Bedford Street) in a section of the cemetery called Author's Ridge. He is buried near the graves of Nathaniel Hawthorne and the Alcotts. His tombstone is marked simply "Henry."

Location: WALDEN POND AND CABIN SITE. Drive south from Concord on Walden Street (Route 126). After crossing Route 2, and approximately one mile from the center of Concord, is Walden Pond State Reservation. There is a car parking lot in the turn-off just beyond two stone posts and a chained fenced gate. Proceed on foot, following the trail marked with the letter "T." When you first glimpse the Pond on the left after about one-quarter of a mile, the trail will turn right at a granite post and you will be able to see the granite posts that mark the site of the cabin. Small admission charge to Walden Pond State Reservation.

Location: THE THOREAU LYCEUM, 156 Belknap Street, Concord, Massachusetts. Small admission charge. Group rates for students.

Location: MUSEUM OF THE CONCORD ANTIQUARIAN SOCIETY, 1/2 mile southeast on SR 2A, 200 Lexington Road, Concord, Massachusetts. Open daily, summer; weekends only during winter months. Guided Tours. Admission charge.

77

NATHANIEL HAWTHORNE
1804–1864

In 1692 in Salem, Massachusetts, an elderly woman named Rebecca Nurse was accused of witchcraft, as were many other unfortunates in the witchcraft mania that swept the small town. Before Rebecca Nurse was put to death, she placed a curse upon Judge Hathorne who had condemned her.

More than a hundred years later a descendant of the judge, Nathaniel Hawthorne (the author changed the spelling of his last name), found himself wondering if the curse was not still afflicting his family. His father, a sea captain from Salem, had died at sea when Nathaniel was four years old. His mother had withdrawn from society and taken her son to live in South Casco, Maine, supported by the charity of a brother. Here the young Nathaniel led a lonely life, where, he said later, he "first got my cursed habit of solitude."

If his father had lived, young Nathaniel would undoubtedly have been a sea captain, too. Instead he was sent to Bowdoin College, in Maine, where he wrote his mother, "I do not want to be a doctor and live by men's diseases, nor a minister to live by their sins, nor a lawyer to live by their quarrels. So I don't see there is anything left for me but to be an author."

After graduating from college, Hawthorne and his mother returned to Salem. For twelve years he lived the life of a recluse in a small, dark, two-room apartment at 12 Herbert Street, painfully and laboriously teaching himself the writing craft. During those years he wrote in despair to Henry Wadsworth Longfellow, who had been a classmate at college, that he "felt like a man who had somehow put himself into a dungeon and could not find the key to let himself out."

Finally he did manage to have published a few short sketches and, in 1837, a collection of his short stories, called *Twice-Told Tales,* followed by another book of stories, called *The Tales of a Grandfather's Chair.*

The income from his writing, though, was modest and in 1839 he left his life of seclusion and took a job at the Boston Custom House. When he lost that job, he joined the Brook Farm Community in West Roxbury (now part of Newton), Massachusetts. Brook Farm, like Bronson Alcott's Fruitlands, was an attempt by Transcendentalists at communal living. Artists and writers like Hawthorne and Margaret Fuller did farmwork part of the day and then spent the rest of the day discussing life and listening to lectures on philosophy.

Although Hawthorne's experiences at Brook Farm served as a background for one of his later novels, *Blithedale*

Romance, the author did not have the temperament for communal living. Also, he had met and fallen in love with Sophia Peabody, sister of Elizabeth Peabody, who was already gaining fame as an educator and writer.

The young couple was married in 1842 and immediately after the wedding went to live in The Old Manse in Concord. Here, Hawthorne continued his writing and his wife painted. Their's was an idyllic marriage, and life at The Old Manse was, Sophia wrote her sister, "a perfect Eden." A daughter was born, and in 1846 Hawthorne finished a delightful collection of short stories and sketches, called *Mosses from an Old Manse.* After three contented years in Concord, however, Hawthorne was once again forced to seek employment. The position he found as a surveyor at the Custom House in Salem was a dull, dusty job he detested.

Yet it was while he was once again living in Salem, at 14 Mall Street, that Hawthorne wrote his most famous novel, *The Scarlet Letter.* The book, published in 1850, scandalized the citizens of the town of Salem. They resented the satirical comments Hawthorne made about them in the preface of the book, and they were shocked at the subject matter of the book—adultery.

The central character in *The Scarlet Letter,* Hester Prynne, Hawthorne always claimed was based on an actual person, a young, beautiful Puritan woman convicted of adultery and condemned to wear a scarlet letter "A" for the rest of her life. Whether true or not, in the old Park Church Cemetery in Boston can still be seen the gravestone of Elizabeth Pain (e), with a faint A as part of the escutcheon on the tombstone. Elizabeth is supposed to have been the Hester Prynne of *The Scarlet Letter.*

After publication of *The Scarlet Letter,* Hawthorne was no longer welcome in Salem, and the Hawthornes moved to Lenox, Massachusetts, in the lovely Berkshire Mountains. It was while he was living in the Red Cottage in the Berkshires that Hawthorne wrote *The House of the Seven Gables.* Published in 1851, the novel, with touches of the Gothic supernatural, tells of the decay of an old Salem family haunted by a curse, much like the Hawthorne family curse. As a setting for his book, Hawthorne choose an actual house in Salem, the Turner-Ingersoll house. Although Hawthorne, of course, invented many of the incidents and scenes in his novel, the Turner-Ingersoll house, ever since the publication of Hawthorne's novel, has been known as the House of the Seven Gables.

In 1852 the Hawthorne family returned to Concord, purchasing the old Alcott home, "Hillside," which Hawthorne rechristened "Wayside." There was a young son as well as a daughter at Wayside, and Hawthorne, who enjoyed writing stories for his children, wrote *A Wonder Book for Girls and Boys,* and the next year, *Tanglewood Tales for Girls and Boys.*

Hawthorne had many friends in Concord, but he still preferred solitude. He would wander by himself through the fields surrounding Wayside, take boat trips on the Concord River, and, when strangers appeared at the house, retreat to a well-worn path along a ridge behind the house.

For a short time, again for financial reasons, Hawthorne accepted a post as United States Consul in England. During his travels, he secured material for yet another novel (Hawthorne preferred to call them romances), this one set in Italy. The book, published in 1860, was called *The Marble Faun.*

The last years of his life Hawthorne returned to Concord and his beloved Wayside. He withdrew more and more from his friends, building a tower onto the house where he did his writing, with a chair sitting upon a trapdoor in the floor to prevent visitors.

Despite his privacy, his writing did not go well. Financial problems were plaguing him again, as well as ill health. His books, although critically well received—Edgar Allan Poe called Hawthorne "a true master of the short story"—were never financial successes.

On a short trip for his health, Hawthorne died suddenly and was buried near his famous author friends on Author's Ridge at Sleepy Hollow Cemetery at Concord.

All his life, Hawthorne was obsessed with the problems of good and evil, guilt and innocence, and haunted by the feeling that the blood of the martyred Salem witches "had left a stain upon him."

These are the themes that run like a scarlet thread through Hawthorne's writings, the destructive effect of sin upon the lives of men and women, the sin of adultery in *The Scarlet Letter,* the sin of avarice in *The House of the Seven Gables,* the sin of alienation in his short story, "Young Goodman Brown." With his searching insight into the darkness of the human heart, Hawthorne has been called America's first psychological novelist, though he wrote before the science of psychology was founded. Yet he wrote equally well in a light-hearted, affectionate vein in his stories for children, which are still being published and read today.

After Hawthorne's death, his widow continued to live at Wayside. Eventually the house passed through several other hands. One of its more prominent owners was a children's author, Margaret Sidney, who wrote the perennially popular *Five Little Peppers and How They Grew* while living at the Wayside in the 1880s.

In 1965 the house was acquired by the National Park Service. For those who visit it, the wide, rambling house with its varying architectural styles clearly reflects the lives of the different authors who have lived there.

Hawthorne's tower study has been carefully preserved and may be visited by means of a steep, narrow staircase through a trapdoor into the lofty room with its vaulted, painted ceiling. Still part of the room are Hawthorne's ink-stand and bookcase and the high desk at which he wrote, standing up.

The Old Manse at Concord, where Hawthorne brought his bride and they spent their happiest years, may also be visited. A specially lovely view of the house may be seen from a canoe on the Concord River. The Old Manse, once owned by the Emerson family, has changed little from the day when Ralph Waldo Emerson's grandfather watched through his study window the British retreat from the North Bridge. There are still mementos in the house of Hawthorne's occupancy, including several loving inscriptions scratched by Sophia Hawthorne with her diamond ring upon the window panes.

In Salem, Massachusetts, the Custom House where Hawthorne worked and received his inspiration for *The Scarlet Letter* may also be visited, although the office in which Hawthorne worked is no longer "cobwebbed and dingy." It was in a room on the second floor of the Custom House, filled with cobwebs and musty old documents, that Hawthorne discovered the "scarlet and gold embroidered Letter A" and the official document that served as the background for *The Scarlet Letter*.

The House of the Seven Gables is open to the public, including a secret staircase behind the thick, central chimney. The blackened walls of the house seem to reflect its "mysterious and terrible past." On the same ground is Hawthorne's birthplace, which was moved to its present site some years ago.

On Charter Street in Salem is the old cemetery described in Hawthorne's unfinished novels, *Dr. Grimshawe's Secret* and *The Dolliver Romance*. The graves of Hawthorne's ancestors, including Judge Hathorne, may be found here. Near a corner of this cemetery is the family home of Hawthorne's wife. Hawthorne also used the somber Peabody house as a setting in his books. The back door of the house is close to the cemetery, and Hawthorne imagined "that the dead might get out of their graves at night and steal into the house and warm themselves at the fire."

The story of Rebecca Nurse, condemned to death for witchcraft by Hawthorne's ancestor, is told at the Salem Witch Museum, along with stories of the other martyred men and women of Salem.

A replica of the Red Cottage in which Hawthorne lived when he wrote *The House of the Seven Gables* is now a part of the Berkshire Music Center at Tanglewood, Lenox, Massachusetts, and contains practice rooms for faculty and students.

The inspiration for one of Hawthorne's most popular short stories, "The Great Stone Face" is a naturally formed profile of a man's face, forty feet high, on a mountainside in New Hampshire.

Location: THE HOUSE OF THE SEVEN GABLES, 54 Turner Street, Salem, Massachusetts. Admission charge.

Location: HAWTHORNE'S BIRTHPLACE, same site as above, Salem, Massachusetts. Open summers only. Admission charge.

Location: OLD CUSTOM HOUSE, Salem Maritime National Historic Site, Derby Street, at the head of the Old Derby Wharf, Salem, Massachusetts. Guided tours, slide shows. No admission charge.

Location: SALEM WITCH MUSEUM, Main Square, Salem, Massachusetts. Admission charge.

Location: WAYSIDE, ½ mile east on Lexington Road (SR 2A) Concord, Massachusetts. Admission charge.

Location: OLD MANSE, Monument Street, Concord, Massachusetts. Open summers only. Admission charge.

Location: NATHANIEL HAWTHORNE'S GRAVE, Author's Ridge, Sleepy Hollow Cemetery, off Bedford Street, Concord, Massachusetts.

Location: THE GREAT STONE FACE is located west of US 3 near Franconia Notch, above Profile Lake, New Hampshire. The face may best be seen from the east shore of the lake 10 A.M. to sunset.

LOUISA MAY ALCOTT
1832–1888

One of the most visited and beloved literary sites in Concord, Massachusetts, is Orchard House, home of Louisa May Alcott and her *Little Women*. Louisa May Alcott wrote her best-selling novel at a desk that may still be seen in her bedroom on the second floor; and wandering through the rooms and passageways of the house, one is constantly reminded of characters and scenes from the book. For although *Little Women* was written as fiction, it is also autobiographical. The March family in the book were Louisa May Alcott's own family, and the March home is Orchard House.

Orchard House was only one of many homes in which Louisa May Alcott lived. In the first twenty-eight years of her life, the Alcott family moved twenty-nine times. Bronson Alcott, Louisa's father, although much adored by his family, was a dreamer, more versed in new theories of education and Transcendental philosophy than he was in the practical aspects of life, such as supporting a family.

In 1843, Bronson Alcott joined with a group of Transcendentalists—a philosophy that encouraged self-sufficiency —and moved his family to one of America's earliest examples of a commune, called Fruitlands. This experiment in communal living was a disastrous failure, and the Alcott family returned to Concord.

The Alcotts, as usual, had very little money, but they were a close, loving family, held together as much by Mrs. Alcott's practical, unswerving strength as Mr. Alcott's gentle idealism. The Alcotts lived in a home called Hillside, and many of the incidents that happened there, as well as the house itself, were pictured in one of Louisa's later books, *Little Men*.

During the years in Concord, it was Louisa and her mother who worked to support the Alcott family, which included Louisa's three sisters. Bronson Alcott had educated Louisa himself and encouraged her to write, but the money she made from her melodramatic suspense tales was not enough to feed six mouths. Desperately, Louisa tried other ways of making money: domestic service, teaching, sewing, anything to earn the much needed dollars. All the time, though, in whatever moments she could spare from her job, she kept writing. Often she wrote late at night until her right hand became painfully cramped, then she would switch to her left hand because she had patiently taught herself to write with both hands.

Louisa never stopped writing, even during the tragedy of her sister Elizabeth's death in 1858. After this there was still another move for the Alcott family, to Orchard House, once the home of the Thoreau family. An old, dilapidated house with fruit trees scattered around it, the house was affectionately called Apple Slump by Louisa.

To the left of the house, Bronson Alcott built a school of philosophy. Although the school was never a financial success, it did bring many famous lecturers to Concord to speak at the summer sessions.

The Civil War interrupted Louisa's writing career. She immediately volunteered as a nurse when war broke out and was sent to a hospital in Georgetown. Ill health, however, forced her to give up nursing and return to Orchard House and her writing.

In 1865 Louisa made her first trip abroad, as a companion to a wealthy young lady. In Europe she met an attractive young Polish refugee, who was to become the hero, Laurie, in *Little Women*. Marriage, though, was not part of Louisa's plan. "I would rather be a free spinster and paddle my own canoe," she would reply when asked about her single state.

Then in 1868 a Boston publisher asked Louisa if she would be willing to write a book for young girls. As always, in need of cash to support her parents and sisters, Louisa replied, "I'll try." She decided to use her childhood experiences in Concord as the background for the book, and her own family for the characters. Louisa's sisters—cheerful Anna, quiet, shy Elizabeth, and artistic May—became Meg, Beth and Amy March. Mrs. Alcott was Marmee, and Louisa, herself, was the prototype for the quick-tempered, tomboyish, warm-hearted heroine, Jo.

The book was begun in May and finished in July. The original title, *The Pathetic Family,* was changed to *Little Women* by the time the book was published in October.

Much to the publisher's and Louisa's surprise, *Little Women* was an immediate, smashing success from one end of America to the other, not just with girls but with adults as well.

The success of *Little Women* meant the end of money worries for the Alcott family. Louisa quickly followed *Little Women* with more novels: *An Old-Fashioned Girl, Little Men, Eight Cousins,* among others, each book more popular than the one before.

In addition to her writing, Louisa became one of the earliest workers for women's rights. She had learned at first hand the harsh conditions under which young women like herself were forced to work in nineteenth century America, and the injustice of being forced to pay taxes from her meager earnings and yet not be allowed to vote.

During her last years, Louisa spent part of each year in Concord and part of the year writing at an apartment at No. 10 Louisbourg Square in Boston. It was in Boston that she died, just two days after the death of her father. Louisa May Alcott was buried in Concord on the Author's Ridge of Sleepy Hollow Cemetery, with the other literary greats of Concord.

Little Women is no doubt Louisa May Alcott's most popular book. The character of Jo, forever young and forever lovable, has a universal appeal that never dims, because Jo reflects the vitality, compassion and understanding of the author, herself.

Wayside House (called Hillside by the Alcott family when they lived there from 1845 to 1848) is today a literary shrine maintained by the National Park Service. Many of the rooms in the house relate closely to the author, Nathaniel Hawthorne, who later lived in the house, but it was Bronson Alcott who added the west wing, where lay the bedrooms used by Anna and Louisa. The Alcott girls acted out their plays written by Louisa in the roomy barn, and on the stairs of the house.

Orchard House, to which the Alcotts moved in 1858, is a two-story frame cottage filled with fascinating nooks and cranies. Sadly rundown when the Alcotts arrived, the house and grounds were refurbished by Mr. Alcott, and May made decorative panels for the walls. Bronson finally had a library where he could hold long philosophical discussions, and Louisa had her own bedroom on the second floor. Her desk and sheets of manuscripts are still there, along with her ink stand and spectacles, her sleigh bed with a quilt sewn by her mother, a painting of a wise old owl by sister May over the mantel. After Louisa started making money, she renovated Orchard House further, although her own bedroom remained modestly furnished.

The Gothic style, dark wooden building to the left of Orchard House is Bronson Alcott's School of Philosophy. He built it for $512.00 in 1880. It was always a "summer school," with such famous lecturers as Margaret Fuller and Elizabeth Peabody coming to speak on Transcendentalism and education. Recently a summer program of lecturers has started there again. An exhibit about Transcendentalism may be seen within the building.

Fruitlands, the eighteenth century farmhouse where Bronson Alcott established his Utopian commune, is another recently opened museum. It was at Fruitlands that Mrs. Alcott labored—cooking, sewing and cleaning—while the men communed with nature and held their philosophical discussions. It is no wonder that when a visitor asked, "Are there any beasts of burden on the place?" Mrs. Alcott replied grimly, "Only one woman!" Fruitlands has been turned into a museum of the Transcendentalist movement and contains memorabilia of the leaders of this movement.

Location: WAYSIDE, ½ mile east on Lexington Road (SR 2A), Concord, Massachusetts. Admission charge.

Location: ORCHARD HOUSE, 1 mile southeast on Lexington Road (SR 2A) Concord, Massachusetts. Open summers only. Small admission charge.

Location: BRONSON ALCOTT'S SCHOOL OF PHILOSOPHY. Next door to Orchard House. Open summers only. Admission charge to Orchard House includes tour of School of Philosophy. Reservations to attend lectures must be made in advance.

Location: FRUITLANDS MUSEUM, Prospect Hill Road, off Route 110, west from Harvard, Massachusetts. Open summers only. Small admission charge.

Location: LOUISA MAY ALCOTT'S GRAVE, Author's Ridge, Sleepy Hollow Cemetery, off Bedford Street, Concord, Massachusetts. Louisa's grave has a star over it, commemorating her service as a Civil War nurse, and the tombstone is marked simply L.M.A.

CONCORD AUTHORS

FROM THE MIDDLE 1800s UNTIL ALMOST THE END OF THE CENTURY, THE SMALL TOWN OF CONCORD, MASSACHUSETTS, WAS AN IMPORTANT CENTER OF LITERARY LIFE IN AMERICA. MANY GREAT AND NEAR-GREAT LITERARY FIGURES LIVED IN CONCORD. THEIR INFLUENCE UPON THE LITERARY HISTORY OF AMERICA STRETCHED FAR BEYOND THE TOWN'S BOUNDARIES.

Literary map of Concord, Massachusetts.

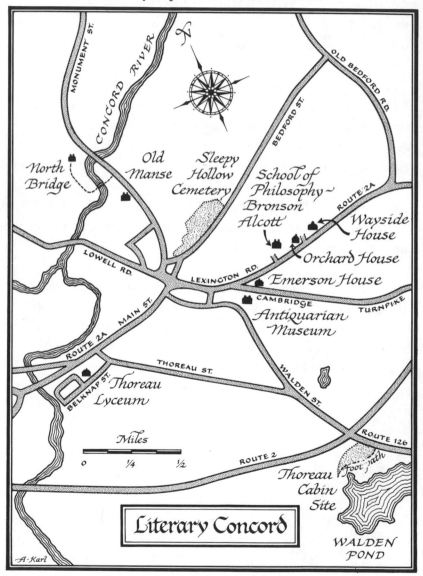

Ralph Waldo Emerson was one of the most important literary figures in Concord. It was Emerson who introduced the new ideas of Transcendentalism in his first collection of essays, *Nature*. Transcendentalism stressed individual self-reliance, appealing to many young people of Emerson's day who made pilgrimages to his square white frame house in Concord. Emerson's home in Concord is open in the summers to the public.
COURTESY RALPH WALDO EMERSON HOME

The Old Manse, overlooking the Concord River, is one of the most familiar literary sites in Concord. It was in the study of the Old Manse that Emerson wrote his first collection of essays. In the same study, but with his desk facing the wall so he would not be distracted by the view, Nathaniel Hawthorne wrote his *Mosses from an Old Manse*. PHOTO BY RICHARD LYNCH

The town of Concord was also the site of one of the first battles of the Revolutionary War. On the base of the famous Minuteman Statue at North Bridge is a poem, "Concord Hymn," written by Ralph Waldo Emerson, commemorating "the shot heard round the world." Emerson's grandfather had watched through the study windows of the Old Manse the British retreat from the North Bridge. PHOTO BY RICHARD LYNCH

Walden Pond, just a mile out of Concord, was where another Concord author, Henry Thoreau, lived for two years alone in a small cabin. He kept a daily journal of his experiences, which, in time, became one of America's most original and influential books, *Walden*. The site of Thoreau's cabin at Walden Pond is outlined by cement posts. PHOTO BY RICHARD LYNCH

The small cabin in which Henry Thoreau lived by Walden Pond no longer exists. However, Thoreau left such a detailed description of the one-room dwelling in his journal that it has been possible for an exact replica to be built. Thoreau's cabin and contents may be seen at the Thoreau Lyceum, Concord. The few possessions Thoreau left at his death are housed at the Antiquarian Museum, Concord. COURTESY THOREAU LYCEUM

One of the most popular writers of Concord was Louisa May Alcott. Her book, *Little Women*, based upon her experiences growing up in Concord, has never been out of print. Jo March in *Little Women* was modeled upon Louisa, and her three sisters served as prototypes of the characters Meg, Beth and Amy March. COURTESY ORCHARD HOUSE

Probably the most popular literary site in Concord is Orchard House, home of Louisa May Alcott. Many scenes from the book *Little Women* took place in this house, and in Wayside House next door, where the Alcott family also lived at one time. Both homes have been restored and are open to the public. PHOTO BY AUTHOR

Nathaniel Hawthorne's best known book, *The Scarlet Letter,* is supposedly based upon the life of an actual young, beautiful Puritan girl, convicted of adultery and condemned to wearing a scarlet letter A for the rest of her life. In the Old Park Cemetery in Boston may be seen the gravestone of Elizabeth Pain(e), who is believed to be the Hester Prynne of *The Scarlet Letter.* A faint "A" may still be seen as part of the engraving on her tombstone. PHOTO BY AUTHOR

Although the author Nathaniel Hawthorne lived for many years in Concord, first at the Old Manse and then at Wayside, he was actually born in Salem, Massachusetts. The House of Seven Gables, shown left, which was the setting for Hawthorne's novel of the same name, still stands in Salem. The seventeenth century house with its "mysterious and terrible past" is a major theme in the book. COURTESY HOUSE OF SEVEN GABLES

Rebecca Nurse, before she was put to death as a witch in 1692, placed a curse upon the judge who condemned her. The judge was an ancestor of author Nathaniel Hawthorne. All his life Hawthorne felt that the blood of the martyred Salem witches "had left a stain upon him," and the themes of sin and guilt run through his writings. Scenes from the Salem witch trials, such as the one shown at left, may be seen at the Witch Museum in Salem, Massachusetts. COURTESY SALEM WITCH MUSEUM

EDGAR ALLAN POE
1809–1849

The small, isolated, low-eaved farm cottage sat in the midst of a grove of cherry trees. Sometimes late in the evening the door of the cottage would open and a man with a pale, intelligent face and lustrous eyes would leave the cottage. Wrapped in a dark greatcape, he would take long moonlit walks through the countryside. It was during these midnight walks that the poet and short story writer, Edgar Allan Poe, composed several of his poems and plotted many of his terror-filled short stories.

Ironically, Edgar Allan Poe's own life was as filled with horror and mystery as the stories and poems he created, with tragedy "following fast and followed faster." After the death of his mother and the desertion of his father, Poe, as a young boy, was reared by the wealthy John Allan family of Richmond, Virginia. The sensitive, handsome young lad led a life of pampered luxury, a life that ended abruptly after Mrs. Allan's death and Mr. Allan's remarriage.

When he was dismissed from the University of Virginia because of his gambling debts, and disinherited by John Allan, the young Poe proudly struck out on his own. He attempted a military career, first as an enlisted man, then as an officer at West Point, from which institution he deliberately got himself expelled in 1831.

Previously, when he was only eighteen years old, Poe had published his first brief book of poetry, *Tamerlane and Other Poems*. Now he published several more books of poetry, which brought him little, if any, financial returns. For one of his most famous poems, "The Raven," the poet received the grand sum of $10.00. Nevertheless, Poe was determined to become a writer. Living in Baltimore with an aunt, Marie Clemm, and her young daughter, Virginia, he began writing short stories, tales of the grotesque and the macabre that set the style for his later works of fiction.

In 1836 in Richmond, Virginia, Poe married his teenage cousin, Virginia, a marriage that was to bring him both happiness and more tragedy. In order to support his young wife, who was stricken with tuberculosis shortly after their marriage, Poe accepted editorial positions on various magazines and newspapers in Richmond, Philadelphia and New York.

Poe showed great skill as an editor, particularly as a knowledgeable, if perhaps too merciless, literary critic, which made him a great many enemies in the literary world. Poe, himself, finally achieved a small measure of fame in 1839 with a collection of short stories, *Tales of the Grotesque and Arabesque,* and his first collection of poetry to win recognition, *The Raven and Other Poems*, published in 1845.

Despite the publication of these works and the critical praise they received, particularly in France, the lack of fame and financial success, to which he felt himself entitled, turned Poe into an embittered, frustrated man. He turned more and more to alcohol and drugs to ease his frustration and unhappiness. There were, in fact, only brief periods of Poe's life when he wasn't fighting off poverty, alcoholism and melancholia, yet he still managed to turn out a great deal of competent work, which at times verged on genius.

In 1846, when a magazine he had tried to start, failed, Poe moved his wife and her mother to a small cottage on what was then the outskirts of New York City. During the bitterly cold winter of 1847, part of the furniture in the house had to be pawned for food, and in her unheated tiny bedroom, Virginia died, wrapped in her husband's old great-cape, with her faithful tortoise cat, Catarina, by her side.

After his wife's death, Poe suffered a physical and mental breakdown. He continued writing intermittently and made a nostalgic visit to his boyhood home in Richmond, finally dying himself two years later under mysterious circumstances in Baltimore.

Only four mourners appeared at Poe's funeral, and it was twenty-seven years before a monument was placed near the grave of one of America's most tragic literary figures.

Unlike contemporary writers of his time, Poe did not choose to reflect the familiar landscape of America in his works. Instead he wrote of the unfamiliar, dark and often haunted landscape of the human heart. In his poetry, also unlike other poets of his day, Poe did not feel it necessary to set forth some great moral lesson. He believed that poems should be brief, their chief aim "beauty, not truth." It was the emotional and musical effect of sound and rhythm that

Poe stressed in such poems as "Ulalume," and "The Bells." In listening to the latter poem, one can almost hear the tinkle of the bells behind the sounds of the words, the lilting rhythm.

It was in the field of the short story, however, that Poe was, and still is, considered the master. Just as his poems, "The Raven" and "Annabel Lee" aroused emotions of terror and grief, so Poe's short stories were deliberately written to create an intense emotional effect on the reader. Stories like "The Tell-tale Heart," "The Pit and the Pendulum," and "The Fall of the House of Usher" produce the single emotional effect of horror. The reader feels that he is actually experiencing the same spine-tingling terror that the character in the story is feeling.

In addition to writing America's first great horror tales, Poe's short stories of mystery—"The Gold Bug," and "Murders in the Rue Morgue," to name only two—have fascinated and puzzled readers for generations. Poe's use of the amateur detective who solves a crime that has defeated all the efforts of the police influenced countless generations of mystery writers. Poe, in fact, created the modern detective story.

Surprisingly, for a man who accumulated few possessions in his lifetime, living mostly in poverty, Poe has four separate literary sites connected with his life.

The home where Poe lived from 1832–1835, after he left the Army and went to stay with his Aunt Clemm, has been preserved and maintained by the Edgar Allan Poe Society of Baltimore. Poe called this two-story brick house, "the little house on the lowly street with the lovely name, Amity." Poe probably used the sparsely furnished attic bedroom as his room. Here he wrote some of his first short stories. An award of $50.00 was given to him for his short story, "Ms Found in a Bottle," in 1833 at the Latrobe House. The house stands on the south side of Mulberry Street in Baltimore, a plaque marking the spot where Poe received the award.

Poe's grandfather was a general in the Revolutionary War and Poe was buried beside his grandfather in Westminster Presbyterian Graveyard, a few blocks from the Amity Street home in Baltimore. Legend has it that when Poe lived at Amity Street, he was inspired to write the first of his macabre tales by wandering around the Westminster Graveyard at night.

While working as an editor and literary critic in Philadelphia, 1839–44, Poe and his wife lived for several years in a house known as Spring Garden Cottage. Virginia had a harp that she played as she sang with a "voice of wonderful sweetness." Poe wrote and entertained visitors in the front parlor, which had a black slate mantel and red carpet—but no mirrors. Poe would not allow mirrors in the house. It was in this house that Poe wrote the first draft of "The Raven" and several mystery stories, including "The Gold Bug." (The background of "The Gold Bug" is Sullivan's Island near Charleston, South Carolina, where Poe was stationed as an enlisted man. The mysterious "gold bug" is a combination of two species of beetles that can be found on Sullivan's Island.)

The small farm cottage in New York where Poe, his wife and his mother-in-law lived from 1846–1849 was once surrounded by open fields. It is now surrounded by urban sprawl. The neat little cottage contains a dark, low-ceilinged parlor, a tiny bedroom, almost filled by the bed upon which Virginia died, and the garret room at the head of a narrow staircase where Poe wrote "The Bells" and, after Virginia's death, "Annabel Lee." In visiting the cottage, one can al-most sense the presence of its one-time occupants: cheerful, talkative Aunt Clemm in her worn dress of rusty black; Virginia with her glossy black hair and wan face; the ele-gant, brilliant-eyed Poe; and perhaps even the ghost of the loyal Catarina!

Although Edgar Allan Poe spent more time in Rich-mond, Virginia, than any other city, there is no actual home site of Poe's in the city. However, the Edgar Allan Poe Museum complex in Richmond is a treasury of documents, autographed manuscripts, pictures and relics of Poe, includ-ing the few worldly possessions he left at his death.

The Raven Room of the museum has an unusual col-lection of illustrations of Poe's famous poem, done by the artist James Carling in the 1880s.

A slide show of Poe's life is presented daily.

Location: EDGAR ALLAN POE HOUSE AND MUSEUM, 203 N. Amity Street, Baltimore, Maryland. The house may easily be reached from the 900 block of West Lexington Street. Evening group candlelit tours with readings from Poe's works may be arranged. Open Saturday afternoons. Small admission charge.

Location: EDGAR ALLAN POE HOUSE, 530 North Seventh Street, Philadelphia, Pa. Small admission charge.

Location: EDGAR ALLAN POE COTTAGE, Poe Park, Grand Concourse and East Kingsbridge Road, the Bronx, New York. By automobile, take Bronx River Parkway to Fordham Road, North on East Kingsbridge Road. The cottage may also be reached by Rapid Transit and bus. Open weekends only. Guided tours. No admission charge.

Location: EDGAR ALLAN POE MUSEUM, 1914–16 East Main Street, Richmond, Virginia. Small admission charge.

HENRY WADSWORTH
LONGFELLOW
1807–1882

Concord, Massachusetts, was not the only literary center in nineteenth century America. The nearby towns of Cambridge and Boston also played an important role in America's literary history. One house, in particular, was the center of literary life in Cambridge, just as Ralph Waldo Emerson's home was the center of literary life in Concord. Called the Craigie House, it was the headquarters for General Washington for ten months during the Revolutionary War. In the mid-nineteenth century, Craigie House was the home of America's most popular and beloved poet—Henry Wadsworth Longfellow.

Longfellow, born and educated in Maine, came to Cambridge when he was 29 years old to serve as a professor of modern languages at Harvard College. His first wife had died while they were traveling abroad, and Longfellow came to the Craigie House to rent bachelor quarters. At first the widow Craigie, thinking that Longfellow with his flowered vest and flowing hair was a student, turned him away. When she learned, however, that he was a professor, she let him rent the two rooms on the second floor that had been the personal quarters of General Washington.

Although Longfellow was a conscientious teacher, his first love was writing. In 1842 he wrote *Ballads and Other Poems,* which included several poems that became so popular they could be recited from memory by almost every schoolchild in America during Longfellow's day. Two of these poems were: "The Village Blacksmith" and "The Wreck of the Hesperus."

Then, after a seven year courtship, Longfellow married the wealthy daughter of a Boston merchant, who gave the couple Craigie House as a wedding present. The marriage was blissfully happy. Craigie House soon became the gathering place for all the well-known literary figures in the area, including Nathaniel Hawthorne, Henry Thoreau and Ralph Waldo Emerson from Concord—although Emerson and Thoreau did not quite approve of the luxurious comforts of Craigie House.

Within Cambridge, itself, a literary circle was formed that had among its members James Russell Lowell, Oliver Wendell Holmes, Margaret Fuller and Richard Henry Dana. In time, this Cambridge-Boston literary group started their own magazine, the *Atlantic Monthly,* which is still being published today.

After his marriage, Longfellow continued his heavy teaching schedule at Harvard. More and more, though, he had become interested in writing historical narrative poems, poems that told a story as well as gave historical information about a people or country. Among the ones he wrote with an American background were: *Evangeline* (1847), *The Song of Hiawatha* (1855), and *The Courtship of Miles Standish* (1858). Each of these poems is based upon some actual or mythical event in American history. Although the historical facts in Longfellow's poems are not always accurate —after all, Longfellow had never met an Indian like Hiawatha or a young Acadian woman like Evangeline—nevertheless he quite literally, with his poems, "created an American past."

Accurate or not, Longfellow's poems were enormously popular, the best-sellers of their day. Over 15,000 copies of *The Courtship of Miles Standish* were sold the first day of publication. By 1854, Longfellow was able to resign from Harvard and devote his full time to writing poetry.

There were five children at Craigie House now, children who inspired another popular poem, "The Children's Hour." Then tragedy struck the Longfellow family. Mrs. Longfellow was killed in 1861 when her dress accidentally caught fire in the parlor of Craigie House.

Longfellow never completely recovered from the loss of his wife, but took refuge in his work. In 1863 he finished writing another collection of story-poems, *Tales of a Wayside Inn,* which included one of his most famous, "The Midnight Ride of Paul Revere."

By the time of his death at Craigie House in 1882, Longfellow was the most popular poet in America. His 75th birthday was celebrated in every schoolhouse in America, and when he visited Europe, it was like a royal tour. After his death, a bust of the poet was placed in the Poet's Corner of Westminster Abbey in London, England, the only American poet ever to be so honored.

Longfellow's popularity is not easy to understand in our day. His poetry seems too sentimental and "preachy." In that respect, though, Longfellow was simply reflecting the tastes of the nineteenth century American reading public, who liked their poetry with simple images and rhymes that were easy to memorize. For all the simplicity of his poems, Longfellow never wrote an awkward or unmusical line, and he had a talent for telling a story, such as "The Midnight Ride of Paul Revere," in verse that "races and rings."

Despite the fact that much of the American history Longfellow immortalized in his poems was more folklore than history, Longfellow often used actual settings for his narrative poems.

The Wayside Inn from Longfellow's Tales of the same name is still an inn, serving wayfarers much as it did in Longfellow's day, when it was called The Red Horse Inn. Longfellow and his friends would often visit the inn in the summer, and sitting by the broad hearth with great beams overhead, tell stories. After the publication of Longfellow's *Tales of a Wayside Inn,* the inn changed its name to Wayside Inn. Today, on the first floor of the inn there are exhibition rooms with replicas of the people and furnishings Longfellow mentioned in his various tales.

Paul Revere's home may be visited in Boston, as well as the Old North Church. It was from a window of the steeple of this church that the signal lanterns flashed, which supposedly started Paul Revere on his famous ride to warn his countrymen that the British were coming.

John Alden and Priscilla Mullins, whose courtship was described by Longfellow in *The Courtship of Miles Standish,* are well represented in the Plymouth National Wax Museum, Plymouth, Massachusetts. John and Priscilla were

Pilgrim ancestors of Longfellow. They actually did marry, although the courtship described in the poem is imaginary. The John Alden home, where the Aldens last lived, the Old Burying Ground where they are buried, and the Miles Standish monument are all located at Duxbury, Massachusetts.

For his poem, *The Song of Hiawatha,* Longfellow was inspired by a picture of the Laughing Water Falls in Minneapolis, Minnesota. The falls are today part of a local park, called Minnehaha Park. Within the park is a bronze statue of Hiawatha, the mythical super-hero of the Ojibway tribe, carrying his beloved Minnehaha, or Laughing Water, in his arms.

The tragic story of the Acadian people, French colonists who were uprooted from their homes in Canada in 1755 and transplanted to Louisiana, is told in Longfellow's long poem, *Evangeline.* The heroine is based upon a real French girl, named Emmeline, who was separated from her lover by the move and never gave up searching for him. In Longfellow's poem, he is an old man when she finds him and he dies in her arms. In actual fact, Emmeline found her sweetheart much earlier, married to another girl, and died of a broken heart. In the village of St. Martinsville on Bayou Teche, Louisiana, there is a statue of Evangeline from Longfellow's poem beside the grave of the broken-hearted Emmeline. Many descendants of the Acadians, called "cajuns," still live in the Bayou Teche area of Louisiana today.

"The Wreck of the Hesperus" was based upon an actual shipwreck, which took place in 1839 on a reef called Norman's Woe, off Gloucester, Massachusetts.

Although Longfellow spent most of his adult years in Cambridge, he always returned to his boyhood home in

Maine for a few weeks each summer. The Longfellow home there is maintained by the Maine Historical Society and contains many mementos of the poet's life, particularly relating to his childhood and boyhood in the house.

The Longfellow-Craigie home in Cambridge would be rich in history even if Longfellow had not lived there. The original Tory owner was forced to flee the country at the outbreak of the Revolution, and General Washington used the house as his headquarters. There is little left to show that Washington once slept there. Instead the home is almost exactly the same as it was when the poet, his wife and children filled the rooms with laughter, music and hospitality. Longfellow did most of his writing in the study on the first floor at an old-fashioned folding desk, or at a standing desk by the window, so the poet could look across the meadows to the Charles River as he worked. Near the fireplace is an armchair made out of the wood of the "spreading chestnut tree" under which the Cambridge village smithy stood, as described in Longfellow's poem. The chair was presented to Longfellow by the children of Cambridge.

Above the study was the playroom for the Longfellow children, "as noisy as young lions," but Longfellow never minded. He allowed the children to play marbles in a corner of the study as he worked and kept pieces of candy for them in his desk.

In 1973 the National Park Service took over the Longfellow home and eventually all eighteen rooms on the three floors will be open to the public.

Location: THE WAYSIDE INN is midway between Boston and Worcester, 2 miles west off US 20 on Boston Post Road,

South Sudbury, Massachusetts. Small admission charge to exhibit rooms.

Location: THE WADSWORTH-LONGFELLOW HOME, 487 Congress Street, Portland, Maine. Open summers only. Small admission charge.

Location: LONGFELLOW NATIONAL HISTORIC SITE (The Longfellow–Craigie Home), 105 Brattle Street, Cambridge, Massachusetts. Small admission charge.

LITERATURE AT MID-CENTURY

BY THE MIDDLE OF THE NINETEENTH CENTURY, AMERICAN LIT-
ERATURE HAD MOVED IN MANY DIRECTIONS. THE POET LONG-
FELLOW, WHOSE WORKS WERE IMMENSELY POPULAR, WAS THE
CENTER OF AN ACTIVE GROUP OF IMPORTANT WRITERS IN
BOSTON. BUT OTHER AUTHORS WHOSE WORKS WERE NOT SO
POPULAR, LIKE POE AND MELVILLE, WERE BEGINNING TO IN-
TRODUCE WHOLLY NEW IDEAS ABOUT WHAT LITERATURE WAS
AND HOW IT SHOULD BE WRITTEN.

One of the most brilliant, as well as the most attacked and defiant, authors among the New England
writers of the nineteenth century was a woman:
Margaret Fuller (1810–1850). Her book, *Woman
in the Nineteenth Century* (1845), with its uncompromising stand for women's equal rights,
caused a storm of controversy, as did her writings
against slavery, harsh treatment of mill workers and
maltreatment of Indians. In addition, she was also
the first woman editor of an important literary magazine, the first woman to serve as a foreign correspondent and the first professional literary critic
of either sex in the United States. Married to the
Marquis Angelo Ossoli in 1847, she fought beside
him in the bloody Italian Revolution of 1848. The
couple and their child drowned on their return voyage to America when their ship sank off Fire Island,
Long Island. COURTESY DICTIONARY OF AMERICAN
PORTRAITS

Almost all the great literary figures of New England, as well as
famous people from all over the world, visited the study, below, in
the Cambridge home of poet, Henry Wadsworth Longfellow.
Longfellow's story-poems, such as *The Song of Hiawatha* and
The Midnight Ride of Paul Revere, had enormous popular appeal,
even if they weren't always historically accurate. Longfellow's
home, for a time the headquarters of General Washington during
the Revolutionary War, is today maintained as a National Historic
Site. COURTESY NATIONAL PARK SERVICE

Edgar Allan Poe overturned tradition by creating poems that existed only for their beauty. He also broke new ground in the field of the short story, writing mystery and horror tales that influenced generations of writers.
COURTESY LIBRARY OF CONGRESS

It was on this bed in a small, unheated room of the Poe cottage that Poe's young wife Virginia died in the bitterly cold winter of 1847. In her memory, Poe wrote the poem, "Annabel Lee." The shock of losing his wife drove the poet further into drugs, alcoholism, melancholia and finally death two years later in Baltimore, Maryland. PHOTO BY AUTHOR

This romanticized etching by F. W. Mielatz of Edgar Allan Poe's home is a far cry from the cottage surroundings as they appear today in the Bronx, New York. In Poe's day, however, the cottage was in the country and the poet delighted in taking long walks at midnight through the surrounding fields. In the garret of this house, now a museum to his memory, Poe wrote such famous poems as "The Bells" and "Annabel Lee." COURTESY METROPOLITAN MUSEUM OF ART

Herman Melville started out writing adventure tales of the South Pacific and ended up writing the greatest sea story of them all, Moby Dick. Readers accustomed to his light adventure novels, however, found Moby Dick and Melville's later books difficult to understand. Melville died many years before he was recognized as one of America's most gifted writers. COURTESY THE BERKSHIRE ATHENAEUM PITTSFIELD, MASSACHUSETTS

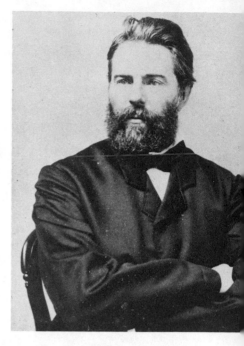

The old Seaman's Bethel, or whaleman's chapel (shown below), at New Bedford, Massachusetts, is the setting for the opening scene of Herman Melville's powerful novel, Moby Dick. The whaling museums at New Bedford and nearby Nantucket give an exciting picture of what life must have been like aboard the Pequod, the whaling ship Melville vividly describes in Moby Dick. COURTESY NEW BEDFORD AREA CHAMBER OF COMMERCE

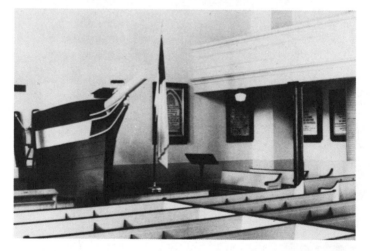

HARRIET BEECHER STOWE
1811-1896

When President Abraham Lincoln was introduced to a short, plump woman at the White House during the Civil War, he is said to have remarked, "So this is the little woman who made this big war."

Whether the incident is true or not, it is certainly true that New England author Harriet Beecher Stowe had written a spectacularly successful anti-slavery book called *Uncle Tom's Cabin*. No other American novel has been so directly responsible for changing the course of human events. And no other book by an American author has been so widely translated and read as Mrs. Stowe's novel.

That Harriet Beecher Stowe hated slavery is not surprising. Her father was the much respected Calvinist minister, Lyman Beecher, and Harriet grew up in Litchfield, Connecticut, listening to him thunder sermons against slavery from his pulpit. Then in 1832, the Beecher family, with 21-year-old Harriet, moved west to Lane Theological Seminary in Cincinnati, Ohio.

It was in Cincinnati that Harriet married the Reverend Calvin Stowe. And it was in Cincinnati, just across the river from the slave state of Kentucky, that she heard and saw at first hand the evils and tragedies caused by slavery. The Seminary itself was a "hot bed of abolitionism" and was occasionally even used as a station on the Underground Railroad, spiriting escaped slaves north.

However, it wasn't until the Stowes moved to Brunswick, Maine, in 1850 that Harriet Stowe determined to write a book "to make the whole nation feel what an accursed thing slavery is." She wrote at the kitchen table at night when her six children were asleep, using brown wrapping paper when she ran out of writing paper. It took her a year to finish the book, and when it was completed, she was sure she had failed, "that nobody would hear, nobody would read, nobody would pity."

She could not have been more mistaken. In 1852 *Uncle Tom's Cabin* made publishing history, not only in America but around the world. A million and a half copies were sold in England alone the first year. In the United States the publisher kept three presses running twenty-four hours a day to answer the demands for the book.

Northern city dwellers and farmers, shopkeepers and factory workers—many of whom had never met a black person—read of the villainous overseer, Simon Legree, the saintly, martyred Uncle Tom, the struggle of the slave couple, George and Eliza, to reach freedom, and were moved to tears and anger against southern slaveholders. For the first time in American literature, black men and women were presented as heroic characters in a book; Mrs. Stowe made her readers feel, as no one had ever done before, how the horror of slavery degraded both the slave and the slaveholder. A popular stage play made from the book brought even more converts to the abolitionists' cause.

Contemporary critics in the North praised the book, calling it "the most valuable addition that America has made to English literature." In the South, though, the book was often banned, or publicly burned, with critics decrying the fact that Mrs. Stowe had never actually lived in the South, and so had no first-hand knowledge of slave life.

After the success of *Uncle Tom's Cabin,* Mrs. Stowe never stopped writing, turning out almost a book a year. The one other book that she wrote with a black as her main character, *Dred* (1856), was not as popularly received as *Uncle Tom's Cabin.*

In her later years Mrs. Stowe traveled a good deal, taking several triumphant tours of Europe. *Uncle Tom's Cabin* had been translated into thirty-seven languages, so she was well-known almost everywhere she went. She lived for a while in Florida, but finally bought a home and settled permanently in Hartford, Connecticut.

In her later books, she used the New England scene as settings for her books, often basing them on her and her husband's experiences growing up in New England. Some critics consider these later books to be better written than *Uncle Tom's Cabin,* catching the humor, spirit and color of early New England life.

Mrs. Stowe died quietly at her home in Hartford in her 85th year, and to the end of her life, she insisted that it was God, and not she, who had written her world-famous novel; that *Uncle Tom's Cabin* had "come" to her in visions.

However it was written, *Uncle Tom's Cabin,* with its Victorian writing style and melodramatic plot, is considered today to be more a literary "oddity" than great literature. Yet, there are many scenes within the novel that have a vitality and power that grip and hold the emotions of the reader and are not easily forgotten.

The home where the Beechers lived when the author first moved to Cincinnati was maintained, until recently, as a museum to Mrs. Stowe and the history of black men and women in the United States. Today the Stowe home is used as a community center with a small exhibit area relating to Mrs. Stowe and the historical significance of the house.

The home in Brunswick, Maine, where *Uncle Tom's Cabin* was written was also, for a short time earlier, the dwelling place of authors Henry Wadsworth Longfellow and Nathaniel Hawthorne, when they were students at nearby Bowdoin College. Today the Brunswick home of Mrs. Stowe is a National Historic Landmark and a charming inn. However Mrs. Stowe, who was a teetotaler, would be shocked to discover that the Victorian-style tavern attached to the inn is called Harriet's Place!

From 1873 until her death, Mrs. Stowe lived at a home she had built at Nook Farm, in Hartford, Connecticut, next door to the home of another famous author, Mark Twain. In addition to writing her many books, Mrs. Stowe took an active interest in interior decoration and painting. She and her older sister, Catharine Beecher, one of America's most important early educators, wrote *The American Woman's Home.* This was the first book written in America on home economics and interior decoration. Many of the ideas incorporated in this book were used by Mrs. Stowe in her Hartford home.

In the small sitting room, next to her unusual ten-sided bedroom, Mrs. Stowe did much of her writing, including *Poganuc People,* based on her childhood in New England. From Mrs. Stowe's bedroom window, she could see the Mark Twain house. In her last years, the two authors became good friends, sharing a mutual bond of humor. Twain reported gleefully that even when Mrs. Stowe was slipping gently into an absent-minded old age, she would still "slip up behind a person who was deep in dreams and fetch a war whoop that would jump that person out of his clothes."

The Stowe and Twain Homes are part of the literary community, known as Nook Farm, and both homes are open to the public.

It is not known which plantation Mrs. Stowe used as the setting for her plantation in *Uncle Tom's Cabin,* whether it was the Shelby plantation she visited briefly in Kentucky, or a plantation her brother visited in the Cane River country of Louisiana. Although there are many typical antebellum restored plantations in the south that are open to the public, the slave cabins, if they still exist on the plantations, reflect only a prettified version of what life was like for blacks during slave days.

To gain an understanding of slave life in the United States, and a background for Mrs. Stowe's novel, a better source would be: the DuSable Museum of African-American History, 3806 South Michigan Avenue, Chicago, Illinois; Museum of Afro-American History, Smith Court, Beacon Hill, Boston, Massachusetts; The Old Slave Mart Museum, 6 Chalmers Street, Charleston, South Carolina; and the occasional exhibits on slavery shown at the Anacostia Neighborhood Museum, 2405 Martin Luther King, Jr. Avenue, S.E., Washington, D.C.

The character of Uncle Tom in Mrs. Stowe's novel was supposedly based on a real slave, Josiah Henson. Unlike the character in the novel, Josiah did not die in slavery but escaped to Canada, setting up a community in Dresden, Canada, where fugitive slaves could support themselves. The Dresden settlement with Uncle Tom's Cabin Museum has been restored and may be visited.

Location: STOWE HOME COMMUNITY CENTER, 2950 Gilbert Avenue, Cincinnati, Ohio. No admission charge.

Location: HARRIET BEECHER STOWE HOUSE, 63 Federal Street, Brunswick, Maine. Now a commercial inn.

Location: HARRIET BEECHER STOWE HOUSE, Nook Farm, 77 Forest Street, Hartford, Connecticut. Admission charge.

Location: UNCLE TOM'S CABIN MUSEUM, Highway 21, Dresden, Ontario, Canada, approximately 60 miles east of Detroit, Michigan. Admission charge.

FREDERICK DOUGLASS
1817–1895

The handsome two story brick house called Cedar Hill stands on a hillside estate overlooking Washington, D.C. Cedar Hill is not only one of America's most interesting literary sites, but an important historical site as well. For Cedar Hill was the home of Frederick Douglass, the remarkable man who started life as an illiterate slave and became the most influential black man in nineteenth century America. It was Douglass's powerful anti-slavery writings that helped bring him to this position of leadership.

Douglass was not the first black person to fight slavery with the pen. In colonial America Phillis Wheatley had protested against slavery in her poetry; and as early as 1829, a free black man, David Walker, wrote a famous *Appeal*, calling upon slaves to revolt against their masters. During the following years, as more and more black men and women escaped north, they began writing and publishing books about their experiences in slavery. Those who could not write themselves told their stories to members of Abolitionist Societies, who wrote them down and saw that they were published. Hundreds of such books were published in the years before the Civil War, stirring the conscience of the North against slavery.

Most of the authors of these slave narratives are all but forgotten today, but Frederick Douglass and the autobiography of his life have become an important part of America's literary heritage.

As a young slave in Maryland, Douglass led a half-starved, brutalized existence. Always rebellious, he was passed from master to master, each new owner attempting to but never succeeding in breaking his spirit. The only happy days in those years were those he spent working for the Auld family in Baltimore, where he was taught to read and write by Mrs. Auld, even though teaching a slave was against the law.

At the age of sixteen, young Frederick was returned by the Aulds to his old master. He tried to escape but his plan failed. He was then sent to work in the shipyards of Baltimore, where he secretly and laboriously continued to teach himself to read and write. When he was twenty-one, he again attempted to escape and this time succeeded.

Frederick Douglass, however, was not content with just achieving freedom for himself. He wanted all black men and women in America to be free. He began speaking at anti-slavery meetings in Massachusetts, although he knew by appearing in public, he faced the danger of recapture. In time he became such a polished, effective speaker that members of his audience doubted he had ever been a slave. To answer these critics, Douglass wrote in 1845 his autobiography called *Narrative of the Life of Frederick Douglass, an American Slave*. The book became so widely known and read that Douglass was finally forced to flee the country in order to avoid being returned south as an escaped slave.

In 1847 his freedom was bought by friends in Great Britain, and he returned to America, settling in Rochester, New York. There he began publishing a newspaper, called *The North Star*, in which he continued his fight for the abolition of slavery. Although there were many other black authors in the abolitionist cause, none wrote as effectively as Douglass. And with the possible exception of the ex-slave woman, Sojourner Truth, none could so skillfully stir an audience to righteous wrath against slavery.

After the Civil War, Douglass held many important government positions, but he never gave up the fight for full equality, not only for black people, but for American women, who, like blacks, were also denied their civil rights.

In 1881 Douglass wrote a second autobiography, *The Life and Times of Frederick Douglass*, which, like Benjamin Franklin's *Autobiography*, is considered by scholars to be one of the classics of American literature.

Douglass spent his later years at Cedar Hill, a spacious brick home, which he purchased in 1877. For many years after his death in 1895, the home was neglected, but through the combined efforts of the National Association of Colored Women's Club, the Douglass Memorial Association and the Federal Government, Cedar Hill is today a National Shrine. The house was completely refurbished and opened to the public in 1972.

Cedar Hill is decorated just as it was when Frederick Douglass lived there, including the library where he worked, his original desk, his canes, and many other personal possessions that were part of his life at Cedar Hill.

Location: CEDAR HILL, the home of Frederick Douglass, 1411 W Street, SE, Washington, D.C. may best be reached by crossing the 11th Street (Anacostia) Bridge to Good Hope Road, turning left on Good Hope Road to 14th Street, and right on 14th Street to W Street. The home is on top of the hill at 14th and W Streets SE. Public transportation is also available. Free guided tours. No admission charge.

ABRAHAM LINCOLN
1809–1865

On November 19, 1863, the President of the United States spoke at the consecration of a military cemetery in Pennsylvania, near one of the bloodiest battlefields of the Civil War. The speech of only ten sentences, spoken in less than five minutes, is one of the most memorable pieces of American literature. The president was, of course, Abraham Lincoln and his speech the Gettysburg Address.

No other American president, with the possible exception of Thomas Jefferson, has been as skilled or lucid a writer as Abraham Lincoln, nor more deserving of a prominent place in any history of American literature.

What makes the literary achievements of Lincoln more remarkable is that he had little formal education. He grew up among simple backwoods people, many of whom were illiterate. Yet somehow Lincoln not only managed to teach himself to read and write, but found time, while working as a farmhand, clerk and rail splitter, to teach himself law.

The law for Abraham Lincoln became a stepping-stone to politics. He served in the Illinois Legislature, was elected to the U.S. House of Representatives, and although defeated for the Senate, eventually won the presidency in 1860.

There is no doubt that Lincoln's political career was greatly helped by his writing and speaking ability. Unlike other well-known orators of his day, he seldom indulged in long, rambling speeches, or the exaggerated, flowery language that confused the audience. "I know what I mean and I do not propose to leave this crowd in doubt," Lincoln once said before one of the famous Lincoln-Douglas debates.

He spoke, as he wrote, directly, simply, with a masterful use of humor, when necessary, to make a point. It was the same backwoods humor he had learned growing up on the Illinois frontier.

Yet Lincoln could also write and speak with great dignity. He was a master of the unforgettable turn of phrase; among the most familiar are: "A house divided against itself cannot stand," which said the United States could not exist half slave and half free; and "with malice toward none, with charity for all . . ." in speaking of the treatment to be accorded the soon to be defeated South at the end of the Civil War. The last sentence of Lincoln's Gettysburg Address is equally memorable for the sweep of its prose: "We here highly resolve that these dead shall not have died in vain; that this nation, under God, shall have a new birth of freedom; and that government of the people, by the people, for the people, shall not perish from the earth."

Perhaps, in the end, it does not matter how Lincoln mastered the art of great writing. Whether it came through the books he read, or the pains he took in writing and re-writing, or it simply reflected the wit, compassion and no-bility of the man himself, the truth is that years after they were written, Lincoln's writings still have "the stamp of great literature upon them."

Five days after Lee's surrender at Appomattox Court House ended the Civil War, President Lincoln was shot by John Wilkes Booth while attending a performance at Ford's Theatre. He died the next day, April 15, 1865.

There are many historic sites around the country that have a close connection with Lincoln's life: the farm in Indiana where Lincoln spent his childhood; the restored town of New Salem, Illinois, where Lincoln grew to young manhood; and the many sites at Springfield, Illinois, where Lincoln practiced law, was married and lived until he left for Washington, D.C. and the Presidency in 1861.

At the Lincoln home in Springfield, the desk where he wrote may still be seen, along with his stove pipe hat and his shawl on a chair beside the desk. It was at the Old State Capitol, also in Springfield, that Lincoln gave his famous "House Divided" speech.

Gettysburg Cemetery, Gettysburg, Pennsylvania, has a monument with the words of Lincoln's address engraved upon it, placed on the site where the president gave his brief, stirring speech that November day in 1863.

Ford's Theatre where Lincoln was shot has now been reopened as a theater with a Lincoln museum on the lower floor.

The most imposing monument to Lincoln, however, is the Lincoln Memorial in Washington, D.C. The colossal statue of Lincoln within the memorial was carved by Daniel Chester French. On the walls of the memorial are carved the words from two of Lincoln's most notable speeches, which have now become a treasured part of our literary heritage: The Gettysburg Address and the Second Inaugural Address.

Location: LINCOLN BOYHOOD NATIONAL MEMORIAL located on SR 162, south of Lincoln City, Indiana. No admission charge.

Location: LINCOLN NEW SALEM STATE HISTORIC SITE is located 2 miles south on SR 97 from Petersburg, Illinois. No admission charge.

Location: LINCOLN SITES IN SPRINGFIELD, ILLINOIS. Most of the sites are located between Capitol and Jackson Streets in Springfield. Lincoln is buried at Oak Ridge Cemetery, 2 miles north of Springfield. No admission charge to Lincoln Home, or Old State Capitol. Small admission charge to Lincoln Museum.

Location: GETTYSBURG CEMETERY in Gettysburg National Military Park, Gettysburg, Pennsylvania. Admission charge to National Park Visitors Center.

Location: FORD'S THEATRE AND MUSEUM, 511 10th Street NW, Washington, D.C. No admission charge to museum.

Location: LINCOLN MEMORIAL is located directly on a line with the Capitol and the Washington Monument, Washington, D.C. Interpretive tours given every 45 minutes. No admission charge.

HERMAN MELVILLE
1819–1891

New Bedford, Massachusetts, in nineteenth century America was a bustling whaling port, with fortunes rising and falling on just one voyage of a whaling ship. In the winter of 1841, a young man named Herman Melville, age 22 years, came to New Bedford to become a crew member on the whaling ship *Acushnet,* bound for the South Seas. Such a venture was not unusual. Many young men sought adventure and their fortunes with the whaling fleet. But the voyage that Melville took aboard the *Acushnet* was to become the best known voyage of any whaling ship. Not only did New Bedford and the *Acushnet* help launch the literary career of Melville, but the voyage itself served as the setting for one of America's greatest novels, *Moby Dick.*

The voyage on the whaling ship was not Melville's first experience at sea. The son of a distinguished but impoverished New York family, he had shipped as a cabin boy from New York to Liverpool, England, in 1839. Later Melville, who had little formal education, was to say that that first voyage at sea was his Yale and Harvard College education.

Returning to New York, Melville tried other jobs, including teaching, but found that he had developed a taste for the sea and an "everlasting itch for things remote." Once signed aboard the *Acushnet,* however, he quickly discovered that a crewman's life aboard a whaler was a cruel and dehumanizing experience. After eighteen months aboard the whaler, Melville jumped ship at the Marquesas Islands in the South Pacific. He leaped, in a way, from the frying pan into the fire, because the natives he landed among in the Marquesas were cannibals. It was several weeks before he made his escape on another whaling ship, this time bound for Australia.

His experiences with the cannibals were only the start of Melville's adventures. He became the ringleader of a mutiny aboard the second whaling ship, once again jumped ship, and became a beachcomber in Tahiti, spent a short time in the Hawaiian Islands, and finally enlisted as a common seaman aboard a U.S. Navy frigate.

In 1844, after four years of travel and adventure, Melville returned to New York but found he still had an "abomination for all honorable respectable toil." Since his family enjoyed hearing him spin tales about life in the South Seas, he decided to write a partly fictionalized account of his life in the Marquesas Islands.

The title that Melville gave his book, *Typee: A Peep at Polynesian Life,* would have tantalized his readers even if nineteenth century Americans weren't already fascinated by travel books about faraway areas of the world. *Typee,* published in 1846, became an immediate, if controversial, best-seller. Missionaries resented its unflattering picture of missionary life, while proper people were shocked at Melville's uninhibited descriptions of native life, including his romance with the dusky, beautiful Fayaway. All the publicity about the book turned Melville into an overnight literary celebrity.

He wrote a second book, *Omoo,* based on his beach-combing life in Tahiti, which again caused a storm of controversy but was also a best-seller of its day. With the popularity of his books, Melville was making enough money to marry and devote his full time to writing.

Within two years he hastily wrote three more books, mostly to make money: *Mardi,* a romance set in the South seas, *Redburn,* based on his voyage to Liverpool, and *White Jacket* (the best of the three), telling of the brutal life of the common seaman aboard a U.S. Navy ship. (Melville, however, was not the first author to point out the cruelties suffered by the common seaman. Ten years before, Richard Henry Dana had exposed the hardships of the sailor's life in his book, *Two Years before the Mast.*)

Then in 1850, Melville moved to Pittsfield, Massachusetts, and began writing a novel based on his experiences aboard the *Acushnet.* The book started out as a simple narrative of the whaling industry and life aboard a whaling ship, but soon became much more than that. Like Nathaniel Hawthorne, an author whose writings Melville greatly admired, Melville had begun looking at the dark side of human nature, puzzling over the origin of evil and seeking the essential truth of life.

For a year and a half Melville was as much obsessed with writing *Moby Dick* as the evil Captain Ahab in the book—

aboard the fictional whaler, *Pequod*—was obsessed with tracking down the great, mysterious white whale. While he was writing the book, Melville felt as if he had "broiled in hell-fire." When he finished, he was physically and mentally exhausted, as if he himself had lived through the terrifying experiences of the character, Ishmael, the narrator of the book and the sole survivor of the voyage of the *Pequod*.

Moby Dick, dedicated to Hawthorne, was published in 1851 and was a failure, critically and financially. Readers who were accustomed to Melville's dashing adventure tales found *Moby Dick* difficult to understand. Even critics friendly to Melville were mystified. And Melville's next published book, *Pierre,* which also explored the dark avenues of the human mind, seemed even more bewildering.

Melville's last published novel within his lifetime, was *The Confidence Man* in 1857, but it too was unsuccessful. Melville was dropped and forgotten by the public as quickly as they had snatched him up.

To support his family, Melville worked as a Customs Inspector in New York. The only writing he did in his last years was poetry, and just before he died in 1891, a brilliant short novel, *Billy Budd*.

Billy Budd was not published, however, until 1924 when Melville's tremendous talent was slowly beginning to be recognized. Today, *Typee* and *Omoo* are still read for the excellent, light-hearted adventure novels that they are, while the story of the foretopsman, Billy Budd, has been dramatized as an opera, play and movie.

As for *Moby Dick,* the book is now accepted as one of the great epic romances of all time. Critics continue to argue over the symbolism of the characters in the novel and try to interpret the several layers of meaning in the book. Is Captain Ahab a villain or a hero? Does the white whale, Moby Dick, stand for Good or Evil, Fate or Nature or God? But even read simply as a robust adventure novel, with vivid descriptions of the whaling industry, the reader cannot help but be swept along by Melville's powerful prose.

In New Bedford today, the scene of the opening chapter of *Moby Dick,* there is a Whaling Museum in honor of the brave and resourceful seamen who manned the whaling ships. In addition to whaling relics, scrimshaw, a cooperage shop and sail-rigging loft, there is a full-rigged, half-size model of an actual whaling ship. Visiting the museum makes the whaling scenes in *Moby Dick* seem even more realistic and exciting. (Other excellent whaling museums may be found at Nantucket, Massachusetts, and Mystic, Connecticut.)

Also at New Bedford is the gray wooden Seamen's Bethel or church, opened in 1832. It was at this Seamen's Bethel that Ishmael in *Moby Dick* heard Father Mapple preach his prophetic sermon. One can still see the black-bordered memorial marble tablets along the wall, dedicated to sailors lost at sea.

The only place Melville lived that is still in existence and open to the public is Arrowhead, his home while he wrote *Moby Dick, Pierre, Piazza Tales, Israel Potter,* and *The Confidence Man.* Since none of these books were financially successful, Melville was forced to sell off portions of the farmland to support his family and pay his debts. The huge square chimney in the center of the old kitchen of the house was the subject of a sketch by Melville, called "I and My Chimney."

The desk at which Melville wrote *Billy Budd,* portraits of the author and his family, and the largest collection of

Melville memorabilia in the country is contained in the Herman Melville Memorial Room at The Berkshire Athenaeum. Guided tours and illustrated lectures on Melville may be arranged for interested groups.

Location: WHALING MUSEUM, 18 Johnny Cake Hill, near the Dock of old New Bedford, Massachusetts. Admission charge.

Location: SEAMEN'S BETHEL, 15 Johnny Cake Hill, New Bedford, Massachusetts. No admission charge.

Location: ARROWHEAD is 3½ miles south of Pittsfield, Massachusetts, on US 7 and 20, then 2½ miles northeast on Holmes Road. Small admission charge.

Location: HERMAN MELVILLE MEMORIAL ROOM, The Berkshire Athenaeum, Pittsfield Public Library, 1 Wendell Avenue, Pittsfield, Massachusetts. No admission charge.

BEFORE, DURING AND AFTER CIVIL WAR

BETWEEN THE YEARS 1830 AND THE CIVIL WAR, THE ONE SUB-
JECT THAT WAS THE MOST CONTROVERSIAL, AND THE MOST
WTITTEN ABOUT IN AMERICA, WAS SLAVERY. HUNDREDS OF
POEMS, PAMPHLETS AND BOOKS, BOTH IN THE NORTH AND
SOUTH, WERE WRITTEN AND PUBLISHED, ARGUING FOR OR
AGAINST THE "PECULIAR INSTITUTION" OF SLAVERY. AFTER THE
CIVIL WAR THE SUBJECT WAS KEPT ALIVE IN SUCH BOOKS AS
BOOKER T. WASHINGTON'S UP FROM SLAVERY.

The most important and influential anti-
slavery book was written by a woman,
Harriet Beecher Stowe. Her novel *Uncle
Tom's Cabin* convinced thousands of
northerners that slavery was an evil that
must be abolished. Women, white and
black, were actively involved in the
abolitionist movement from the beginning. One of the first controversial anti-
slavery tracts was written in 1833 by
Lydia Maria Child, entitled "An Appeal
in Favor of That Class of Americans
called Africans." COURTESY OHIO
HISTORICAL SOCIETY

In the years after the Civil War, Harriet Beecher Stowe also wrote
excellent short stories and novels about New England in her Hartford, Connecticut, home, shown below. The home, open to the
public, is very reminiscent of the charm and character of its
author-owner. COURTESY STOWE-DAY FOUNDATION, HARTFORD

INCIDENTS

IN THE

LIFE OF A SLAVE GIRL.

WRITTEN BY HERSELF.

"Northerners know nothing at all about Slavery. They think it is perpetual bondage only. They have no conception of the depth of degradation involved in that word, SLAVERY; if they had, they would never cease their efforts until so horrible a system was overthrown."   A WOMAN OF NORTH CAROLINA.

"Rise up, ye women that are at ease! Hear my voice, ye careless daughters! Give ear unto my speech."   ISAIAH XXXII. 9.

EDITED BY L. MARIA CHILD.

BOSTON:
PUBLISHED FOR THE AUTHOR.
1861.

NARRATIVE

OF

WILLIAM W. BROWN,

A

FUGITIVE SLAVE.

WRITTEN BY HIMSELF.

————Is there not some chosen curse,
Some hidden thunder in the stores of heaven,
Red with uncommon wrath, to blast the man
Who gains his fortune from the blood of souls?
COWPER.

BOSTON:
PUBLISHED AT THE ANTI-SLAVERY OFFICE,
No. 25 CORNHILL.
1847.

The earliest black authors in America were ex-slaves who had escaped North and wrote books about their experiences in slavery. Hundreds of these books (frontispiece of two shown above) were published in the thirty years before the Civil War. The influence of these slave narratives in rousing the conscience of Americans against slavery makes them a unique, if little known, part of America's literary heritage. COURTESY ST. LOUIS COMMUNITY COLLEGE AT MERAMEC LIBRARY

The best-known slave narrative was written by Frederick Douglass, fugitive slave from Maryland. Douglass became one of the leaders in the abolitionist movement and the most influential black man in nineteenth century America. He was the editor and publisher of the *North Star,* an abolitionist newspaper in Rochester, New York. COURTESY NATIONAL PARK SERVICE

In the study of his home, Cedar Hill, in Washington, D.C., Frederick Douglass wrote his autobiography in 1888, *The Life and Times of Frederick Douglass.* The book, like Benjamin Franklin's *Autobiography,* has become a classic in American literature. Today, the Douglass home is a national shrine for Americans of all races. COURTESY NATIONAL PARK SERVICE

Speech-writing was a form of literature very popular in nineteenth century America. Abraham Lincoln was not only a master orator, moving his audience as easily to laughter as to tears, but his speeches, which he wrote himself, are prose writing at its very best. Engraved in the walls of the Lincoln Memorial, Washington, D.C., are two of Lincoln's most famous speeches, the Gettysburg Address and the Second Inaugural Address. COURTESY NATIONAL PARK SERVICE

Abraham Lincoln's home in Springfield, Illinois, along with other sites connected with Lincoln's Springfield years, are open to the public. In the study of his home may be seen the desk where he did his writing. Lincoln painstakingly wrote and rewrote before he gave a speech. COURTESY ILLINOIS OFFICE OF TOURISM

The famous black educator and author, Booker T. Washington, was born in this cabin on the Burroughs Plantation, before the Civil War. Washington's autobiography, *Up from Slavery,* was a "rags to riches" success story. Although Washington worked to improve the lot of southern black men and women by building Tuskegee Institute, in his writings he did not deal as effectively with the problem of racial injustice as did other black authors.

The Burroughs Plantation, with Washington's birthplace, is now the Booker T. Washington National Monument and a "living history" farm, open to the public. COURTESY BOOKER T. WASHINGTON NATIONAL MONUMENT

WALT WHITMAN
1819–1892

In 1855 a slim book of poetry entitled *Leaves of Grass* was written by a then unknown poet, Walt Whitman. Although only a few copies of the book were sold, a second edition of the book, published the next year, stirred up a storm of controversy that has not died down more than a century later. Critics called the unusual, formless, or free verse, style of the poetry, with its rude vocabulary drawn from the man on the street . . . "An impertinence towards the English language." Even more shocking to critics and readers alike was the sensual imagery used in the poems. The poet's exultation of the human body, his frank allusions to sex, even touching upon homosexuality, were forbidden subjects in nineteenth century American literature.

Distinguished contemporary authors such as Whittier,

Lowell and Holmes were scandalized by the book. Whittier was so disgusted he threw his copy into the fire. One critic, though, who read the first edition of *Leaves of Grass*, and who glimpsed the genius behind the poetry was Ralph Waldo Emerson. He wrote Whitman a prophetic letter in which he said, "I greet you at the beginning of a great career."

It was a career that was late in starting. Whitman, born at the family home on Huntington, Long Island, was 36 years old when *Leaves of Grass* was first published. Before that time the poet had done some writing on conventional subjects but had spent most of his time moving restlessly from job to job, from printer's devil to country schoolteacher, from editor of several small Brooklyn newspapers to working as a carpenter with his Quaker father in Brooklyn.

Most of the time he wandered around the Long Island countryside, from Brooklyn to Montauk Point, when Long Island was still open fields and beaches. But he also haunted the theaters and Bohemian quarters of New York City. Wherever he wandered, he talked with all sorts and classes of people: farmers, clam diggers, bus drivers, ferry pilots, free blacks and bound servants. It was during these restless years that Whitman described himself as "simmering, simmering, simmering."

The simmering came to a boil in 1855 with the publication of *Leaves of Grass*. Not only did Whitman write the poetry, he assisted in the printing and publishing of the book at his own expense. He was also his own best public relations man, writing and publishing anonymous critical reviews of his poetry. Naturally, the reviews were all extremely favorable!

The third revised edition of *Leaves of Grass*—Whitman continued revising and adding additional poems to the book through nine editions—was published just before the Civil War. Whitman's Quaker upbringing kept him out of combat, but he spent three years caring for wounded soldiers from both the North and South in hospitals in and around Washington, D.C. It was while he nursed mutilated and dying soldiers that Whitman wrote one of the best collections of war poetry ever written, *Drum Taps*, in 1865. That same year President Lincoln, a man Whitman greatly admired, was assassinated. In Lincoln's memory, Whitman added two poems to a new edition of *Drum Taps*, "When Lilacs Last in the Courtyard Bloomed" and "Oh Captain! My Captain!" In these two poems, Whitman's poetry is said to have reached its full maturity.

Although Whitman called himself "the poet of the people," and was personally well-liked, unfortunately, "the people" did not understand or buy his poetry. To support his mother, brother and himself, he took a job as a clerk in the Indian Bureau, but was fired when his supervisor discovered Whitman had written that "indecent book."

With each new edition of *Leaves of Grass*, more controversy swirled around the book. In 1882 the Society for Suppression of Vice condemned *Leaves of Grass*, and a criminal lawsuit was brought to stop publication. Nevertheless, Whitman continued his writing, not only of poetry but several excellent books of prose, including a collection of sketches of his boyhood called *Specimen Days and Collect*.

In 1873, Whitman suffered a paralytic stroke, brought on by the strain of his years of nursing during the Civil War. He moved to Camden, New Jersey, buying a small, weather-beaten house where he lived with "a black cat, a spotted dog, a parrot and a canary."

His poetry never brought him a great deal of money, and he was often supported by gifts from admirers of his poetry in England. He had faithful and loyal admirers in America, too, who visited his Camden home to pay homage to the "good, gray poet" as Whitman became known in his last years. He died in Camden in his 73rd year and is buried at Harleigh Cemetery in Camden in a family vault he designed himself.

From the beginning, Whitman broke with the conventional rules for poetry, which insisted that verse must rhyme and scan. Whitman chose instead to write his poetry in a formless, irregularly lined free verse, using simple, easily understood words, seeking a "perfect, transparent clearness."

He also wrote some poetry, like "Out of the Cradle Endlessly Rocking," to be chanted aloud. The reader was intended to catch the long, rolling rhythm of the lines, like the rhythm of waves rolling onto a beach.

Despite the controversy that surrounded Whitman's poetry, not all his poems had controversial themes like those in "I Sing the Body Electric." He celebrated all aspects of American life in "I Hear America Singing," and the teeming mass of American people in "Song of Myself." In the latter poem, Whitman is actually speaking not for himself but for every man and woman . . . "for every atom belonging to me as good belongs to you." In his later works, Whitman's poetry became less sensual and less nationally oriented. He moved from glorifying the body and soul to a more mystical outlook on life and from celebrating America to celebrating universal man.

Like Herman Melville, a contemporary of Whitman,

the recognition of Whitman's genius came many years after death, and his reputation has grown with each passing year. Today, his poetry, once condemned as vulgar and indecent, has been described by one critic as "original and revolutionary and indisputably American."

Whitman's boyhood home in Huntington, Long Island, was a great influence on his work. Even after his family moved to Brooklyn, he would return to his grandparents' home in Huntington to visit and roam the surrounding countryside. The sea, Whitman felt, was his mystic "savage old mother" and he "spent many hours on Turtle Hill by the old lighthouse on the extreme point, looking out on the ceaseless roll of the Atlantic."

In *Specimen Days,* Whitman describes a visit to the family home, the simple frame house built by Walt's father in 1810 with its borning room, Walt's schoolmaster's desk, the sturdy, simple furnishings and, near the house, the kitchen garden, the ancient oak tree, grove of black walnut trees, and the burial ground of the Whitman family nearby.

Many of the old trees are now gone, but the Whitman home still stands, open to visitors, with many of the furnishings Whitman described present in the rooms. The second floor of the house has been turned into an exhibit and library area for Whitman's works, with copies of his manuscripts and photographs and portraits of the poet on view.

Whitman's last home at Camden is also open to visitors, thanks to the Walt Whitman Association and the state of New Jersey. The house, even in Whitman's lifetime, was simply furnished: an iron stove in the kitchen, a stuffed parrot in the front room, Whitman's collection of walking canes and his seashell collection, a stepping stone in front of the house with the initials "W. W." There has been added to the house a photograph of the poet, inscribed with the lines from one of his own poems . . . "at the last, tenderly."

Location: WHITMAN FAMILY HOME, 246 Walt Whitman Road, Huntington, Long Island. Follow SR 110 to Huntington and turn left Norwich Road to Whitman Road (SR 25) for ½ mile. No admission charge.

Location: WALT WHITMAN HOME, 330 Mickle Street, Camden, New Jersey. From Ben Franklin Bridge, go south on Broadway to Cooper Street, straight on Cooper to 3rd Street, left on 3rd Street to Mickle Street. Small admission charge.

LEW WALLACE
1827-1905

In the western Indiana town of Crawfordsville is tucked an exotic jewel of a temple, as if a bit of Arabian Nights had dropped into the midst of the rural Indiana countryside. This pavilion-like structure was the study of Lew Wallace, author of *Ben Hur,* one of the most popular and best-selling novels of all time.

A native of Indiana, Lew Wallace traveled widely and had a varied and distinguished career, first as a lawyer then as an Army officer in the Mexican and Civil War, rising to the rank of General. After the war, he lived for a while in Mexico, served as Governor of New Mexico and as U.S. Minister to Turkey. It was while he was Governor of the Territory of New Mexico that he began writing *Ben Hur,* for which he had done research during his travels in the Holy Land. It is said that while he was writing his book, he had to keep his windows shuttered at night because his life had been threatened by the renegade, Billy the Kid, who was roaming New Mexico at the time.

Although *Ben Hur* was not Lew Wallace's first book, the novel, which has been called "an amazing mixture of melodramatic adventure and scholarly research" brought the author lasting fame and fortune. A historical romance, it is set in Jerusalem at the time of Christ, and the chariot race between the character, Ben Hur, and his long time enemy, Messala, is undoubtedly one of the most exciting scenes in any novel ever written. Over the years *Ben Hur* has been read by millions of people all over the world. Millions more have seen the dramatization of the novel on the stage, screen and television.

In 1896, General Lew Wallace was once again living in Crawfordsville, Indiana, and personally designed the building that became his study on the grounds of his home. The study is a bizarre combination of Byzantine, Greek and Italian architecture with a domed roof, tower, piazza, fountains and a lagoon. A wall surrounds the structure, with sculptured scenes from Wallace's novels.

Calling the study "a pleasure house for my soul," Lew Wallace spent his last years writing his autobiography, surrounded by the mementos of a rich and varied life.

Today, *Ben Hur* is still read and enjoyed for its dramatic, swiftly moving story as well as its carefully researched historical background, while the pavilion-study of the author is still a delight to visit, reflecting the varied interests and unusual life of one of America's most popular writers.

Location: BEN HUR MUSEUM, East Pike Street at Wallace Avenue, Crawfordsville, Indiana. Open summers only. Small admission charge.

EMILY DICKINSON
1830-1886

The spacious two-story brick mansion with the well-tended lawn and garden has an open and friendly look. Yet behind the sedate walls of this house lived Emily Dickinson, a poet whose life and genius have been one of the most puzzling, unsolved mysteries in the history of American literature.

The outward facts of Emily Dickinson's life are well-known. She was born in what was then the small, conservative New England village of Amherst, Massachusetts. Her mother was a semi-invalid, her father a respected, well-to-do attorney, a somewhat austere man who provided his bright young daughter Emily with books to read, then worried that they might joggle her mind. In spite of her rather restricted homelife, Emily had a happy, normal childhood, enjoying a circle of friends and the social activities that Amherst provided its young people.

She adored her sharp-tongued sister, Vinnie, and her handsome brother, Austin, who would often sneak books into the house for his sisters to read that Mr. Dickinson would not have considered proper for young ladies. At age fifteen, Emily even had dreams of someday becoming the belle of Amherst, but several years later realized sadly that with her plain appearance, she would always remain "the same old sixpence."

Emily was educated at a young woman's seminary. Refusing to conform to the harsh, puritanical religious concepts taught at the school, Emily displayed the streak of rebelliousness that for all her shyness never lay far beneath the surface. Her father took her home and, except for brief visits to Boston, Washington, D.C. and Philadelphia, Emily remained at home for the rest of her life.

So far Emily's life was not unlike that of many other dutiful daughters and New England spinsters of her day. She helped with the household chores, gardened, entertained occasionally and tended her invalid mother. Then, when she was around twenty-three years old, Emily's life gradually began to change.

As limited as Emily Dickinson's social life had been, it became more narrow. She withdrew more and more from social contact with everyone but members of her family and close friends. By the age of thirty, she had become almost a complete recluse. "I do not," she wrote a friend, "go from home." She refused to see visitors, and when her sister or brother entertained, she would listen, unseen, to the conversation in the parlor from a dark middle passageway or pantry off the front hall.

She took to wearing white clothes only, and at night curious townspeople would sometimes glimpse Emily flitting like a white moth through the Dickinson garden, disappearing like a startled ghost into the house if anyone appeared.

There have been various reasons given for Emily Dickinson's cloistered life. Some of her biographers say a blighted romance with a married man she had met briefly in Philadelphia turned her into a recluse. Other critics blamed her domineering father. Others believed that Emily deliberately chose her seclusion so that she would not drain herself in social encounters, but save her energy for the writing of poetry. For it was the writing of poems that occupied Emily long into the night in her bedroom-workroom.

Whatever the reason, and more than likely it was a combination of all of the above, in the years between 1859 and 1865, Emily wrote an astonishing quantity of poems, almost one a day. She wrote the poems on backs of envelopes, on pieces of brown paper bag, scraps of discarded bills, finally sewing the poems into paper packets. She continued writing after 1865, but at a decreased rate. And during all those years, only seven of her poems were published, those anonymously.

In 1862 Emily sent four of her poems to a well-known literary critic with the cryptic note, "Are you too deeply occupied to say if my verse is alive?" Emily's unorthodox formless poetry, the liberties she took with meter and rhyme must have dismayed the critic. In any case, his discouraging answer convinced Emily that her poetry was far in advance of its time. She never tried to have her poetry published, for fear it would not be accepted by the reading public.

During the last years of her life, Emily Dickinson was a semi-invalid, and she died in 1886 as quietly and uneventfully as she had lived. On a May day her white coffin, covered with violets, was carried out the back door of the Dickinson Homestead, across the field to the West Cemetery, with only a few friends and neighbors following.

It was her sister, Vinnie, sorting through Emily's possessions after her death, who discovered the stacks of poems hidden in a cherry bureau in her sister's bedroom. Over the next months she discovered other poems hidden around the room. In all, approximately 1775 poems of Emily's were uncovered. Emily had requested that her writings be destroyed after her death, but Vinnie could not bring herself to burn the poems. She did, however, destroy Emily's letters, which were extensive—and in doing so, destroyed forever any hope of untangling the riddle of Emily Dickinson's secret life.

Perhaps, though, the most bewildering mystery is not why Emily Dickinson became a recluse, but how a young woman, living in almost complete seclusion, with little first-hand experience of life, could write poetry of such sharp intensity, power and passion. Emily once wrote that in reading poetry, "if I feel physically as if the top of my head were taken off, that is poetry." Reading a Dickinson poem gives much that effect.

Many of her poems are short, some less than twelve lines, but in a few simple, concentrated sentences, she captures the very essence of the great themes of life—love, death, nature, immortality. With her use of the imperfect or eye-rhyme, her fresh, startling images, her unconventional grammar and rhythm, Emily Dickinson, along with Walt Whitman, has been called America's most original and inventive poet. But it is impossible to compare the Amherst poet with any other poet. She is separate, unique.

Because of family quarrels over ownership, the first of Emily Dickinson's poetry wasn't published until several years after her death, the last poems in 1945. With each new edition of her poetry, Emily Dickinson's reputation has grown, until today she is regarded as one of the finest poets that America has produced.

The house in Amherst, a large brick house behind a hemlock hedge, in which the poet wrote the majority of her poems—and which was almost the complete circumference of her life—is now owned by Amherst College. Emily's bedroom was on the second floor on the right at the front of the house. From her bedroom window, she would sometime lower a basket of gingerbread to the children playing in the yard below.

Upon awakening, Emily once described the scene that always met her eyes, "A distant hill, a steeple with a weather vane and a chimney." Some of the original pieces of Emily's furniture are still in the room today, as well as one of her famous white dresses. The original cherry bureau, where Emily's poems were hidden, is now lodged at the Harvard College Library, Cambridge, Massachusetts.

The Dickinson Homestead may be visited by the public on Tuesday afternoon from three to five p.m., by reservation only. Appointments to visit the home may be made through the office of the Secretary of Amherst College. Since the house is now a faculty home, only Emily's bedroom may be visited.

Location: DICKINSON HOMESTEAD, Main Street, Amherst, Massachusetts. No admission charge. Guided Tour.

EMILY DICKINSON AND WALT WHITMAN

THE SECOND HALF OF THE NINETEENTH CENTURY PRODUCED
TWO OF AMERICA'S MOST ORIGINAL AND FINEST POETS—EMILY
DICKINSON AND WALT WHITMAN. ALTHOUGH THEIR LIFE STYLES
WERE POLES APART, BOTH POETS BROKE NEW GROUND IN
POETIC TECHNIQUES WHICH GREATLY INFLUENCED TWENTIETH
CENTURY POETS.

Emily Dickinson was a shy New
England recluse, who seldom left her
home in Amherst, Massachusetts,
and whose poetry, hidden in her
room, was not discovered until
after her death. COURTESY
DICTIONARY OF AMERICAN PORTRAITS

The family home where Emily Dickinson cloistered herself is now
owned by Amherst College. The bedroom where Emily wrote and
some of her personal belongings may be seen on weekday afternoons, by appointment only. COURTESY AMHERST COLLEGE
AMHERST, MASSACHUSETTS

Walt Whitman was undoubtedly the most controversial author in nineteenth century America. The sensual imagery in his poetry shocked the Victorian morals of mid-nineteenth century America, just as his imaginative free verse annoyed critics and confused readers. Whitman thought of himself as a poet of the people. In this picture the poet looks the part in jeans, shirt sleeves and red flannel undershirt. This is the picture he chose for the frontispiece of the first edition of *Leaves of Grass*.

The kitchen of the Walt Whitman home on Long Island shows the schoolmaster's desk used by Whitman during his schoolteaching days on Long Island. The rural life of Long Island, the farms and woods and beaches, appear again and again in Whitman's poetry. His home at Huntington, Long Island, and his last home at Camden, New Jersey, are both open to the public. PHOTO BY AUTHOR

THOMAS BAILEY ALDRICH
1836–1907

In 19th century America, books written for children followed more or less the same pattern. The girl in the story was a model of sweetness and decorum; the boy a dull, obedient paragon of virtue. Louise May Alcott's rebellious, headstrong Jo in *Little Women* helped change the image for girls. And Thomas Aldrich's humorous story of young Tom Bailey in *The Story of a Bad Boy,* published in 1870, changed the pattern for boys.

The Story of a Bad Boy is actually the story of incidents that happened to Thomas Aldrich as a lively young boy growing up in Portsmouth, New Hampshire. The town became "the rusty, delightful old town of Rivermouth" in Aldrich's book. The mischevious pranks of Tom and his companions, burning up an old stagecoach, firing off a battery of ancient cannon, Tom's romantic crush on an older girl—seem mild to young readers today. In 1870, however, such misbehavior written up in a humorous fashion was frowned upon. After all, it might set a bad example for young boys who read the book!

Nevertheless, the success of Aldrich's book started a new trend in American literature. Other authors were influenced to write humorously and realistically of childhood. George Peck wrote *Peck's Bad Boy,* Booth Tarkington's popular *Penrod* was published in 1914, and the outstanding humorist writer of them all, Mark Twain, created his unforgettable boyhood characters, Tom Sawyer and Huckleberry Finn.

In later life, Thomas Aldrich became the distinguished editor of the *Atlantic Monthly Magazine,* yet his more serious writings have now been forgotten, and it is his amusing nostalgic account of his boyhood that is still remembered and read today.

The house where Thomas Aldrich was born and grew up, which was the background for his book, is furnished down to the minutest detail exactly as it is described in the book. Each room brings back memories of characters in the book: Tom's bedroom with Tom's clothes stretched across the quilt-covered bed; the jar of marbles on the bureau; Aunt Abigail's knitting needles in the front parlor. The table is set for dinner in the dining room and the kettle is on in the kitchen, as if at any moment the family will return.

In the rear of the house is a memorial to Thomas Aldrich, with his manuscripts, autographs, first editions and paintings.

Location: THOMAS BAILEY ALDRICH MEMORIAL, 386 Court Street, Portsmouth, New Hampshire. Open summers only. Small admission charge.

SAMUEL CLEMENS (Mark Twain) 1835-1910

One of the most visited literary sites in America—second only to Concord, Massachusetts, in popularity—is the small town of Hannibal, Missouri, boyhood home of Mark Twain, or Sam Clemens, as he was known in Hannibal.

Thousands of visitors come to this bustling river town each year to visit sites that are as familiar to them as scenes from their own childhood. For it was Hannibal that Mark Twain used as the setting for the adventures of two of the most unforgettable characters ever created in American literature—Tom Sawyer and Huckleberry Finn.

Although Samuel Clemens was actually born in Florida, Missouri, in the same year that Halley's Comet flashed across the sky, his father, a footloose wanderer, moved his family to Hannibal when young Sam was four years old. His growing-up years in Hannibal, the people and homes and streets of the town, the fascination the young boy felt for the robust Mississippi River rolling by Hannibal's front door, were an inexhaustible mine of material for his future writing. Many of the incidents that happened to Tom Sawyer and Huckleberry Finn were real adventures that had happened to Sam Clemens in Hannibal, and many of the characters in the books were neighbors and friends of the Clemens family.

When Sam was twelve his father died, and he went to work as a printer at his brother's newspaper; but there was too much of his father's wandering spirit in young Sam for him to stay. At age eighteen he left Hannibal to seek his fortune as an itinerant printer in New York and Philadelphia.

Eventually he drifted back to the Midwest, and still fascinated by the romantic spell of the Mississippi River, he became a river pilot. Clemens always said his years of steamboating were his real schooling, where he "got acquainted with all the different types of human nature." Later he was to write *Life on the Mississippi,* using his colorful experiences on the river in his book. He also picked up his pen name, Mark Twain, from an expression river pilots use when testing the depth of the river channel.

When the Civil War shut down river traffic, Clemens found himself out of a job. He tried soldiering and didn't like it, then traveled west by stagecoach with his brother to Virginia City, Nevada, experiencing adventures used later in his book *Roughing It.*

In the 1860s Virginia City was a rough, boisterous mining town. Clemens was unsuccessful in finding gold, but he discovered something more valuable. The humorous pieces he wrote for the Virginia City newspaper were popular enough to be picked up by eastern newspapers. After years of trying various careers, Sam Clemens at last had found his true profession; he was a writer.

San Francisco beckoned him next. The Bay City already had an active literary community, led by western writer, Bret Harte. Although the two men eventually ended up detesting each other, Harte did help Clemens through the apprentice stage of writing. In San Francisco, Clemens found he had another talent. He was a born comedian. He could set an audience to roaring with laughter when he told them the humorous stories he had picked up from his years on the river and in the mining towns of the west. This ability to hold the attention of an audience while carefully building a funny story to its climax was a talent Sam Clemens transferred successfully to his writing.

In 1867 Clemens traveled with a group of Americans to Europe. The articles he wrote about the experiences of the tourists were gathered in a book in 1869, called *The Innocents Abroad*. Most travel books in Clemens's time were written with respectful awe of the wonders of Europe. Sam Clemens, however, could not resist poking fun at the sights he saw on the trip, as well as his fellow travelers. The book was a great success, establishing Samuel Clemens as America's leading humorist writer.

Now Sam Clemens could devote all his time to writing, and he could also move East and marry Olivia Langdon, a young woman he fell in love with after only seeing her picture in a locket.

The books Samuel Clemens wrote during the next quarter of a century fall roughly into three types. There were his humorous travel books, such as *The Innocents Abroad, Roughing It, A Tramp Abroad,* and *Following the Equator.* His novels varied between humorous and, at times, bitter satires of nineteenth century society, such as *The Gilded Age,* and highly romanticized tales set in the past, like, *The Prince and the Pauper* and *A Connecticut Yankee in King Arthur's Court.* Lastly, there were Clemens' most important books, written from his Hannibal years: *Tom Sawyer* and *Huckleberry Finn.*

Samuel Clemens made a great deal of money from his writing. In 1873 he built in Hartford, Connecticut, a three-story, thirty-room mansion for his family, where he lived and entertained lavishly. Unfortunately Clemens also invested recklessly. By 1894 he was bankrupt. To pay off his debts, he went on an extended lecture tour abroad. While he and his wife were out of the country, their daughter, Suzy, died. Mrs. Clemens, herself, became seriously ill and died several years later.

Samuel Clemens never stopped writing, but his books after Mrs. Clemen's death tended to be written in haste and fatigue and were more and more tinged with bitterness beneath the humor. Although in a few of his later books, such as *Pudd'nhead Wilson,* flashes of Clemens' lively wit can be found, the golden age of Samuel Clemens was past.

As the author had prophesized years before, he died on a day when Halley's Comet once again blazed across the sky, on April 21, 1910.

The books that Samuel Clemens wrote can be classified as "local color" stories, but they were much more than that. He had a remarkable talent for creating and bringing characters to life in just a few short sentences. It was a talent he took great pains to cultivate, never using an unnecessary or wrong word. The difference he always said between using the right and the almost right word in a sentence was the difference between "the lightning and the lightning bug." Most important, Sam Clemens was and still is America's greatest humorist. He took native American humor—the tall tale of the frontier, the Negro roustabout's story, the miner and riverboat gambler's roisterous stories—and raised it to a high art.

The home where Sam Clemens was born, as well as exhibits from his life, is now contained within a museum at Mark Twain State Park, Florida, Missouri.

The town of Hannibal is much changed from the days when young Sam roamed its streets. A section of the town near the river, however, has been kept much as it looked when Clemens first described the town in his books, calling it St. Petersburg instead of Hannibal.

The Mark Twain boyhood home is across the street from the Becky Thatcher House, where Tom Sawyer's boyhood sweetheart lived. There is even a white board fence, descendant of the fence that Tom tricked his friends into painting for him. Nearby is No. 4 Hill Street, the law office young Sam crept into one night to sleep and found he was sharing a room with a dead man. There is Cardiff Hill (called Holliday's Hill in *Tom Sawyer*), a favorite rendezvous for Sam Clemens and his playmates. Also on Hill Street is the Mark Twain Museum and further down the street, the Tom Sawyer dioramas with scenes from *Tom Sawyer* and *Huckleberry Finn*.

Two miles south of Hannibal on Route 79 is the cave in which Tom Sawyer and Becky were lost and where Injun Joe died. As a young boy, Sam actually got lost in this cave. The cave is open daily to the public from 8 a.m. to dusk.

One of the mining camps at which Twain stayed during his early days in the West was Angels Camp. He had a cabin at nearby Jack Ass Hill, and it was on one of his jaunts into town that he heard the story of the jumping frog, which he later turned into one of his funniest short stories, "The

Celebrated Jumping Frog of Calaveras County." The third weekend of May each year, a Jumping Frog Competition is held at the Calaveras Fairground, near Angels Camp, in honor of Sam Clemens.

Samuel Clemens's home at Hartford is part of the Nook Farm complex, which also includes Harriet Beecher Stowe's home. The Clemens house has many unusual details, designed by the author himself: a fireplace with a window above it so he "could watch the flames leaping to meet the falling snowflakes,"; a dressing room that resembles the pilot house of a Mississippi River steamboat; and a porch that looks like the deck of a river steamer. Although an elaborate study was built where the author could write, he chose instead to write in the huge third-floor billiard room. Twain also liked to write in bed, a large carved bed that he had imported from Venice.

Location: MARK TWAIN STATE PARK MUSEUM is ½ mile south on SR 107, Florida, Missouri. Small admission charge.

Location: HANNIBAL, MISSOURI, boyhood home of Mark Twain, is located on State Highway 79 and US 36 on the Mississippi River. Small charge to Mark Twain Cave and dioramas. No admission charge to Mark Twain home and museum.

Location: ANGELS CAMP, SR 49, approximately 40 miles east of Stockton, California.

Location: MARK TWAIN MEMORIAL HOME (Nook Farm), 351 Farmington Avenue Hartford, Connecticut. Admission charge.

BRET HARTE
1836–1902

Hidden in the foothills of the Sierras in California, along Highway 49 and the Stanislaus River, a few old gold mining ghost towns still survive. This was the region that the writer Bret Harte used as the setting for many of his exciting western tales, so many stories, in fact, that the area from Angels Camp to Table Mountain has become known as Bret Harte country.

Strangely enough, Bret Harte, the author who is credited with having invented the western short story, was actually an Easterner, born in Albany, New York. Harte went to California in 1854 when he was eighteen years old, along with a great many other gold-seekers. He spent two years in the gold mining camps in the foothills of the Sierras, but at heart he was always the greenhorn who found frontier life "hard, ugly, unwashed, vulgar and lawless."

When his gold-hunting was unsuccessful, Bret Harte tried teaching school, rode shotgun for Wells Fargo, and finally drifted into journalism. He worked for a short time as a newspaperman in Union, California, but was driven out of town by vigilantes who objected to an editorial Harte wrote, condemning the massacre of a group of Indians by local townspeople.

Returning to San Francisco, in time Harte became editor of the *Overland Monthly*. As an editor, and a writer, he became a leader in the small literary world of San Francisco. One of the young writers he "trimmed and trained" was an ex-riverboat pilot from Missouri, with the pen name of Mark Twain.

For his magazine, Bret Harte encouraged the writing of "local color" stories, that is, stories with a local background. In Harte's case, this meant stories about California. Using his own experiences in the primitive gold mining settlements, he wrote "The Luck of Roaring Camp" in 1868. Since the characters in his story were drifters of the type that inhabited gold mining camps, as well as prostitutes and gamblers, Californians were outraged when the story was published. They were sure it would damage public morals and stop people from emigrating to California. However, when the story was reprinted in the East, it created a literary sensation. Overnight Bret Harte was lifted from obscurity to national fame.

In the next several years, Harte wrote other stories about California and the men and women of the gold mining camps, the most famous being "The Outcasts of Poker Flat" and "Tennessee's Partner." His stories were eagerly read by Easterners, curious about the glamorous, little-known wild west. So successful were Harte's stories that the author, who had never really felt at home in the West, promptly and triumphantly headed back East.

In staid Boston, the western author was received with much fanfare by the greatest authors of the day. Bret Harte, who always had thought of himself as an Easterner, suddenly delighted in playing the role of the "Westerner" to the hilt.

Unhappily, Bret Harte's fame was short-lived. He continued writing his stories with western backgrounds and using the stock western characters he had invented, the heroes and the bad men, the sheriff and the posse, the New England school marm, the good-hearted lady of ill repute, and the gentleman gambler. But eventually he was only repeating himself in his stories. He never developed as a writer beyond his early "local color" stories of the West.

Eventually Harte moved to England and spent the last years of his life as an expatriate. He made a modest living churning out his western stories, but never returned to the United States or the West that had brought him his brief days of glory.

Although only a few of Harte's stories are still read today, in his best short stories he created flamboyant characters who sprang to life the moment they came upon the scene. And single-handedly he created a new form of literature, peculiarly and uniquely American—the western. The influence of Bret Harte and his legends of the West may still be seen in popular western motion pictures and television shows.

Most of Bret Harte's stories were drawn from actual people, events and places he knew at first hand, but the gold mining camps, the roisterous, brawling towns found in his short stories, have long since crumpled into ruins. However, one old gold mining camp in the Stanislaus River area that could be a prototype of the camps that Harte described so vividly in his stories is Angels Camp. Today, sections of the town look very much the same as they did in the early days of the Gold Rush. At Angels Camp Museum may be seen a large variety of equipment, supplies and rolling stock used by the miners during the frenzied gold rush days of '49.

Location: ANGELS CAMP is located approximately 40 miles east of Stockton, California, on SR 49. Small admission charge to museum.

JOHN BURROUGHS
1837–1921

A wildlife sanctuary near the Hudson River, 80 miles north of New York City, is a little-known literary site. It was at a rude, slabside cottage within this wooded sanctuary that John Burroughs, one of America's first great nature writers, lived and worked.

Even as a young boy living on a farm near Roxbury, New York, John Burroughs spent a great deal of time studying the birds around the farm, particularly the great army of passenger pigeons, which have now become extinct. In school, Burroughs came under the influence of the nature writings of Thoreau and Emerson. So great was their influence that when Burroughs wrote and sold his first nature essay, the publisher, at first, suspected the essay was stolen from Emerson's writings.

The second great influence in Burroughs's life was the

poet Walt Whitman. Burroughs met Whitman while he was working in Washington, D.C., and it was Whitman who encouraged Burroughs to continue his nature writings.

In 1871 Burroughs gathered his nature essays into a book, called *Wake Robin,* and later into a second book, *Winter Sunshine.* No longer could Burroughs be accused of writing like Emerson. Critics praised Burroughs's fresh poetic style and his keen, sensitive gift for observation. One critic said about *Wake Robin* . . . "the dusk and cool and quiet of the forest seem to wrap the reader. It is sort of a summer vacation to turn its pages."

Burroughs now spent all his time studying and writing about nature. Although he himself was not a trained botanist, in his travels and numerous lectures around the country, he spoke out strongly against fake nature writers who made up facts as they went along. In many ways, Burroughs was part of the new realist tradition in literature, insisting upon "straight seeing and straight thinking" in his writing.

During the last years of his life, Burroughs returned to his native mountain country, where he built a home called Riverby, and about a mile from that home, an isolated cottage in the woods, called Slabsides. As remote as Slabsides was, Burroughs, nevertheless, was visited by admirers from all over the country. Many of his readers regarded Burroughs as a sage and a prophet as well as a naturalist.

Because of John Burroughs and his popular nature books, thousands of Americans began to be interested in the life outside their doors. Perhaps in no other period of American history was there so much interest in nature talks and nature writing. Nature courses began to be offered in schools, and many Americans became amateur naturalists. From the standpoint of literature, John Burroughs took the nature essay and made it a permanent, vital part of American literature.

Today, the cottage, Slabsides, still stands surrounded by 175 acres of wilderness, a wildlife sanctuary owned and maintained by the John Burroughs Memorial Association. The sanctuary is open to visitors for nature study at all times of the year. The cottage itself is open twice a year on the third Saturday in May and the first Saturday in October. For groups from clubs and schools, the cabin is open at other times by appointment.

Woodchuck Lodge on the original Burroughs homestead, where the author-naturalist spent his summers writing, is being restored. At the present time it is open to the public the first Sunday in June, and at certain other times during the summer by arrangement.

Location: SLABSIDES, John Burroughs Sanctuary, West Park, New York. Drive west on Floyd Ackert Road from 9W to intersection with Burroughs Drive. No admission charge.

Location: WOODCHUCK LODGE, Roxbury, New York, is located 2 miles off SR 30. No admission charge.

JOHN MUIR
1838–1914

No author has a more impressive monument than the 550 acres of towering redwood trees on the slopes of Mt. Tamalpais, California. The redwood trees have been named Muir Woods in memory of author–conservationist, John Muir.

Like another author–naturalist, John Burroughs, Muir had a lifelong, passionate interest in the natural world around him. In college he studied trees and glaciers, and in 1867 he walked from Indiana to the Gulf of Mexico, keeping a daily journal of the flowers and trees, as well as the people, he met along the way. (The journal was published in 1916 under the title of *A Thousand-Mile Walk to the Gulf.*) From the Gulf, John Muir continued his trek on foot until he reached Yosemite Valley in California in 1868. Here, with only a packet of tea, a sack of bread and a hand axe, he built a sawmill, where he lived and studied the Yosemite Valley for six years.

His first article, published in 1871, proved that Yosemite Valley was created by glacial erosion and brought Muir to national attention. In the years that followed, John Muir became an authority on the lands, forests and wilderness of North America. He walked the length and breadth of the country from the Sierras to Alaska, from the midwest to Florida. And always on his journeys, he kept extensive journals. Like Henry Thoreau, an earlier author–naturalist whom Muir admired, Muir used his journals as material for his articles and books.

Almost from the beginning, Muir's writings were concerned with conserving and saving the American wilderness. During his travels, he had seen how the great forest and wilderness regions of America were being "sold and plundered and wasted at will," by lumbermen and cattlemen and a growing, indifferent population. Through Muir's writings, Americans became aware of the urgent need to conserve the country's natural resources for future generations. It was books like Muir's *The Mountains of California,* published in 1894, that helped spread Muir's philosophy of conservation, and finally led to the establishment of our National Park System.

John Muir's writings reflected his knowledge and love of the trees and forests of America and the delight and great joy he found in life itself, but they also display his anger at those who would destroy the life of a forest or wilderness area. It was said that in Muir's writings, "his words bubble and dance," but when he is fighting the foes of conservation, they are as "hot as flying sparks."

In 1880 John Muir married and moved to a fruit farm in California. He succeeded so well at fruit farming, developing new strains of pears and grapes, that within ten years he was able to retire and spend the rest of his life writing and fighting for the preservation of our forests and wilderness. The John Muir home is now a historic site, open to the public. The eight acres of land surrounding the house have been restored to show what the vast orchards and vineyards that once made up the farm were like. A film about Muir's life and philosophy is shown hourly.

Although Yosemite National Park, as well as other national parks that came into being because of John Muir, are all monuments to the conservationist, the most beautiful monument is still Muir Woods. Several of the redwood trees within the woods have grown to the awesome height of 240 feet with a diameter of 13 feet.

Location: JOHN MUIR NATIONAL HISTORIC SITE, SR 4 and Alhambra Avenue, Martinez, California. Small admission charge.

Location: MUIR WOODS NATIONAL MONUMENT is 17 miles northwest of San Francisco, California, on the southwest slopes of Mount Tamalpais. The woods may be reached via Golden Gate Bridge and SR 1. Small admission charge.

JOAQUIN MILLER
1839-1913

One of America's most unusual literary sites is a grove of redwood, pine and eucalyptus trees on a hillside overlooking Oakland, California, and San Francisco Bay. Behind a small cottage built into the hillside may still be seen the stone funeral pyre upon which the western poet Joaquin Miller requested he be cremated after his death with his ashes scattered over the High Sierras.

This bizarre last request was a fitting climax to the life of a man who may not have been America's greatest poet, but was certainly one of the most colorful. The actual facts of the poet's life are vague because the poet had a tendency toward exaggeration when giving out facts about himself. It is known that he took his first name from the famous California stagecoach bandit, Joaquin Muretto.

Joaquin Miller claimed to have been born in a covered

171

wagon headed west, and it is true that his family took the Oregon Trail west to Oregon from Liberty, Indiana. Joaquin was fourteen when he ran away to the California goldfields. He made no big strikes and turned to running a road house, living and fighting with the Modoc Indians and finally practicing law in Oregon, as he always claimed, "with one law book and two six shooters."

Becoming interested in journalism, he bought a newspaper in Eugene, Oregon, lived a while in Canyon City, and at last took his literary talents to San Francisco in 1870. The leaders of that city's literary community were not impressed with Miller's poetry.

Undaunted, Miller moved to London, England, where his collection of poetry, *Songs of the Sierras* (1871) about the miners and mining camps of California made him an immediate, if short-lived, celebrity. Miller was invited into the best homes, where he appeared, costumed in a red shirt, buckskins and a bearskin flung over his shoulders. If his poetry hadn't caused a sensation, his flamboyant appearance certainly would have!

When he returned to America, he purchased the hillside near Oakland, California, which he called The Hights. Here he built a small cottage, which he called The Abbey, and planted groves of pine, redwood and eucalyptus trees. The poet always spent his mornings, wrapped in fur, writing poetry to the sound of rain on the roof. It was a sound he particularly liked and provided for himself by special water pipes he had built on the roof.

Near the house, he built stone pyramids to the memory of explorer John C. Fremont, and in honor of Moses, and a large stone tower in tribute to the English poet Robert Browning. One of the poet's last projects was the building of his own funeral pyre, upon which he wanted to be cremated. However, when Joaquin Miller died, this was not allowed. Instead a portion of his ashes were brought to the pyre and then scattered to the winds to be carried over the High Sierras that he loved.

Although only a few of Joaquin Miller's poems, among them "Columbus," are remembered today, he was one of the most authentic voices of the Old West. There are moments in his poetry when he catches the heroism of the pioneer men and women of the old frontier West when, as he wrote, "there were giants in the land."

Today, the tiny trees that Miller planted at The Hights are giants themselves. Miller's home, The Abbey, still stands, part of the Joaquin Miller Park. It was acquired by the city of Oakland after Miller's death. In another section of the park is a collection of trees dedicated to California authors Jack London, John Muir, Bret Harte, Mark Twain, and Joaquin Miller, among others. A statue of Joaquin Miller on horseback stands near an entrance to the park.

Joaquin Miller's cabin at Canyon City, Oregon, where he lived from 1864–1870 has been restored and furnished in the style it was when the poet lived there.

Location: JOAQUIN MILLER CABIN, Herman and Eliza Oliver Historical Museum, 2 miles south of John Day in Canyon City, Oregon, on Highway 395. Open summers only. Small admission charge.

Location: JOAQUIN MILLER PARK, The Hights, is located on Joaquin Miller Road, Oakland, California. Park open to public but The Abbey is open by appointment only.

SIDNEY LANIER
1842–1881

Along the southeast coast of Georgia, in the county of Glynn, great silver-green marshes stretch toward the Sea Islands. The marshes held an enduring fascination for the poet, Sidney Lanier. When he lived near Brunswick, Georgia, he visited the coastal area daily, stopping at a favorite spot by an inlet under an ancient, moss-hung oak. His study of the play of light and shadow across the marshland later became part of a famous poem called "The Marshes of Glynn."

Sidney Lanier, however, was not only a poet but a talented musician. He had planned a career in music and literature, but the Civil War put an end to his dreams. When he returned to Georgia after four years in the army and six months in a prisoner of war camp, he found the war-ravaged South offered little opportunity for either poets or musicians.

To earn a living, he clerked in a hotel, taught school,

wrote an unsuccessful novel, and after his marriage in 1868, helped his father in his law office at Macon. Music and poetry though were never completely out of mind.

In 1874 Lanier finally found a job as a flutist with a symphony orchestra, and in 1875, "Corn," his first poem to win critical acclaim, was published. Both accomplishments brought him recognition but little money, and his life became a continual struggle against poverty. Gradually, however, the two great interests in Lanier's life, music and poetry, came together.

Lanier began experimenting with creating pure musical sounds through the medium of verse. In his poem, "The Symphony," also written in 1875, he succeeded so well that by listening carefully, one can almost hear in the poem various musical instruments, the lilting flute, the melting clarinet, the bold brass horn. When in 1878 Lanier wrote his best-loved poem, "The Marshes of Glynn," the poem was described as a symphony without musical score.

Not all of Sidney Lanier's poetry was equally successful in becoming "essentially music." And critics of Lanier's day did not always appreciate Lanier's new experimental poetry. Yet he struggled to keep writing, even though he now knew he was racing against time and a fatal illness. He died at the age of 39 from the tuberculosis contracted in the prisoner of war camp. His last poem, "Sunrise," written while he was dying, is one of his finest. Words from that poem, "I am lit with the sun," appear on Lanier's tombstone.

Sidney Lanier today is considered one of the major poets to come out of the South after the Civil War, and his poem, "The Marshes of Glynn" one of the few great American poems. Lanier's birthplace, a modest little Victorian gabled cottage, is maintained by the Middle Georgia Historical Society as a shrine to his memory.

Perhaps an even more fitting tribute to Georgia's most famous poet is the Marshes of Glynn themselves with all their haunting beauty. The moss-hung oak tree under which Lanier was inspired to write his poem is marked with a plaque, and named Lanier's Oak in the poet's memory.

Location: SIDNEY LANIER COTTAGE, 935 High Street, Macon, Georgia. No admission charge.

Location: LANIER'S OAK is less than a mile north on US 17, near Brunswick, Georgia.

GEORGE WASHINGTON CABLE
1844-1925

In the old French Quarter of New Orleans stands an eighteenth century Creole home called Madame John's Legacy. The galleried house with its L-shaped courtyard and dormered windows was already almost a century old when George Washington Cable, intrigued by the romantic legends associated with the house, used the home as a setting for his short story, "Tite Poulette."

Everything about the Creole people—French-speaking descendants of early French and Spanish settlers of New Orleans—interested George Washington Cable. It was a case of opposites attracting. Although he had been born in New Orleans, the sober, industrious Cable was not at all like the indolent, luxury- and pleasure-loving Creole society.

At age fourteen, when his father died, the young Cable had become the chief support of his mother and two sisters.

He held several jobs, fought for four years in the Confederate Army during the Civil War, then, after the war, worked briefly for a New Orleans newspaper and as a bookkeeper for a New Orleans cotton firm. As part of his job for the cotton firm, he had to dig into old French and Spanish records kept in the city archives. In doing so, Cable uncovered the history of the Creole people. Hot-blooded and proud, the Creoles often settled their quarrels with duels, as well as adding grace, wit and romance to historic old New Orleans. Reading these old records with an author's eye, Cable felt it was a pity that such rich, exotic material should go to waste.

Quitting his job at the cotton firm, he devoted himself full-time to writing. His first short story with a Creole background to gain national recognition was "Sieur George," published in 1873. Other stories quickly followed.

The late 1800s was a period in American literature when local color or regional stories were very popular. Readers were fascinated by Cable's romantic stories of exotic New Orleans. By 1879 Cable's popular Creole tales had been gathered in one volume, called *Creole Days*. Two of his best known stories, "Tite Poulette" and "Belles Demoiselles" were included in that collection. The following year Cable wrote a romantic, historical novel about New Orleans called *The Grandissimes,* and then in 1881, another novel, *Madame Delphine.*

Although Cable's writings were popular in the northern states, they were not as popular in New Orleans. The Creoles resented the rather unflattering picture Cable drew of them. And when Cable spoke out against racial injustice in the South in his book, *The Silent South,* Cable and his family were forced to leave New Orleans. He and his family lived in Massachusetts for the rest of his life, although occasionally

Cable toured the country reading his Creole stories aloud and singing the lovely, drawling Creole melodies.

Cable was one of the first authors to write realistically about black people and their social conditions in the South; he was also a leading author in the local-color literary movement. Although his story plots are at times overly complicated, George Washington Cable caught the flavor of historic New Orleans, its virtues and vices, beauty and ugliness, as no other writer ever has.

There is no better introduction to the old French Quarter of New Orleans than one of George Washington Cable's stories. Cable often described and used actual places and houses as settings for his stories. The house he described in his story "Sieur George," although not open to the public, is at 640 Royal Street. However, the home Cable used in "Tite Poulette" is not only open to the public but is called "Madame John's Legacy" after the name Cable gave the house in his tale.

Madame John's Legacy is today the property of the Louisiana State Museum and has been furnished in the style of the fine Creole residence of the eighteenth century. Visiting the home with its exquisite French furniture, porcelains and china, one can almost imagine the heroine of Cable's story, the tragic Madame John and her beautiful daughter Poulette moving gracefully through these elegant rooms.

Location: MADAME JOHN'S LEGACY, 632 Dumaine Street (in the old French Quarter) New Orleans, Louisiana. No admission charge on Fridays.

JOEL CHANDLER HARRIS
1848–1908

One of the oddest literary sites to be found anywhere is a monument to a rabbit—not just any rabbit, but the cunning Br'er Rabbit, known to everyone who has read the *Uncle Remus Tales*. Br'er Rabbit's statue stands in the courthouse square of Eatonton, Georgia, the home town of his creator, Joel Chandler Harris.

A shy, freckle-faced, red-haired boy, young Joel was only fifteen when he went to work as an apprentice printer at Turnwold Plantation, before the Civil War. When he wasn't working on the plantation newspaper, Joel liked to visit the slave cabins and listen to the stories that the older slaves told. Joel particularly liked the stories about clever Br'er Rabbit, who by his wits alone outdid stronger animals like Br'er Fox and Br'er Bear.

What the young apprentice didn't realize was that he

was actually listening to folk tales that the slaves had brought with them from Africa. The African countries have a long tradition of oral rather than written literature, passing their folk stories by word of mouth from one generation to the next. This tradition was continued by the black slaves in America. Some of the characters in the stories, however, had changed somewhat during their trip from Africa. The trickster hare of the African Housa tribe and the cunning spider of the Ashanti people became the American Br'er Rabbit. Animals native to Africa, such as the leopard and the zebra, became the more familiar American buzzard and woodpecker. The powerful African Sky God, Nyame, became the plantation owner.

The Civil War brought an end to the publication of the plantation newspaper, and Joel Chandler Harris had to find other employment. After working for several newspapers in Louisiana, he finally ended up as the chief editorial writer on the Atlanta *Constitution*. In addition to his editorial work, Harris wrote sketches and stories for the newspaper. Remembering the stories he had heard from the slaves on the Turnwold Plantation, he decided to write them down, using the black dialect as he remembered it from his days on the plantation.

The first Uncle Remus tale, "The Story of Mr. Rabbit and Mr. Fox" was published in the *Constitution* in 1879. To the editor's surprise, delighted readers wrote in, demanding more such stories. Next, Harris wrote down the famous tar baby story. Many other tales of Br'er Rabbit, Br'er Fox and "other critters" followed in rapid succession.

In 1880 the stories Harris had written were collected in a book, *Uncle Remus: His Songs and His Sayings*. In the book, the stories were told to a small boy by Uncle Remus, a shrewd, elderly black man, modeled after Uncle George Terrell and several other slaves Harris had known.

Nine more Uncle Remus collections followed, each more popular than the last. Joel Chandler Harris lived the last years of his life at his home, called the Wren's Nest, in Atlanta, Georgia. Shy and retiring, he always insisted that none of his Uncle Remus stories were made up by him, but that all were tales told to him by black Georgian men and women.

Harris was one of the first writers to recognize the literary possibilities in the lives of southern black men and women. And unlike the over-sentimentalized faithful slaves so often portrayed in stories written before and after the Civil War, Harris's Uncle Remus was shrewd and independent, devoted to the underdog.

In Turner Park, near Eatonton, Georgia, there is a log cabin reconstructed from two original slave cabins. The cabin and furnishings represent the setting of the Uncle Remus stories. One end of the cabin has an old-fashioned fireplace with a cane rocker, looking as if it were waiting for Uncle Remus to arrive and tell his stories to the Little Boy. All the articles in the cabin are from the time Uncle Remus is supposed to have lived and are mentioned in the Uncle Remus stories.

The rambling, gabled house in Atlanta where Joel Chandler Harris lived took its name from a family of wrens that nested in the mailbox. There is an old-fashioned veranda where Mr. Harris sat in his rocker in the evening. Although a second-floor room was designed for a study, with rocking chair and desk, the author preferred to write his tales at the round library table where he could be near his wife and children.

Location: UNCLE REMUS MUSEUM in Turner Park is ½ mile south of Eatonton, Georgia, on U.S. 129 and 441. Admission charge. BR'ER RABBIT STATUE in Courthouse Square, Eatonton, Georgia.

Location: WREN'S NEST, home of Joel Chandler Harris, 1050 Gordon Street, S.W. Atlanta, Georgia. Admission charge.

BOOKER T. WASHINGTON
1856–1915

On the Burroughs Plantation in the Blue Ridge foothills of southwestern Virginia are several crude one-room cabins. In one of these cabins in 1856 a boy was born who was listed on a property inventory of the plantation as simply "One negro boy, Booker, $400." Yet it is because of the accomplishments, both literary and non-literary, of this slave boy that in 1957 the Burroughs farm was restored by the National Park Service and called The Booker T. Washington National Monument.

The Burroughs plantation was a frontier plantation, and the few slaves that John Burroughs possessed slept on rags on dirty floors and ate, as Washington recalled in later life, "a piece of bread here and a scrap of meat there." After the Civil War, the young ex-slave took the last name of Washington and went to work in salt furnaces and coal mines, with only a few months education a year.

The turning point in Washington's life was his admittance to Hampton Institution in Virginia. The school had been started by General Armstrong, "to lift the colored race by a practical education that shall fit them for life." Booker T. Washington was greatly influenced by General Armstrong. When he graduated from Hampton and started a school for black students in Tuskegee, Alabama, in 1881, he followed Armstrong's philosophy. His school at Tuskegee was a vocational school, teaching agricultural skills, as well as the ability to teach those skills to other black people.

Later Washington was criticized by black intellectuals, such as W. E. B. DuBois, for refusing to educate black students beyond the status of laborers, and for meekly accepting racial injustice at a time when blacks were being deprived of all their civil rights.

Nevertheless, Washington did a remarkable job of building what is today one of the outstanding black colleges in the country, starting from a shanty and a handful of students. By the turn of the century, Booker T. Washington, with his establishment of Tuskegee Institute, his speeches and writings and his friendships with prominent Americans, was the acknowledged unofficial spokesman for black America.

In 1901 Washington wrote his autobiography, *Up from Slavery*. He wrote the book "on board trains, or hotels or railroad stations while I have been waiting for trains or during the moments that I could spare from my work while at Tuskegee." *Up from Slavery* is a dramatic story, simply told, of the rise of a slave child to a position of power in America. In its own way, Washington's autobiography was a typically American book in the popular "rags to riches" style that Benjamin Franklin had made popular in his *Autobiography*. And it was the first book by a black author to reach hundreds of thousands of readers, both black and white, in the United States and abroad.

Washington wrote twelve books in his lifetime, including a biography of another famous black leader, Frederick Douglass. At the time of his death at Tuskegee, the institute had grown to over a hundred buildings, including The Oaks, the home in which Washington lived on campus.

The Burroughs plantation on which Booker T. Washington was born and spent his childhood is now a "living history" plantation. Visitors may see life as it was actually lived on such nineteenth century farms, including the kitchen cabin which doubled as a home for Booker, his mother, brother and sister. The facilities of the plantation include a visitors center, museum, movie of Washington's life and a self-guiding trail through the plantation.

Visitors are also welcome at Tuskegee Institute where Booker T. Washington's study in his home, The Oaks, has been restored to look as it did when Washington lived and wrote there. The George Washington Carver Museum and Art Center on the campus houses many mementos of Washington's life and work. The museum is dedicated also to the life of the famous black scientist, George Washington Carver, who was brought to Tuskegee by Booker T. Washington.

Location: BOOKER T. WASHINGTON NATIONAL MONUMENT is 16 miles northeast of Rocky Mount, Virginia, via SR 122N and 20 miles southeast of Roanoke via SR 116S and 122N. No admission charge.

Location: BOOKER T. WASHINGTON'S STUDY AT THE OAKS, Tuskegee Institute, Tuskegee, Alabama. Free guided tours of the campus are available. No admission charge.

EDWARD BELLAMY
1850–1898

Men and women have always dreamed of creating a better world—a Utopia. In 1888 a writer by the name of Edward Bellamy created such a fictional Utopia here in America in an unusual novel, entitled *Looking Backward*. In his book Bellamy created an imaginary United States in the year 2000 in which all poverty, social ills and injustices have been eliminated because the wealth of the country has been distributed with exact equality among all its citizens. Bellamy made several other fascinating prophecies in his book. He foresaw the coming of the airplane, radio, television, paper fabric for clothing, electrical heat—all unknown in 1888.

To readers of the late nineteenth century, Bellamy's book must have seemed a sort of impossible science fiction. And in a way Edward Bellamy was one of America's first science fiction writers. His earliest works of fiction included tales of interstellar space travel and visits to the planet Mars, as well as tales of psychic phenomena.

But Edward Bellamy's main passion in life was not writing science fiction. As a young man he had traveled widely and seen hovels in the great cities of Europe, as well as the slums in America's cities, and the "extent and consequences of man's inhumanity to man." Like many other liberals of his day, he became involved in trying to find a solution to the economic problems facing America at the turn of the century. In his novel, *Looking Backward*, Bellamy presented a socialistic solution to those problems.

Even Edward Bellamy, though, could not have foreseen the success of his novel. Many thousands of Americans read *Looking Backward* and decided that the society it described was much preferable to the capitalistic form of government. Bellamy Clubs were organized, a new People's Political Party was formed, and Bellamy lectured widely across the country, gaining new converts.

Bellamy, of course, was not the only social reformer of his day to turn to literature to present his ideas to the American public. Hamlin Garland described the hardships and injustices suffered by the pioneer families in the middle border states in his *Main-Travelled Roads;* Frank Norris did the same for the wheat farmers in California in *Octopus;* Upton Sinclair exposed the cruelties of the Chicago stockyards in *The Jungle;* Lincoln Steffens in his *Shame of the Cities* focused on the problems and corruption in American cities.

Edward Bellamy, though, did not only expose social injustice, in his highly readable novel, he also set forth plans for a new social and economic order, which would come about not through violent revolution, but peaceful persuasion. Bellamy's improbable dream of converting America to his own vision of Utopia lasted only a few short years. His health was destroyed by overwork, and he was forced to retire to his home in Chicopee Falls, Massachusetts, where he died in 1898.

Recently, the Edward Bellamy Memorial Association has been formed with the goal of opening to the public on a permanent basis the Edward Bellamy Homestead, which contains several hundred items of Bellamy memorabilia. At present it is open by appointment only.

Location: EDWARD BELLAMY MEMORIAL ASSOCIATION, 6 Center Street, Chicopee Falls, Massachusetts. No admission charge.

SARAH ORNE JEWETT
1849–1909

The picturesque southern coast of Maine with its small green islands, salt inlets and lonely houses facing the sea was used as setting for what has been called "the best piece of regional fiction produced in the nineteenth century." The author was Sarah Orne Jewett, and the book, *The Country of the Pointed Firs.*

A native of South Berwick, Maine, Sarah, as a young girl, would accompany her doctor father on his visits to patients around the southern Maine countryside. Since the frail, intelligent girl was "subject to instant drooping whenever she was shut up in school," she received much of her education from her father on those carriage rides. He told her stories of the families living at the salt-water farms they visited, and the colorful history of the decaying harbor areas where descendants of wealthy sea captains still lived. Riding with her father, Sarah learned to be observant, to notice the exact color of the marsh rose, the rich scent of bayberry and recognize the notes of the song sparrow. Her father taught her that "nothing is uninteresting if you look at it long enough."

Sarah Orne Jewett stored up all the knowledge she learned on those carriage rides and used it later in her stories about the southern Maine coast. For very early in her life, Sarah had determined to become a writer. She had read the stories Harriet Beecher Stowe had written about New England, and decided she would write stories about her own beloved Maine coast.

At age nineteen, she sold her first story with a Maine background, and by 1877 she had written enough stories to be collected in a book. Entitled *Deephaven*, after the fictitious name she gave the town in which the stories took place, Deephaven was, in fact, Miss Jewett's own home town of South Berwick.

Deephaven received immediate critical acclaim; and at age 28, Miss Jewett was recognized as one of the foremost writers in New England. Although she always insisted she could only write her stories while actually in Maine, she began to travel widely, believing "you must know the world before you can know the village."

But it was the villages, the people of Maine, who never ceased to hold her devotion, and it was to South Berwick she constantly returned from her travels. And, despite her success, she wrote as carefully and precisely as she had when she first started writing, "nibbling" as she herself said, "around her stories like a mouse."

In her lifetime she wrote several collections of stories, as well as three novels. Her masterpiece, however, was a collection of Maine stories, *The Country of the Pointed Firs,* published in 1896.

Miss Jewett never married. Writing always took first place in her life, writing and the large white mansion that had belonged to her seafaring grandfather and where she lived her whole life. Miss Jewett once said of her home, "I was born here and I hope to die here, leaving the lilac bushes still green and growing and all the chairs in their places." She died, as she wished, at her home in South Berwick.

Miss Jewett's stories of Maine, her descriptions of the quiet villages and weathered farms, have never been excelled. The characters in her stories always rang true, doughty, courageous, independent New Englanders with a strong sense of duty. She was particularly successful in catching the shrewd and eccentric old Maine village women, such as are found in one of her best short stories, "The Durham Ladies." Miss Jewett once laughingly said that her head was full of old houses and old women and that when the two got together in her brain with a click, she know a story was underway.

The whole southern coast area of Maine from the coast towns of Wells and York, inland to South Berwick, served as the setting for Miss Jewett's writings, as well as the big old house in which she was born. Today the house has been restored, with Miss Jewett's bedroom study carefully arranged as she left it.

Another lovely old home in South Berwick, the Hamilton House, was used as the highly romantic background in a Jewett novel, *The Tory Lover,* a historical romance of John Paul Jones and Revolutionary War days in Maine. The house is open to the public and furnished as a magnificent example of a nineteenth century Georgian mansion.

Location: JEWETT HOUSE, Route 236, Main and Portland Streets, South Berwick, Maine, located in the center of town next to the South Berwick Public Library. Open summers only. Small admission charge.

Location: HAMILTON HOUSE, Vaughan's Lane, South Berwick, is ¾ miles south on SR 236, then 1 mile via Vine Street and right on Brattle St. opposite the junction with Route 91. Open summers only. Small admission charge.

JAMES WHITCOMB RILEY
1849-1916

The Riley homestead in Greenfield, Indiana, is a typical old white country house with a large back porch, a white picket fence and green shutters at the windows. But to thousands of readers who have enjoyed the humorous poetry of James Whitcomb Riley, the Riley home is special. For the white clapboard house is the setting for two of his most popular poems, "Little Orphant Annie" and "The Raggedy Man Who Works fer Paw."

Growing up in Greenfield, young James had a happy, carefree childhood much like other small-town boys of his generation. He had his favorite swimming and fishing hole and liked to hang around the courthouse with his lawyer father and listen to the town gossip. His father wanted him to become a lawyer, too, but James was more interested in poetry, drama and music. When he was sixteen years old, he ran away from home, joining a traveling medicine show where he recited his own poetry and played the banjo to draw customers.

Later he came back to Greenfield, and then after he began to earn his living by his pen, finally settled in Indianapolis. In 1883 his first book of poetry, *The Old Swimmin' Hole and 'Leven Other Poems,* was published. Catching the humor, sentiment and tang of country life, and using the speech patterns of rural Indiana, Riley's poems were immensely popular with readers in nineteenth century America.

In addition to writing hundreds more such dialect poems, Riley, who was a born mimic and showman (despite acute cases of stage fright), toured the country, reciting his own verses. He was so successful that he became known as "the poet of the people." His poems about Little Orphant Annie, who said "the goblins'll get you if you don't watch out," and the Raggedy Man were favorites of children all over America. Public schools celebrated a "Riley Day" in honor of the Hoosier poet.

In his later years, Riley maintained two homes, one, his family home in Greenfield, and a second home, with friends, in Indianapolis. Although he occasionally attempted more formal poetry, he was much more at home with homespun rhymes that caught the flavor of rural America.

James Whitcomb Riley's childhood home is maintained with its original family belongings; the old Melodeon-type organ in the parlor; an ancient peacock fly-shooer and an old pie-safe. Around October 7, each year, a James Whitcomb Riley Festival is held in Greenfield, and a Raggedy Man shows up at the Greenfield house to entertain visiting children.

Next door to the house is the Riley Museum and just

east of the city is Riley Park, containing the Old Swimming Hole made famous by Riley's poem. The Riley Hiking Trail winds through farm and forest along the lovely Brandywine Creek where young James Whitcomb Riley used to swim and fish.

The Lockerbie Street home, where the poet spent the last twenty years of his life, was purchased by a group of Riley's friends after his death, refurbished and opened to the public. Riley was a familiar figure in Indianapolis. Despite his age and dignified appearance, he would often stop to throw snowballs with the neighborhood children. The Lockerbie home reflects Victorian city life at the turn of the century, just as the Riley homestead in Greenfield preserves rural and small town life in nineteenth century America.

Location: JAMES WHITCOMB RILEY BOYHOOD HOME, 250 West Main Street (U.S. 40) Greenfield, Indiana. Open summers only. Small admission charge.

Location: JAMES WHITCOMB RILEY LOCKERBIE STREET HOME, 528 Lockerbie Street, near downtown Indianapolis, Indiana. Small admission charge.

EUGENE FIELD
1850-1895

Many literary sites in America have been destroyed forever by the wrecker's ball. One such site, the boyhood home of the children's poet, Eugene Field, was saved at the last minute by the combined efforts of civic-minded citizens and $2,000 contributed in pennies and nickles from children in the St. Louis Public School system.

Although Eugene Field was born in the tall, narrow row house on South Broadway in St. Louis and lived there as a young boy, he and his brother were sent East to live with an aunt after his mother's death. Eventually, Eugene Field returned to Missouri to attend college then traveled abroad in a grand manner, rapidly running through the inheritance left to him by his father. Always, throughout Eugene Field's life, money had a way of slipping lightly through his fingers.

Marriage, when his bride was only sixteen and he was

twenty-two, meant that the young man had to find a way to make a living. He worked at editorial jobs on newspapers throughout the Midwest and in 1883 joined the staff of the Chicago *Morning News,* where he remained the rest of his life.

At the *Morning News* Eugene Field started writing a popular column for the newspaper, entitled "Sharps and Flats." In his column he combined sentimental childrens' poems with caustic, satirical prose. As a critic said, "Field dipped one pen in sugar, the other in astringent."

Today, Eugene Fields' satiric prose is largely forgotten. His sentimental poems for and about children, however, are still being read. Poems such as "Little Boy Blue," and "Wynken, Blynken and Nod," have become classics.

The original Eugene Field boyhood home was part of a section of row houses built in 1845. With donations from hundreds of St. Louis school children, the house was saved from destruction and restored as a shrine to the children's poet. Personal belongings of the poet may be seen in the house, the skullcap he always wore when he was working, handwritten manuscripts of his poems, even a collar belonging to Field's pet fox terrier, Jessie. Field once said that he always tried out his poems on Jessie and she "always liked them!"

Of special interest on the second floor of the house is an exhibit of toys, some over two-hundred years old, that Field collected. The collection even includes the famous gingham dog and calico cat about which Field wrote.

Location: EUGENE FIELD HOUSE AND TOY MUSEUM, 634 South Broadway (three blocks south of Busch Stadium, St. Louis, Missouri. Small admission charge.

PAUL LAURENCE DUNBAR
1872–1906

Phillis Wheatley was the first published black poet in America. The poet, however, who became known in his time as the "Poet Laureate of the Negro Race" was Paul Laurence Dunbar.

Born and educated in Dayton, Ohio, Paul Laurence Dunbar's parents and grandparents had been slaves on plantations in Maryland and Kentucky before the Civil War. While young Paul was growing up in Ohio, the Dunbar family had very little money, but Mrs. Dunbar had a great gift for song and story-telling, which she passed along to her son. Many of her stories were of the plantation days before the war.

When he was only seven years old, Paul wrote his first poem. In high school, despite the fact that he was the only black student in the school, he was elected editor of the school newspaper.

At twenty-one he paid to have published his first book of poetry, *Oak and Ivy*. Then he personally sold copies of his book to passengers on the elevator he operated, the only job he could find, as a black, after graduating from high school. A second volume of poetry, *Majors and Minors*, was published in 1895 and caught the attention of editor and literary critic, William Dean Howells. Howells gave the book of poetry a glowing review in his magazine and the young poet's literary career was made. Howells wrote that Paul Laurence Dunbar was "the first writer of African descent to feel the Negro life aesthetically and to express it lyrically." Within the next ten years, Paul Laurence Dunbar became one of America's most popular poets.

Dunbar wrote rapidly and prolifically, not only books of poetry such as *Lyrics of Lowly Life* in 1896, but also short stories, articles, novels and lyrics for a musical play. He also read his poetry aloud to audiences around the country in his rich, musical voice.

Although Dunbar's professional life was successful, his personal life was not as fortunate. He married after a triumphant tour of England; but in 1903 when his marriage broke up, largely because he was ill, he returned to Dayton to live. He continued writing, literally working himself to death while fighting a losing battle against tuberculosis. Paul Laurence Dunbar died at age thirty-three at his home in Dayton.

A great deal of Dunbar's poetry was folk poetry, so lyrical in style that forty of his poems were set to music. In poems like "When Malindy Sings" and "The Party" Dunbar skillfully caught the speech patterns of southern black men and women and children, as well as describing with humor and pathos, the warmth and closeness of black family life "down home." But the bulk of what he wrote was in standard English and expresses the yearnings, joys and sorrows of every person.

Dunbar has been criticized for presenting in his poetry a too-happy picture of plantation days in the south, but at times the poet did write such poems as "We Wear the Mask," expressing the more bitter side of black life in America.

After the poet's death, his mother lived in their home in Dayton, preserving carefully her son's books and manuscripts and keeping the furnishings in his study exactly as he left them. After Mrs. Dunbar's death in 1935, the State of Ohio purchased the property along with the poet's personal possessions. The house is now maintained as a State Memorial to the poet, the first such memorial in America dedicated to a black author.

Location: PAUL LAURENCE DUNBAR HOME, 219 N. Summit Street, Dayton, Ohio. Small admission charge.

HAMLIN GARLAND
1860–1940

Near La Crosse and West Salem, Wisconsin, is a beautiful region of green hills, ridges and deep ravines, or coulees. On a farm at Green's Coulee, the author Hamlin Garland was born and spent his childhood. Later, in one of his best-known books, *A Son of the Middle Border,* he described the farm as "crumpled against the wooded hills and lay well upon a ridge to the west . . . over the height to the north was the land of the red people, and small bands of their hunters used occasionally to come trailing down across our meadow."

Green's Coulee was a pleasant place for a young boy, but unfortunately Hamlin's father was not content with the Wisconsin farm. Like many other farmers of his day, he was drawn westward, seeking the promise of rich land to homestead along the middle border states of Iowa, Nebraska and the Dakota territory. He moved his family west to a homestead near Osage, Iowa, and then on again to a pioneer sod homestead on a bleak plain near Ordway, South Dakota.

For young Hamlin there was little happiness in the pioneer life. Although he found beauty in the rolling prairie land and the wide blue western skies, farm life itself was sheer, relentless drudgery. There were freezing winters and searing summer droughts, along with grinding poverty. And in the end, the homesteaders were often deprived of any profits from their land by the exploitation of the railroads and eastern banks.

Hamlin was twenty-four before he managed to break free of the farm. Disenchanted with the west, he moved back east to Boston and, having no money for school tuition, embarked upon a system of self-education at the Boston Public Library. He was particularly influenced by the writings of William Dean Howells, and the new "realism" in Howells' novel, *The Rise of Silas Lapham*. In his novels, Howells spoke out strongly against social injustice in America. Soon Hamlin Garland was caught up in the various reform movements sweeping the country, protesting political corruption and the exploitation of the small farmer and workingman by large industrialists and eastern bankers.

In 1887 Garland returned to South Dakota to visit his parents. He found his mother "in a small cabin on the enormous sunburnt, treeless plain, with no expectation of ever living anywhere else." His mother's health had been broken; his father was old before his time from the years of backbreaking farmwork. Angered and depressed by the waste of his parents' lives, Garland sat down in that hot little farmhouse and in one afternoon wrote his first short story, a sketch of pioneer life as it really was, with all its hardships and dehumanizing drudgery.

The story, entitled "Mrs. Ripley's Trip," was published by *Harpers Magazine.* Soon other stories followed, and in 1891, a collection of Garland's stories were gathered in a book called *Main-Travelled Roads.* Although basically local-color stories, describing pioneer life in the middle border states, Garland's stories were much more realistic and bitter than other regional stories written during this period. A later novel, *Rose of Dutcher's Coulee,* exposed the tragic barrenness and heroic endurance of the life of the pioneer woman.

Although local-stories were popular with nineteenth century Americans, they did not like grimly realistic stories like Garland's. The author had married, and in order to support his family, he began writing the sort of sentimental western story that magazines were eager to buy and that people were eager to read.

It wasn't until 1917 that Garland once again began to write of his boyhood. His autobiography, *A Son of the Middle Border,* exploded the romantic myths of pioneer life and won critical acclaim as one of the finest regional works American literature had produced. A sequel to his autobiography, *Daughter of the Middle Border,* won the Pulitzer Prize for literature in 1921.

Hamlin Garland wrote many more books in his long lifetime, but his fictional *Main-Travelled Roads* and the autobiographical *A Son of the Middle Border* are considered his two greatest works. They are important not just for their savagely truthful picture of pioneer life, but because they were the forerunners of the new realism in American literature.

The log cabin in which Hamlin Garland was born in

Wisconsin has long since disappeared, but the countryside around La Crosse and West Salem, Wisconsin, played a prominent role in Hamlin Garland's Middle Border books. Near West Salem is Gill's Coulee where Rose of Dutcher's Coulee lived, while nearby Green's Coulee was the site of one of Garland's best known stories, "Return of a Private."

In 1893 Hamlin Garland persuaded his parents to leave their homestead in the Dakotas and bought them a home in West Salem. Garland divided his time between this home and his home in Chicago. In 1973 the Garland home was designated a National Historic Landmark. Restoration of the house to make it as it was during the period when the author lived there was begun in 1975, and the home today is maintained and operated by the West Salem Historical Society.

Location: HAMLIN GARLAND HOMESTEAD, 357 West Garland Street, West Salem, Wisconsin. Open summers and by appointment in winter. Small admission charge.

WILLIAM PORTER (O. Henry)
1862–1910

By the turn of the century, New York City had become the literary center of America, with more writers gathered there than any place else in the country. One such writer was William Porter, better known by his pen name, O. Henry.

In the latter part of his life, William Porter lived in a furnished room in New York at 55 Irving Place near Gramercy Park. He would haunt the streets and parks of the city in his slouch hat and black bowtie, talking to men and women from all walks of life—bums, shop girls, bell boys, starving actors, painters and musicians. Porter was fascinated by a city that teemed with what he called "four million mysterious strangers." And each stranger had a sometimes sad, sometimes happy story to tell. In time Porter probably knew the city of New York better than any writer before or since. And he used his knowledge in the short stories he wrote with New York City as his favorite setting.

William Porter, however, was not a native New Yorker. He was born near Greensboro, North Carolina, and went to work in his uncle's drugstore when he was only fourteen. When his health failed, he went to live in Texas, first on the Hall Ranch near San Antonio, and then in Austin where he eloped with a young Austin girl and took a job in a bank. Writing, though, was always more interesting to Porter than banking. For a while he contributed columns to several Texas newspapers, even starting his own newspaper in Austin, called *The Rolling Stone*.

Then in 1896 Porter was arrested for an alleged embezzlement of funds from the bank in Austin where he had formerly worked. Although there was little evidence to back up the charges, Porter feared imprisonment and fled the country. For a year he drifted around Central and South America, hobnobbing with other exiles running away from the law. When he received word that his young wife was dying, however, he promptly returned to Austin, where, after his wife's death, he was arrested and sentenced to five years in prison.

By an odd twist of fate, the years in prison gave Porter the time he needed to master his writing skills. Some of the men he met in prison showed up later as characters in his stories. When Porter was released from prison, he went to New York to begin a new life.

In New York, Porter began writing at an amazing pace. He churned out as many as one or two stories a week, seldom stopping to polish or rewrite. His short stories sold quickly and were so popular that in time, Porter or O. Henry, his pen name, became the most widely read author in the nation. Eventually his stories were collected into a number of books, among them *The Rolling Stone, The Four Million* and *The Voice of the City*. In his lifetime, it is estimated that Porter wrote over six hundred pieces of original fiction.

Although Porter used all the various places he had lived as background material for his stories, his best stories were the ones written with a New York background, the city that never ceased to fascinate the author. It was in New York City that he died at age 48 and was buried from The Little Church Around the Corner, not far from the Gramercy Square area he knew and loved so well. '

William Porter's stories are often called local-color stories because they caught the special feeling of New York City. It was the little people of the city, though, for which he had the greatest compassion and understanding, the unknown men and women who lived in furnished rooms with ill-paying jobs. These were the people in such stories as "The Gift of the Magi," "The Furnished Room," and "The Last Leaf." Porter's greatest talent as a writer, however, was in his plotting, particularly the surprise twist at the end of the story, which became O. Henry's trademark.

The drugstore in which Porter worked as a young man is now part of the O. Henry-Richardson Memorial Room in the Greensboro Historical Museum, along with some of William Porter's original manuscripts, letters and displays depicting his life.

While living in San Antonio, Porter often stayed at a small house on South Press Street. It was here he wrote one of his best stories of the West, "A Fog in Satone," which had a setting of San Antonio. The house has been moved to the grounds of the Lone Star Brewery and renovated as part of the Buckhorn Museum Complex.

Porter and his wife also lived for three years at a small cottage in Austin, Texas. It was during this period that he published his weekly humorous newspaper, *The Rolling Stone,* in which his own short stories often appeared. Unfortunately it was also during this period that his wife's health failed and Porter faced the embezzlement charges which eventually sent him to prison. The home today contains personal effects of the author and has been placed on the National Registry of Historic Sites.

In the area around Irving Place where Porter lived in New York City, many of the restaurants, hotels and bars found in Porter's stories still exist. The house in which O. Henry lived at 55 Irving Place is no longer as it was, however. The building has been remodeled, and a restaurant now occupies the front parlor in which O. Henry would sit and write at his bay window while watching the passing street scene.

Location: GREENSBORO HISTORICAL MUSEUM, with Porter Drugstore and displays of Porter's life, 130 Summit Avenue, Greensboro, North Carolina. No admission charge.

Location: O. HENRY HOUSE, Buckhorn Hall of Horns Museum, 1½ miles south on US 281 on ground of Lone Star Brewery, San Antonio, Texas. Small admission charge.

Location: O. HENRY MUSEUM, 3 blocks west of I-35, at 409 East 5th Street, Austin, Texas. No admission charge.

LOCAL COLOR OR REGIONAL AUTHORS
AFTER THE CIVIL WAR

LOCAL COLOR OR REGIONAL STORIES AND POETRY WERE VERY POPULAR AFTER THE CIVIL WAR. THE COUNTRY WHICH HAD SPLIT VIOLENTLY APART WAS NOW BACK TOGETHER AGAIN. AMERICANS WANTED TO READ ABOUT REGIONS OF THE COUNTRY OTHER THAN THEIR OWN. SOUTHERNERS WERE CURIOUS ABOUT NEW YORK CITY. NEW YORKERS WERE FASCINATED BY STORIES OF THE ROMANTIC FAR WEST. AS ONE CRITIC SAID IN 1894, "EVERYBODY WRITES 'LOCAL' STORIES NOWADAYS; IT IS AS NATURAL AS WHOOPING COUGH."

Bret Harte and Joaquin Miller, with their stories and poetry of life in the California gold mining camps, were two of the more popular western local-color writers. This scene is an illustration from an early edition of "The Iliad of Sandy Bar," a Bret Harte story. Although most of the gold mining camps have long since crumpled into ruins, historic Angels Camp, California, looks much like the setting for one of Bret Harte's tales of the West and may still be visited today. COURTESY WASHINGTON UNIVERSITY LIBRARY

In the Midwest, local-color authors wrote nostalgically about a rural way of life that was already vanishing, such as the one-room schoolhouse seen left. The Indiana poet, James Whitcomb Riley, of "Lil Orphant Annie" fame, attended the above school in Greenfield, Indiana, where his home still stands as a historic literary site today. Edward Eggleston (1837–1902), another well-known local-color writer, was from Vevey, Indiana. His popular novel, *The Hoosier Schoolmaster,* might have taken place in just such a schoolhouse.

The lovely coastal marshland near Brunswick, Georgia, was the setting for Sidney Lanier's famous poem, "The Marshes of Glynn." Shown at right is Lanier's Oak, named in honor of the southern poet-musician, whose poetry combined local color with his love for music. COURTESY SOUTHERN RAILWAY

The writer who has been called the "best regional author of the nineteenth century" was Sarah Orne Jewett of Maine. Her book, *The Country of the Pointed Firs,* might have taken place in a coastal setting much like the one shown on the right. Miss Jewett's home in West Berwick, Maine, was also used as a setting for many of her stories and today has been restored and is open to the public. COURTESY LIBRARY OF CONGRESS

Madame John's Legacy was the setting for one of George Washington Cable's popular local-color Creole stories, which took place in the Old French Quarter of New Orleans. The house, today, has taken its name from the Cable story and is open to the public as an excellent example of Creole architecture. COURTESY LOUISIANA STATE MUSEUM

Although O. Henry (William Porter) is best known for his local-color stories of the Greenwich Village and Gramercy Park area of New York City, he also wrote stories with a Texas background. O. Henry had lived in Texas as a young man and he began his literary career there, a career unhappily interrupted by a term in prison for embezzlement. There are two memorials to O. Henry in Texas, one in Austin (shown above) and one in San Antonio. COURTESY O. HENRY MUSEUM

Among the works of Paul Laurence Dunbar were poems about the plantation South. Dunbar's home in Dayton, Ohio, has been restored and is open to the public. COURTESY OHIO HISTORICAL SOCIETY

Although Paul Laurence Dunbar wrote of plantation life in the South, he was actually born in Dayton, Ohio, where his study, or "loafing hole" as he called it, may be visited in his home. COURTESY OHIO HISTORICAL SOCIETY

Mark Twain (Samuel Clemens) was America's greatest humorist as well as a skillful local-color writer. Wherever he lived gave him material for his books: his boyhood home at Hannibal, Missouri; his piloting days on the Mississippi; and his gold mining days in Virginia City, as well as his many trips abroad. COURTESY MARK TWAIN MEMORIAL, HARTFORD, CONN.

One of the best known scenes in Mark Twain's *Tom Sawyer* is Tom and Becky becoming lost in a cave. A modern day "Tom and Becky" are shown below in what is now called Mark Twain Cave, near Hannibal, Missouri. The cave, which is the same one Mark Twain wrote about in his book, is open to the public year round. COURTESY HANNIBAL CHAMBER OF COMMERCE

Another familiar scene from *Tom Sawyer* is the one where Tom
tricks his friends into taking over his chore of whitewashing a
fence. The scene is recreated each year on the fourth of July,
in a fence-painting contest in Hannibal, Missouri.
COURTESY MISSOURI DIVISION OF TOURISM

Mark Twain made a great deal of money from his writing, but
he spent it just as fast. One of his greatest extravagances was his
home in Hartford, Connecticut, shown below, now restored and
open to the public. Twain helped design the house himself, including a room that resembles the pilot house on a riverboat and the
palatial billiard room where he did his writing. COURTESY MARK
TWAIN MEMORIAL, HARTFORD, CONN.

STEPHEN CRANE
1871–1900

The battle of Chancellorsville, Virginia, was one of the hardest-fought battles of the Civil War. Thirty years later a young man who had never fought in the battle—or any battle for that matter—was to write one of the most realistic war novels ever published, using the Chancellorsville battle as the setting. The author was Stephen Crane, and the novel was *The Red Badge of Courage*.

As a young boy growing up in New Jersey, Stephen Crane took easily to writing, and during his year at Syracuse University worked as a correspondent for the New York *Tribune*. College ended with his mother's death in 1890, and Crane began the struggling life of a writer in New York City.

Although he worked occasionally as a newspaper reporter, he spent most of his time prowling the tenements and saloons of the Bowery, the poverty-ridden slums of New York City in the 1890s. In 1892 he published, at his own expense, *Maggie, a Girl of the Streets,* which presented an honest picture of the brutal and sordid life of men and women forced to live in the Bowery. The book, although now considered by critics as America's first "naturalistic" novel, was too grimly written to attract many readers.

The following summer, while living in an artist's studio at 143 East 23rd Street, Crane wrote his short novel, *The Red Badge of Courage.* Although Crane had no first-hand knowledge of battle, he secured background information for his book by talking with Civil War veterans, reading books about the war and studying the Civil War photographs of Matthew Brady. The result was a book that told with remarkably fresh and true images the terror of a young boy's first experience in battle. And at age twenty-two Stephen Crane was famous.

Later, Crane did experience warfare when he covered the Spanish–American war in Cuba as a war correspondent. While he was sailing to Cuba, Crane's ship was sunk, and he endured several days in a lifeboat, an experience he vividly described in his short story, "The Open Boat." Earlier, he had taken a trip west as a newspaper correspondent, and, after surviving a bandit attack, used the western setting for two of his best known short stories, "The Blue Hotel," and "The Bride Comes to Yellow Sky."

Crane continued to use the naturalistic approach in his writing, that is, describing people and events in his stories as they actually occur in real life with no attempt to make moral judgments about his characters. This realistic approach to writing, in addition to the unconventional life Crane led, made the young author a controversial figure. He became so controversial that he finally left America and went to live in England.

Stephen Crane died when he was only twenty-nine years old, but within the short span of his life, his writings filled twelve volumes. A brilliant and innovative author, he is still considered one of America's most powerful writers and one of the greatest influences on twentieth century authors. As one critic said, with the publication of *Maggie,* "modern American fiction was born."

The battlefield of Chancellorsville, which was the setting for *The Red Badge of Courage,* is today part of the Fredericksburg and Spotsylvania National Military Park. The National Park Service provides a visitor center which features exhibits and a documentary film, with special programs interpreting soldier life during the war. A visit to the battlefield helps make the setting and action of Crane's novel come to life.

Location: FREDERICKSBURG AND SPOTSYLVANIA NATIONAL MILITARY PARK (which includes Chancellorsville Battlefield) are all within a seventeen-mile radius of Fredericksburg, Virginia. The Visitor Center to the battlefields is at the corner of Lafayette Blvd., (US 1) and Sunken Road. Self-guided and conducted tours begin here. No admission charge.

JACK LONDON
1876–1916

In the foothills of the Sonoma Mountains in northern California stands a massive, fire-blackened ruin. Crumbling walls and chimneys are all that remain of Wolf House, Jack London's dream of a baronial home that he said proudly, "would last one thousand years." Wolf House lasted just one day. The twenty-six room mansion was destroyed by fire within hours of its completion.

Yet the fact that Jack London could build such a lavish home using only money earned from his writing was in itself something of an impossible dream. As a young boy in Oakland, California, Jack London worked twelve to sixteen hours a day in a cannery to help support his impoverished family. At fifteen, he became an oyster pirate, engaged in the dangerous and illegal business of raiding oyster beds in San Leandro Bay. At seventeen, he went to sea aboard the *Sophie Sutherland*.

Returning to California in 1893, he found America in the depths of a depression. Unable to find work, he rode the rails, leading the life of a hobo, from one end of the country to the other. Finally he joined the gold rush to the Klondike in Alaska and wintered in the Yukon when he was twenty-one years old.

Jack London's education was sketchy and gained mostly from his own reading in the Oakland Public Library. One book was to influence his life more than any other; the *Communist Manifesto*. It was this controversial book, along with London's own knowledge of the oppressive conditions under which working men and women lived in nineteenth century America, that turned London into a Socialist.

After failing to find any gold in the Yukon, Jack London returned to Oakland, determined to make a success of his life through writing. From the very beginning of his writing career, he disciplined himself to write at least one thousand words a day, without fail, every day of his life.

At first, he sold only a few stories a year, mostly stories about the Yukon. Then in 1903 he wrote a short novel, *Call of the Wild,* which brought his first fame and financial success. Many critics still consider it London's finest work. In writing the story of Buck, the dog from civilization who finally reverts to the wild, London used a pattern he followed in all of his future writings; he based his story on experiences from his own life.

The year he spent in the Yukon became the background not only for *Call of the Wild,* but also for *White Fang* (1906) ; his experiences as a seaman furnished the material for *The Sea Wolf* (1904) ; the difficulties he encountered as a young writer became the semi-autobiographical *Martin Eden* (1909) ; and his struggle to overcome alcoholism became *John Barleycorn* (1913) . London's "protest novels" mirrored his involvement in the socialist cause. The struggles of the working man and woman, and the danger of Facism in America became the themes of the novels, *Valley of the Moon* (1913) and *The Iron Heel* (1907).

With each book, and short story, Jack London became more and more successful, becoming, in time, the most popular and highly paid author of his day. Success, however, brought disillusionment as well. Although London became a colorful, romantic figure on the American scene, noted for being as fast with his fists as he was with words, he was often depressed and began drinking heavily.

He had married in 1900 and was separated from his wife in 1903. His books, which more and more stressed London's belief in white, Anglo-Saxon superiority, began to turn many Socialists against him. As a matter of fact, London with his powerful sense of individualism, his desperate drive and need for money, never did fit well into the conventional Socialist mold.

In 1905 he married a second time, a young woman who loved the adventurous life as much as London did. Together they set sail around the world on their yacht, *The Snark,* a voyage made hazardous by the fact that neither London nor his sailing master had any knowledge of navigation! The adventures of that 27-month voyage were excitingly recorded by London in his *Cruise of the Snark* (1911).

After London and his wife returned to California, his chief interest became his 1500-acre ranch situated in the rich, green Valley of the Moon and the home he was building there. He had dreams of the ranch becoming the center of a great scientific experiment in farming. London poured a fortune into his ranch, but his experiments in scientific farming ended in failure, and his redwood and volcanic stone mansion burned within twenty-four hours of its completion. He was forced to write more and more short stories and books in a hurry—"hackwriting" London called it—to support the ranch. Within the space of sixteen years, he turned out more than fifty books and his income rose to $75,000 a year. Because of the expenses of the ranch, however, and his generosity to friends and strangers alike, he was always in debt.

During the last years of his life, London was in ill health but never stopped working hard and living exactly as he pleased, despite the doctors' orders to take it easy. "The proper function of man is to live, not to exist . . ." London insisted stubbornly. "I would rather that my spark should burn out in a brilliant blaze than that it should be stifled by dry rot."

Jack London died on the morning of November 22, 1916, from an overdose of morphine, whether accidentally or deliberately taken has never been determined.

Many of Jack London's books and short stories were too hastily written in his never-ending need for money to have any great value, but his best works, *Call of the Wild, The Sea Wolf,* and *Martin Eden,* are still considered minor classics. Primarily a storyteller, London will be best remembered for his adventure tales. However, it should be noted that he was one of the first American authors to write sympathetically and realistically of working class Americans. Along with Stephen Crane and Frank Norris, Jack London was a trailblazer, introducing new themes and a realistic style of writing into American literature.

Jack London's wife, Charmian, outlived her husband by forty years, and at her death, her home in the Valley of the Moon, called The House of Happy Walls, was turned into a memorial to her husband. The museum houses a replica of Jack London's study, his priceless collection of South Seas articles and other fascinating memorabilia. In 1959 the Jack London State Historical Park was created from a portion of the land that was once the author's ranch. The site now includes the museum, Jack London's gravesite and the impressive ruins of Wolf House.

In the city of Oakland, California, in Jack London Square, the First and Last Chance Saloon, where the young Jack London celebrated his "oyster swag," still stands. A portion of the original cabin where London stayed in the Yukon has been brought to the Square and restored to look as it might have during Alaska Gold Rush days.

The Oakland Public Library, where Jack London spent many hours as a boy, has a Jack London Room, containing books, pictures and clippings about the author. A short film on Jack London is shown in this room several afternoons a week.

Location: JACK LONDON STATE HISTORIC PARK is located midway between Sonoma and Santa Rose, at Glen Ellen, California off State Highway 12. Small admission charge to museum.

Location: JACK LONDON SQUARE, foot of Broadway, Oakland, California.

Location: OAKLAND PUBLIC LIBRARY (Jack London Room), Fourteenth and Oak Streets, Oakland, California.

ZANE GREY
1875-1939

The Wild West has had an irresistible fascination for the American reading public since the days of James Fenimore Cooper's frontiersman novels. The writer, however, who did the most to make the western novel one of the most popular forms of American literature was Zane Grey.

Like Bret Harte, another early western writer, Zane Grey was not a native-born westerner. His home was Zanesville, Ohio, which his ancestor, Ebenezer Zane, a celebrated Indian fighter, had founded when Ohio was still frontier territory. By the time Zane Grey was born, Zanesville was a thriving, civilized community. His father was determined that his son should become a dentist, and a dentist was what Zane Grey became.

Dr. Grey, however, much preferred playing semi-professional baseball and fishing to dentistry. After his marriage, he gave up dentistry completely, and he and his wife moved to Lackawaxen, Pennsylvania, where he began to write for a living. His first book, which his wife paid to have published, was *Betty Zane,* the story of the founding of Zanesville, Ohio.

The book did not sell, nor did other stories Zane Grey wrote. Discouraged, he would have given up writing if it had not been for his wife's encouragement. Then the struggling young author was given a chance to visit the Far West. Traveling with one of the last of the plainsmen, Buffalo Jones, Grey hunted mountain lions in the Grand Canyon, joined a party of wild horse hunters from Utah, crossed the Painted Desert of Arizona with a Mormon caravan, and even lived for a while with the Texas Rangers.

When he returned home, he wrote, in 1910, *The Heritage of the Desert,* using as a setting the "lonely purple land of sage and rock." With this book Zane Grey was on the road to success. His second novel, and his most popular book, *Riders of the Purple Sage* (1912), with a setting in Kanab, Utah, sold more than two millions copies and is still being sold today. In all, Zane Grey wrote 54 books, many of them still eagerly read.

When he wasn't writing, Grey traveled the West, hunting, fishing, exploring, gathering material for his novels. One of his favorite spots was an almost inaccessible cabin in the wilderness near Payson, Arizona, below the "Mogollon Rim." He used this region as a setting for many of his novels, although in his books he called it the "Tonto Rim."

As with other best-selling novelists of his day, Zane Grey was more popular with readers than with literary critics. His stories of heroic cowboys with nerves of steel, rustlers, Indians and villainous gunmen were called "violent, bloody and crudely written." Yet even the critics had to admit that Grey's books had swiftly moving, inventive plots, and his western settings were colorful and authentic down to the last detail.

The cottage in which Zane Grey and his wife lived in Pennsylvania, much enlarged since he struggled to become a writer there, is today the Zane Grey Inn. The room in which he wrote is now a museum with mementos from the author's life, including the Morris chair in which he always wrote, longhand, on a lapboard across the chair arm.

Near Zanesville, Grey's boyhood home, is the National Road–Zane Grey Museum, which houses a reconstruction of the Zane Grey study. There are also exhibit cases containing copies of Grey's original handwritten manuscripts, some of his western clothing, guns and knives and other articles from the author's life.

Perhaps the most fitting memorial for Zane Grey is his lodge in the Mogollon Rim area of Arizona. The Rim is a forested cliff 2,000 feet high, overlooking the Tonto basin in the Tonto National Forest. It was in this region that Zane Grey felt most at home, and he often used it as a setting for his novels. After his death, the lodge fell into disuse; but it was completely renovated in 1963, to make it look as it had when Grey lived there. Today the lodge is visited by countless fans of Zane Grey books, not only from America but from around the world.

Location: ZANE GREY HOUSE/INN, Lackawaxen, Pennsylvania. Open summers, April through October. Admission charge.

Location: NATIONAL ROAD–ZANE GREY MUSEUM, 8850 East Pike, is 10½ miles east on US 22 and 40, east of I-70, exit 65. Zanesville, Ohio. Admission charge.

Location: ZANE GREY LODGE is located 17 miles east of Payson, Arizona (Gila County), then north along the Tonto Creek in the Tonto National Forest. Small admission charge.

GENE STRATTON PORTER
1868–1924

In the early 1900s, it was unusual for a woman to enter, much less be successful in, a profession. Gene Stratton Porter, however, managed to achieve success in two careers. She not only won acclaim as a naturalist, but her romantic novels were best-sellers in their day.

A tomboyish upbringing on an Indiana farm, where she was allowed to roam freely, early introduced her to the fascinations of nature study. It was an interest she never outgrew. After she married in 1886 and moved with her husband to Geneva, Indiana, they built a cabin at the edge of the great Limberlost Swamp, where Mrs. Porter became a serious student of the local wildlife and wildflowers.

Photography was a new invention at the turn of the century, but Gene Stratton Porter soon saw the possibilities in photographing birds and plant life in their natural habitat.

Soon Mrs. Porter became a familiar sight around Geneva with her little black horse and her buggy loaded with camera equipment. She waded shallow rivers, fought quicksand, worked for days in the slime of swamps and marshes to get a photograph of the first dove in March or the last migrant bird in October.

Her early writings were nature articles, illustrated with her own photographs, which she developed in the family bathroom. Then one day when she was tracking down the nest of a black vulture, she conceived the idea for a romantic novel, using the great Limberlost Swamp as a setting. The success of *Freckles,* published in 1904, encouraged her to write more novels in the same romantic veih, the most popular being *A Girl of the Limberlost,* in 1909.

Although Mrs. Porter continued writing her nature books, it was her novels that brought her enormous popularity. Ten million copies of her novels had been sold by the time of her death. Those Americans who had not read the Porter novels saw them on the screen when they were made into movies.

Like other popular novelists of her day, Mrs. Porter's plots and characters were overly sentimental. Her descriptions of the nature settings, though, the serene beauty of woodland and swamp, were written by Mrs. Porter with a sure, authentic touch.

Mrs. Porter's home at Geneva, Indiana, the cedar-logged Limberlost Cabin where she did much of her early writing, was presented to the state of Indiana in 1947. The house contains many mementos of the author, including her priceless moth and butterfly collection. Parts of this house and the surrounding countryside served as background for her novels, and visitors to the house often ask to see

"Freckle's window," or "the Limberlost girl's bedroom."

In 1913, the Limberlost Swamp was drained, and Mrs. Porter built another, more lavish home near Sylvan Lake. She wrote her later books on the large screened porch of this home, and her photographic darkroom on the first floor of the house, as well as her large library, may still be seen. The area around the house is a bird and wildflower sanctuary with the garden containing over 3,000 trees, shrubs, vines and wildflowers, which Mrs. Porter had planted.

Location: LIMBERLOST CABIN, 200 East 6th Street, Geneva, Indiana. Small admission charge.

Location: GENE STRATTON PORTER STATE MEMORIAL is located 1 mile south on SR 9, then 1 mile east, near Rome City, Indiana. No charge to garden area. Small admission charge to house.

HAROLD BELL WRIGHT
1872–1944

One hot July day in 1904 a man pitched a tent on a high point of land overlooking the valleys and ridges of the Ozark Mountains of Missouri. For the next three months Harold Bell Wright lived in the tent, writing a novel about the Ozark region and people. The novel, *The Shepherd of the Hills,* was published in 1904 and became such a phenomenal best-seller that special freight trains were required to carry the books to stores all over the country.

Harold Bell Wright had planned to become a minister. When his money and health ran out after two years in college, he went west to Missouri in 1897. He served as a minister to small churches in Missouri and Kansas, and, late at night, began writing. But he pushed himself too hard, and once again his health failed.

Moving to an area of the Ozarks, near Branson, Missouri, of which he was particularly fond, Wright pitched his tent overlooking a spectacular view. Here he could watch the mist rise in the morning from the valleys and a blue dusk creep across the hills at sunset. He settled down to write his novel, *The Shepherd of the Hills,* about the proud and occasionally violent people who inhabited the Ozark hills, scratching a living out of the rocky soil.

Wright's next two novels, *The Calling of Dan Matthews* (1909) and *The Winning of Barbara Worth* (1911) were also best-sellers. In all, Wright wrote nineteen novels, which sold over ten million copies.

The popularity of Wright's books bewildered literary critics, who found his books sentimental and melodramatic. Wright, however, never claimed his books were great literature. He wrote in a clear, readable style and captured the essence of the Ozark people and region better than anyone before or since.

Because of the popularity of Wright's books, the Ozark area of Missouri extending through Stone and Taney Counties, the setting for Wright's most popular novel, has taken the name, "The Shepherd of the Hills Country."

Today, visitors still tour the Shepherd of the Hills Farm, visiting Old Matt's cabin, where one of the main characters in the book lived. A jeep train has been provided, which tours the historic points used as incidents in the book, including the mysterious Pete's cave, and traveling "the trail that is nobody knows how old." The tour also visits Inspiration Point where Wright pitched his tent and wrote his book.

In the evening, under the stars at an outdoor amphitheater on the farm, an exciting dramatization of *The Shep-*

herd of the Hills is presented during the summer and early fall months.

Location: THE SHEPHERD OF THE HILLS FARM is located 7 miles west, just off SR 76, from Branson, Missouri. Old Mill Theatre is located on the grounds. Admission charge.

JOHN FOX, JR.
1863-1919

When John Fox, Jr. came to live in the Cumberland Mountains of Virginia at the turn of the century, the families in the isolated settlements still lived by a code of behavior and way of life that their forefathers had brought with them generations before. Feuds between families, some so old that the original cause was forgotten, were not uncommon. Law enforcement was practically non-existent.

John Fox Jr. moved to Big Stone Gap, Virginia, hoping to make a fortune in the booming coal industry. Although an Easterner, and a graduate of Harvard, young Fox soon began to feel at home among the mountain people. As he was to write later, "I slept with the people, ate and drank with them, and even fought against them."

When his mining ventures failed, Fox turned to writing for a living. And it was the people of the Cumberland mountains he wrote about, describing the ruggedly beautiful country in which they lived, and detailing how encroaching civilization was slowly destroying their primitive, natural way of life.

Fox's stories sold slowly at first. Gradually, however, he attracted more and more readers. The novel for which he is best known is *The Trail of the Lonesome Pine,* written in 1908 and still read today.

Like other popular writers of the early 1900s, such as Harold Bell Wright and Gene Stratton Porter, John Fox's novels were overly sentimental. *The Trail of the Lonesome Pine* is no exception. The story of the romance between the young mountain girl, June Tolliver, and an eastern engineer and the feud between the Tolliver and Falin family (based upon an actual incident) is saved from complete sentimentality, however, by John Fox's sure instinct for storytelling and his intimate knowledge of the ways of the mountain people.

During the summer months, *The Trail of the Lonesome Pine* is recreated as an outdoor musical drama at the June Tolliver Playhouse in its actual locale, Big Stone Gap, Virginia. The June Tolliver House and a small John Fox, Jr. Museum, with mementos from the author's life, is also open to the public, with guided tours available.

Location: JUNE TOLLIVER PLAYHOUSE AND JUNE TOLLIVER HOME, Jerome and Clinton Streets, Big Stone Gap, Virginia. Admission free to house; admission charge to June Tolliver Playhouse performance.

Location: JOHN FOX, JR. MUSEUM, Shawnee Avenue, Big Stone Gap, Virginia. Open summers, afternoons only. Small admission charge.

BEST-SELLING NOVELISTS, 1901–1915

BETWEEN THE YEARS 1901 AND 1915 MORE AMERICANS WERE READING NOVELS THAN EVER BEFORE. THE NOVELS THEY LIKED TO READ WERE ADVENTURE NOVELS LIKE JACK LONDON'S *Call of the Wild*, OR ROMANTIC NOVELS LIKE GENE STRATTON PORTER'S *Freckles*, AND ESPECIALLY WESTERN NOVELS LIKE ZANE GREY'S *Riders of the Purple Sage*.

Jack London became America's best-selling writer and "literary celebrity" with his adventure novels set in the Yukon. Although his books were extremely popular, London did not write in the overly sentimental style common to other best-selling authors of his day. COURTESY JACK LONDON STATE HISTORIC PARK

Jack London used his ranch in the Sonoma Valley of California as a setting for several of his novels. Below is a photograph of the ruins of Jack London's home, Wolf House, shortly after it was destroyed by fire. The ruins of Wolf House, a Jack London Museum and a portion of his ranch now constitute the Jack London State Historic Park. COURTESY JACK LONDON STATE HISTORIC PARK

Several literary sites that may be visited honor Zane Grey: the Zane Grey House/Inn, Lackawaxen, Pennsylvania; the National Road–Zane Grey Museum in Zanesville, Ohio; and the author's hunting cabin (shown here) in the ruggedly beautiful Tonto National Forest, Arizona. The author used the Mogollon Rim area of Arizona as the background for several of his novels. PHOTO BY BILL GOETTL

Zane Grey, shown with his horse, Night, sold millions of copies of his western novels. Another popular western novelist of this time was Owen Wister (1860–1938), whose best-selling book was *The Virginian* (1902). Although these western writers were scorned by critics, they fulfilled the dreams of millions of city dwellers back east, and in time made the cowboy a respectable character for serious literature. COURTESY OHIO HISTORICAL SOCIETY

A few cowboys wrote their own autobiographies or stories of the West as they knew it first-hand. One of these was Nat Love. Born in slavery, he went west as a young man to work the cattle drives, winning the title of Deadwood Dick because of his marksmanship. In 1907 he wrote *The Life and Adventures of Nat Love,* the only book-length autobiography of a black cowboy. COURTESY NEBRASKA HISTORICAL SOCIETY

One of the popular romantic
novelists of this period was
former minister, Harold Bell
Wright. His best-selling *Shepherd of the Hills*, was set in the
Ozark region, near Branson,
Missouri. One of the characters
in his novel, Uncle Matt, lived
in the cabin shown above right,
now located within the Shepherd of the Hills Farm. The
novel has been turned into an
outdoor spectacular drama,
shown each summer in an amphitheater on the farm. A scene
from the *Shepherd of the Hills*
dramatization is also shown.
COURTESY MISSOURI DIVISION OF
TOURISM

Cowboy and Indian western
stories were very popular in the
early twentieth century. Unfortunately, the Indians could
not write their own side of the
story as their tradition in literature was oral, or spoken,
rather than written. The Cherokee Indian, Sequoya, shown
right, did invent the Cherokee
alphabet and a system of writing
in 1821, but most of the history
and myths of Indian tribes
were handed down by word of
mouth. A few American writers
at the turn of the century, Mary
Austin (1868–1934) and her
The Land of Little Rain (1903)
and nature writer, Ernest
Thompson Seton (1860–1946),
wrote realistically of Indian life.
Most western writers of the
period, however, either overromanticized the Indian or made
him into a brutal, uncivilized
savage. COURTESY BUREAU OF
AMERICAN ETHNOLOGY SMITHSONIAN INSTITUTION, DICTIONARY OF
AMERICAN PORTRAITS

VACHEL LINDSAY
1879-1931

Just a few blocks from Abraham Lincoln's home in Springfield, Illinois, is another house, equally historic, though not as well known. This is the home of Vachel Lindsay, America's "vagabond poet," who, like an early day flower child, tramped across America spreading his gospel of beauty and trading his poetry for bread.

Born into a moderately well-to-do Springfield family, the son of a physician father and an extremely religious, artistic mother, young Vachel early showed an interest in art and poetry. Although his parents would have preferred that their son become a minister or doctor, it was the pursuit of beauty that was to dominate Vachel Lindsay's life.

He studied art, first in Chicago, then in New York, but his artistic talent was not great enough to bring him financial success. So he concentrated instead on writing poetry, which turned out to be equally unprofitable. Then in the spring of

1906, out of work and out of money, but filled with missionary zeal, Lindsay started on a tramping trip through the South. He was determined to bring art and poetry into the lives of those who had never had the opportunity to read poetry or see great masterpieces of art. He pitched hay or chopped wood for a night's lodging or "traded rhymes for bread." Often hungry, wet and tired, he still could write in his diary, "If I cannot beat the system, I can die protesting."

Vachel Lindsay took several such vagabonding trips through the country, but in between his trips, he always returned to his home in Springfield. His parents were bewildered by his unconventional way of life, as were his neighbors in Springfield. To them a tramp was a tramp, and not a vagabonding troubadour intent upon erasing ugliness from the face of America.

It was during Lindsay's last walking trip west in 1912 that he wrote one of his best-known poems, "General William Booth Enters into Heaven," on the occasion of the death of General Booth, founder of the Salvation Army. The poem was accepted by *Poetry* magazine, a new Chicago magazine founded by the driving force and genius of Harriet Monroe.

Like Vachel Lindsay, Harriet Monroe was determined that poetry should become an accepted part of American life. Most of all, she wanted to break with the old traditional forms of poetry and introduce a "new poetry" to America. Through her magazine she found and introduced many unknown poets to American readers. Three she introduced were the so-called "prairie poets" from the Midwest: Vachel Lindsay, Edgar Lee Masters and Carl Sandburg.

Vachel Lindsay's poems certainly did break with tradition. In his poem about General Booth he included directions for musical instruments to be played as accompaniment to the poem. The rhythm of the poem caught the beat of the "Boom-Boom-Boom-Boom-Boom" of the Salvation Army drum, as well as the banjos, flutes and tambourines played in a Salvation Army band.

Lindsay's most famous poem, and equally non-traditional, was "The Congo," a blend of rhyme, religious revival sermon and the ragtime beat of the cakewalk, a popular dance in 1914 America. Although Lindsay also wrote poetry in a more conventional style, as for example in "Abraham Lincoln Walks at Midnight," he won his greatest popularity with his poetry that was meant to be half-sung, half-recited.

Not only did Lindsay's poetry become well known, but the poet himself came to be in great demand, reciting his works to audiences all over the country. Audiences swayed in sympathetic excitement, as the poet mounted the stage and chanted and shouted the lines of "The Congo," rocking on the balls of his feet, his eyes blazing, arms pumping like pistons, lifting his voice to a high, jubilant shout, then dropping to a whisper on the last line. So successful were his poetry readings that in 1920 Vachel Lindsay was the first American asked to recite his poetry at Oxford University in England.

Lindsay continued what he called his "high vaudeville" tours until almost the end of his life. The tours, however, more and more exhausted him and took away time and energy he might have devoted to his writing. The poems he did manage to write later in life were more lyrical, less raucous and exuberant, and never achieved the originality and popularity of his earlier works.

During his last years, and in between tours, Lindsay

lived in Springfield. He had married late in life, and the income from his poetry and recitations barely supported his wife and family. Ill-health finally caused a mental breakdown. Always eccentric and undisciplined emotionally, Lindsay's eccentricities became more pronounced. Depression set in, and in 1931 he was dead by his own hand, in the house and bed in which he had been born.

The Vachel Lindsay home in Springfield originally belonged to Abraham Lincoln's sister-in-law. Lincoln and his family were often entertained there. Today the house, maintained by the Vachel Lindsay Association with volunteer help from high school students, remains much as it was when Lindsay lived there. In the dining room, where the poet held many readings of his poetry for visiting college students, neighbors and friends, is housed a valuable collection of phonograph records of the poet reading his own poetry, in his own special style. At the top of a steep oak staircase is the tiny room where the poet wrote at a plain wooden table, overlooking the governor's mansion next door. The poet always claimed he could not write as well anywhere else. Nearby is a large bedroom with an old four poster bed where the poet was born—and died.

One of Vachel Lindsay's dreams, to bring beauty to his home town, was partially fulfilled. Through his influence, a beautiful man-made lake may now be found south of the city of Springfield. Over the lake is a bridge named for the poet, and a bronze statue of Vachel Lindsay stands at one end of the bridge.

Location: VACHEL LINDSAY HOME, 603 South Fifth Street, Springfield, Illinois. Open summers only. Small admission charge.

EDGAR LEE MASTERS
1869–1950

In 1915 a book of poems, called *Spoon River Anthology*, was published, which used the poet's home town, Petersburg, Illinois, as a background. The book brought its author Edgar Lee Masters instant national fame, but so shocked and angered the people of Petersburg that for many years the poet was no longer welcome there. Actually Edgar Lee Masters had lived in Petersburg only as a young boy. When he was eleven years old, his father had moved the Masters family to nearby Lewistown, Illinois. As he grew up, although he clearly showed a literary bent and talent as a poet, his father insisted that his son should become a lawyer because there was no money in writing poetry.

As a lawyer, Masters joined the liberal law firm of Clarence Darrow in Chicago, a firm that was noted for defending the poor and oppressed. Masters was a successful lawyer, but he soon left the law firm, convinced that the law could not bring about the social reforms needed in America.

And becoming a lawyer had not, as his father had hoped, stopped him from writing poetry. In 1914 a noted literary magazine in St. Louis, *Reedy's Mirror,* published a collection of poem/epitaphs in free verse written by Edgar Lee Masters. The next year the poems were published in book form, the now famous *Spoon River Anthology.* The poems in the book were supposedly epitaphs written by the dead of Spoon River. In their epitaphs they finally tell the real truth about themselves, with all their meanness and hypocrisy, their successes and failures, their bitter frustrations, exposed.

Critics hailed *Spoon River Anthology* as a masterpiece, "the most original piece of imaginative literature ever written," as well as "intense and moving drama." The citizens of Petersburg and Lewistown, however, felt otherwise. They recognized at once that the fictional town of Spoon River was a combination of the towns of Petersburg and Lewistown. And the dead in the poems were just as readily recognized as being based upon actual people, ancestors of families who were still living in the two small towns.

Masters's book was bitterly denounced from the pulpits and the streets, as was Masters, himself. And it didn't help matters any when in 1931 the poet wrote a biography of Abraham Lincoln, called *Lincoln, the Man,* which denounced Illinois's greatest hero as an opportunist politician.

After Masters left law, he devoted his full time to writing. He was one of the leading members of the Chicago literary group and a supporter of Harriet Monroe's *Poetry* magazine in Chicago. Over the next thirty-five years he wrote novels, biographies, plays, histories and poetry, but no matter how hard he tried, he was never able to produce another masterpiece like *Spoon River*.

It wasn't until 1936 that Petersburg forgave Masters; he was then invited to speak at the town's centennial. The years had mellowed Masters so that he could say . . . "my heart has always remained here . . . I am one of you . . . I am prouder that I am sprung from this land than of anything else in my life . . ."

When Masters died in New York City, he requested that he be buried in the Oakland Cemetery at Petersburg, surrounded by tombstones bearing names of men and women that he had written about in his *Spoon River Anthology*. His own grave is not far from the tombstone of Anne Rutledge, Lincoln's supposed childhood sweetheart. On Anne Rutledge's tombstone may be seen the epitaph that Edgar Lee Masters wrote for her in his book.

The poet's small frame childhood home in Petersburg is now maintained in his memory by the people of Petersburg. The house contains mementos from Master's early life as well as his desk where he did his writing in later life, and where he always kept a copy of Walt Whitman's poetry and a picture by Rembrandt. The Masters family was not wealthy, and the small house is typical of the period, with no running water, simple furniture, and heated only by a stove in the winters.

One room of the house contains manuscripts and books written by Masters, as well as posters and phonograph records of the many stage dramatizations made from *Spoon River Anthology* over the years.

There is an actual Spoon River, a small, meandering stream, that runs between Petersburg and Lewistown.

Location: OAKLAND CEMETERY (Setting for *Spoon River Anthology*) Oakland Avenue, Petersburg, Illinois.

Location: LEWISTOWN CEMETERY (Setting for *Spoon River Anthology*) Lewistown, Illinois.

Location: EDGAR LEE MASTERS MEMORIAL MU-SEUM, Eighth and Jackson Streets, Petersburg, Illinois. Open summers only. No admission charge.

WILLA CATHER
1873-1947

Nestled in the midst of the rolling grasslands of southern Nebraska is a small midwestern town that has been used more often as a setting for novels and short stories than any other town of its size in America. This town is Red Cloud, and it was the childhood home, and also source of inspiration, for one of America's most distinguished authors, Willa Cather.

Willa Cather's father moved his family from the green valleys of Virginia to a ranch in Nebraska in 1883, when Miss Cather was ten years old. Nebraska was frontier country then, with trails still marked by the Indians and the buffalo. The young Willa was lonely and homesick, but also curious about this new, raw land, so different from Virginia. She soon became acquainted with their immigrant farm neighbors: Bohemian, Czech, and German families. These people were struggling to survive in a harsh land and alien culture, far removed from the life they had known.

Miss Cather wrote later, "The ideas for all my novels have come from things that happened around Red Cloud when I was a child. I was all over the country then, on foot, horseback, in farm wagons. My nose went poking into nearly everything . . . by the end of the first autumn that shaggy grass country had gripped me with a passion I have never been able to shake . . ."

In 1885 the Cather family moved into the town of Red Cloud. Willa attended high school and took Greek and Latin lessons from a shopkeeper, and even worked for the local newspaper. But as much as Willa loved the prairie land, she was eager to escape the restrictions of small-town life. She attended the University of Nebraska, planning to become a scientist, but it was the literary life that won her in the end.

In 1906 she joined the staff of *McClure's* magazine in New York City, becoming after a few years managing editor of the magazine. Although successful as an editor, Miss Cather eventually left the magazine to devote all her time to writing. Her friend, the well known author from New England, Sarah Orne Jewett, advised her to write about the Nebraska region she knew so well.

Willa Cather took the advice. She remembered the pioneer immigrant families she had known as a young girl. Many of the families had been broken by the harsh farm life, but others had triumphed over the land. From these memories, she wrote *O Pioneers* in 1913. This was the first of her novels to use her home town of Red Cloud (called Hanover in her novel) as a setting. The success of *O Pioneers* put Nebraska on the literary map.

Of all Miss Cather's novels that use Red Cloud and the

people of Red Cloud as background material undoubtedly the best known is *My Antonia*. Published in 1918, the novel is a lovingly drawn portrait of an immigrant pioneer woman and is based upon a Bohemian hired girl that Willa Cather had known as a child. Many of the people in the book are taken from the author's own family and some of the incidents from Willa Cather's own childhood. However, the book is not only a story of the courageous, enduring Antonia, but a biography of the land, itself.

Not all of Miss Cather's novels used Nebraska as a setting, however. From summers she spent at Mesa Verde and Taos, New Mexico, the author gained material for a book that some critics consider her masterpiece: *Death Comes for the Archbishop* (1927). In her story of two dedicated missionary priests (based upon actual historic figures), Miss Cather caught the landscape, people and culture of New Mexico with the same sensitivity she had captured the red grass plains, hills and skies of Nebraska. Miss Cather's best books were always written against the sweep of the land, with her characters caught up in the conflict between themselves and the environment.

Fiercely devoted to the craft of writing, Miss Cather never married. She loved her freedom too much, she once said, and firmly believed that a writer "must give self absolutely to his material." And although she lived the last years of her life in the East, her roots always remained deep in the Nebraska soil.

Unlike several authors who wrote at the same time, Willa Cather did not like to use excessive details in her novels. She preferred what she called an "unfurnished" style of writing, leaving the reader free to concentrate on the characters in her novels. Her writing, often loosely plotted, seems simple but is in fact a fine art; it brought Miss Cather the Pulitzer Prize for literature. Perhaps most important, with her ability to remember so vividly scenes from her childhood, Miss Cather recreated the history of the immigrant pioneers in America.

Today the town of Red Cloud is much as it was when Willa Cather grew up there. The Republican River, which she often wrote about, still flows parallel to the Burlington railroad tracks "between fringes of cottonwood and willows." The Willa Cather house has been restored and refurbished, as well as other homes and buildings in the town that play a part in Miss Cather's novels.

Miss Cather described her childhood home as "a low story and a half house . . . everything a little on the slant, roofs, windows and doors." When the Cather family first moved into the house, seven children crowded into the small rooms and leaky attic. Willa finally got the ell-shaped gable wing partitioned off to give her a private room for her writing. It is unplastered, lined with soft pine, with a ceiling so low it can be reached with the palm of the hand. She worked in the drugstore to earn money to buy the wallpaper with red and brown roses that still may be seen in the room, though now faded and stained.

Not far from the Cather home is the Willa Cather Pioneer Memorial Museum and Archives, which houses exhibits honoring Nebraska's most famous writer.

Of special interest are two free tour maps available to visitors. One map takes the visitor on a tour of the town of Red Cloud, identifying literary sites that may be found in Miss Cather's novels. The second map takes visitors on a tour of the region around Red Cloud, pointing out where incidents in various novels took place. Personally conducted tours are available, at a fee, through the town of Red Cloud and the surrounding countryside, starting from the Memorial Museum.

Location: WILLA CATHER CHILDHOOD HOME, 3rd and Cedar Streets, Red Cloud, Nebraska.

Location: WILLA CATHER PIONEER MEMORIAL MUSEUM, Webster Street, Red Cloud, Nebraska. Both sites open only in the summer, except by appointment. Combined small fee to both buildings. Tours of Red Cloud and "Cather country" start from the museum.

LAURA INGALLS WILDER
1867-1957

The winters are long and hard in South Dakota, and the winter of 1880–1881 was particularly severe. The freezing weather and blizzards forced Charles Ingalls to move his wife and daughters from their sod house on the prairie into the town of De Smet. But even living in town was not easy that winter. The railroad couldn't move through the snowdrifts that blocked the tracks. Cut off from all outside help for seven months, food and fuel running low, the Ingalls family barely managed to survive. Many, many years later one of the Ingalls children, Laura, was to describe that winter and the town of De Smet in a book that she called simply, *The Long Winter.*

Like another noted American author, Willa Cather, Laura Ingalls was born into a restless pioneer family, constantly moving west in search of new lands, new opportunities. And it is the story of the Ingalls family, as well as other courageous pioneer families who tamed the raw frontier land of Wisconsin, Minnesota and the Dakotas, that Laura immortalized in her popular Little House books.

Laura's first novel in the Little House series, *Little House in the Big Woods,* was published in 1932 when the author was sixty-five years old. The novel tells of Laura's earliest memories, and takes place when the Ingalls family, was living in an isolated "little house in the woods" near Pepin, Wisconsin. The book then follows the Ingalls family in a prairie schooner as they cross Minnesota, Iowa, Missouri and into Indian territory in Kansas. Kansas became the setting for Mrs. Wilder's second book, *Little House on the Prairie.*

Dispossessed by the government, who gave the land the Ingalls family owned back to the Indians, Charles Ingalls moved his family again, this time to western Minnesota where they settled near Walnut Grove, the setting for *On the Banks of Plum Creek.*

Several years later Mr. Ingalls (the Pa in Mrs. Wilder's books) once again became restless and moved his wife and daughters, Mary, Laura, Carrie and baby Grace further west into Dakota territory where he staked a claim *By the Shores of Silver Lake.* It was while they were living on this claim in the Dakotas, that the terrible winter of 1880–81 forced the Ingalls to leave their claim and move for safety into town. And it was during *The Long Winter* in De Smet that Laura, still a young girl, met Almanzo Wilder, later to become her husband. (Laura told the story of Almanzo's family in a book called *Farmer Boy.*)

After that bitter winter the Ingalls stayed on in De Smet, and it was in this small prairie town that Laura received most of the little formal education she had. At age fifteen, Laura began teaching school herself. Her sister Mary had gone blind, and Laura grew accustomed to acting as her sister's eyes. In doing so, her own descriptive powers developed, and she began to see everything around her with a sharp clarity. This ability to observe closely and describe what she saw exactly proved invaluable to Laura years later when she wrote down her impressions of pioneer life. The Ingalls family experiences in De Smet, and Laura's growing up years are told in *Little Town on the Prairie. These Happy Golden Years* and *The First Four Years* tell of Laura's marriage to Almanzo.

The early years for the young couple were not easy. There was illness, hailstorms and drought, the loss of a baby son and finally, happily, the birth of a baby daughter, Rose. At last, discouraged, the Wilders decided to move to the Ozark area of southern Missouri. Here they bought a piece of land and once again began farming. The move, recorded in Laura's diary, later made into the book *On the Way Home,* was a fortunate one. The Wilders made a success of their farm, and Laura began writing articles for farm magazines to earn extra money.

Her daughter, Rose Wilder Lane, eventually became a well-known writer. Rose Wilder Lane's best-known book, *Let the Hurricane Roar,* was based on stories of pioneer life she had heard from her mother. Rose encouraged her mother to write the story of her own life, and at age 64 Mrs. Wilder sat down and began to write of her frontier childhood, thriftily using both sides of an ordinary school tablet as her manuscript paper. The stories that finally emerged were told through the eyes of young Laura Ingalls. But it is the whole Ingalls family that comes alive in Laura's *Little House in the Big Woods,* one of the most engaging and beloved families in American literature.

Mrs. Wilder had planned to write only one book, but

her first book was so popular that publisher and readers begged for more. Mrs. Wilder continued writing her books, in a tiny room off the bedroom, while still managing her household and farm chores. Each book in the Little House series can be read separately, but together they form a lively, authentic picture of pioneer life. Readers feel as if they are members of the Ingalls family, taking part in their day by day chores, adventures, hardships and joys.

Today the Rocky Ridge farm near Mansfield, Missouri, where Laura Ingalls Wilder lived and wrote her books is open to the public. The farm is a combined home and museum of Mrs. Wilder's life and writings, as well as those of her author-daughter, Rose Wilder Lane. Almanzo built the small frame house, using stone from the land for the foundations and fireplace. In the kitchen can be seen the old-fashioned stove where Laura baked her famous gingerbread; the organ in the front room, which Laura helped buy for her blind sister, Mary; the tiny room and desk where Laura did her writing; and the large front parlor with the wide arm chair that Almanzo built. Laura and Almanzo are so much a part of this simple yet lovingly fashioned home that one can almost feel their presence.

In the museum next to the house are fascinating exhibits of items mentioned or described in the Little House books; Pa's fiddle, the needlework Laura loved to do, a painting by Laura to show baby Grace what trees looked like. In addition there are the orange-colored school notebooks that are the original handwritten manuscripts of the Little House books, in Laura's careful handwriting.

The town of De Smet, South Dakota, the setting for five of Laura's books, has honored Mrs. Wilder by restoring several of the sites mentioned in her books, including the Surveyor's House where the Ingalls family lived from 1879–

1880, and the last Ingalls home on Third Street, where they lived from 1887–1928. There are eighteen sites in all that may be visited, including Laura's first school and the Ingalls and Wilder homesteads. Daily tours of the area are conducted. Each summer, the last weekend in June and first two weekends in July, the "Long Winter Pageant" is performed on a tract of land adjoining the Ingalls homestead, in sight of the cottonwoods that Pa planted.

All that remains of the Ingalls dugout home *On the Banks of Plum Creek* is a depression in the ground, but the prairie grasses and flowers grow much as they did in Laura's time and the small spring still flows nearby. There is a plaque marking the site, a mile and one-half north of Walnut Grove, Minnesota.

Location: LAURA INGALLS WILDER–ROSE WILDER LANE HOME AND MUSEUM, Rocky Ridge Farm, Mansfield, Missouri. The home and museum are located 1¼ miles east of Mansfield on U.S. 60 business route. Open summers only. Admission charge.

Location: INGALLS HOME, on Third Street, between Poinsett and 1st Avenues, De Smet, South Dakota. Tours of the Laura Ingalls Wilder sites start at the Surveyor's House on First Street. Summers only. Rest of year by appointment. Small admission charge.

Location: LAURA INGALLS WILDER PARK, MASTER'S HOTEL. The Master's Hotel in Iowa is where the Ingalls family lived for a brief time. The hotel, in the process of restoration, is located on Highway 52, 10 miles north of Decorah at Burr Oak, Iowa.

SINCLAIR LEWIS
1885–1951

Main Street, U.S.A. Almost every American town has one, but the street and town that served as the setting for Sinclair Lewis's award-winning novel, *Main Street,* was the author's own hometown, Sauk Centre, Minnesota.

The son of a country doctor, young Lewis was an awkward, freckled, red-haired youth, and his boyhood in Sauk Centre was not a particularly happy one. He had few friends, and even at an early age was more interested in writing than in the usual boyish pursuits. His stern, undemonstrative father wanted his son to become a doctor, but Sinclair Lewis rebelled against following in his father's footsteps. At Yale University his main interest was writing for the college literary magazine, and for a short time he dropped out of college to join a Socialist commune, run by another well-known author, Upton Sinclair.

After graduating from college, Lewis tried to make his

living at various literary and journalistic enterprises, including newspaper work, advertising and editing magazines. Then he went West, lived at a bohemian writing community near Carmel, California, and began writing novels.

Sinclair Lewis's early novels had little to distinguish them from other run-of-the-mill novels of his day, written to please the general reading public. Then in 1919, he decided to write a novel to please himself. The result, in 1920, was *Main Street,* a novel that outraged much of America, even as it sent thousands rushing to libraries and bookstores to read the book.

Set in the fictional Midwest town of Gopher Prairie, Minnesota, *Main Street* is a devastating, satirical attack upon the dullness and cultural drabness of small-town life in America in the 1920s. Sinclair Lewis, of course, was not the first writer to shatter the myth of the "friendly village" in America. Edgar Lee Masters's *Spoon River Anthology,* and Sherwood Anderson's *Winesburg, Ohio* had also attacked the meanness and shallowness of small-town life. Nor was Lewis the only author "debunking" America between World War I and World War II. No other author, however, achieved the immense popularity that Sinclair Lewis did. Within a short time, he became the voice of the rebellious younger generation, striking back at the establishment. And because *Main Street* was translated into almost every European language, the author became a noted world figure as well.

Sinclair Lewis continued his attack upon American life and culture with his novel *Babbitt* in 1922. Set in the fictional town of Zenith (actually Minneapolis), *Babbitt* ridiculed the greedy materialism and pomposity of the American businessman of that period, who "knew the price of everything and the value of nothing." The title of the novel, taken from the main character, businessman George Babbitt, even

added a new word to the American language . . . a babbitt
—an uncultivated, narrow-minded person whose only interest in life is money and social success.

Although Sinclair Lewis wrote fifteen novels between
1920 and his death in 1951, his fame rests on five novels:
Main Street; Babbitt; Arrowsmith, (1925) which attacked
the medical profession; *Elmer Gantry* (1927), which exposed the hypocrisy of the clergy; and *Dodsworth* (1929),
which satirized American women.

Sinclair Lewis received the Pulitzer prize for *Arrowsmith.* Although he refused the award, he did receive and
accept in 1930 the Nobel Prize for distinction in world literature, the first American to receive this award. However, by
1930 the author's most important writing had been done.
His later novels, although he still attempted to expose what
he felt was fraudulant and provincial in American life, never
achieved the satirical brilliance of his early novels.

Despite the fact that Sinclair Lewis achieved his literary
success by making fun of rigid, small-town life, he, himself,
was never able to reject completely his own beginnings in
Sauk Centre. Like those he satirized in his novels, he was
eager to get ahead in the world and loved gadgets and material comforts. And all his life he maintained an attachment
to his hometown. One critic has said that Lewis loved the
town of Sauk Centre "so much that he hated it for not being
all he wanted it to be and knew it could be."

He died alone in Rome, Italy, but had asked to be
buried in Sauk Centre between the graves of his parents.
And this was done.

Sinclair Lewis's novels have been criticized for being
sociological studies, rather than novels. It is true that his
characters are types rather than individuals, and he used an
excessive amount of detail in his books. But in his best

novels, Lewis has the journalist's easy-to-read style and an unerring talent for mimicking the speech patterns of the Midwest. He also was able to capture in words, as faithfully as a photographer, the exact setting of his novels so that in reading *Main Street,* one can almost see and touch and smell the town of Gopher Prairie.

It was said that Sinclair Lewis's father never forgave his son for writing *Main Street.* The citizens of Sauk Centre were not too happy with the book either, because they felt it held their town up to public ridicule. However, the home in which the author grew to adulthood has been carefully restored to look as it did during the turn of the century years when Lewis lived there with his parents and two brothers. It is a "sober, comfortable, middle class house," and one has a hard time imagining a "fiery, honest, impatient" man like Sinclair Lewis growing up in such a place.

In addition to the home, there is also a Sinclair Lewis Museum, now housed in the Sinclair Lewis Interpretive Center in Sauk Centre. The museum has exhibits on the author's life, including a mini-slide show, focusing on the story of the town and Sinclair Lewis. The exhibits go into the writing methods of the author, as well as the importance of the town as a source of background material for Lewis's novels.

Location: SINCLAIR LEWIS BOYHOOD HOME, West Sinclair Lewis Avenue, Sauk Centre, Minnesota. Open summers only. Small admission charge.

Location: SINCLAIR LEWIS INTERPRETIVE CENTER is located at a highway rest stop at the junction of Interstate 94 and US 71 at Sauk Centre, Minnesota. No admission charge.

REFORM MOVEMENT,
END OF NINETEENTH CENTURY,
BEGINNING OF TWENTIETH CENTURY

AT THE END OF THE NINETEENTH CENTURY, AND WELL INTO THE TWENTIETH, AMERICA WAS FACING A MULTITUDE OF SOCIAL ILLS. FARMERS WERE BEING CRUSHED BY EASTERN BANKERS; THE LABORING MAN, WOMAN AND CHILD WERE BEING EXPLOITED BY BIG BUSINESS; THE CITIES WERE GHETTOS OF POVERTY AND POLITICAL CORRUPTION, AND BLACK AMERICANS WERE STILL FIGHTING FOR THEIR CIVIL RIGHTS. WRITERS LOOKING AT THIS PERIOD THEN AND LATER, TURNED TO LITERATURE TO SHOW WHAT LIFE WAS REALLY LIKE. CALLED REALISTS, THEY POR-TRAYED AMERICAN LIFE IN THE CITIES AND ON ITS FARMS AS IT REALLY WAS, WITHOUT SENTIMENTALITY OR ROMANTICISM.

Hamlin Garland in his books, *Main-travelled Roads* and *Son of the Middle Border* described scenes much as above: farm families living in sod huts on the bleak, windswept plains. Hamlin Garland's home in West Salem, Wisconsin, although far removed from the rude log hut in Green Coulee, Wisconsin, where he was born, has recently been restored and is open to the public. COURTESY SOLO-MON D. BUTCHER COLLECTION NEBRASKA STATE HISTORICAL SOCIETY

Theodore Dreiser (1871–1945), raised in poverty himself, could sympathize with the heroines of his novels, *Sister Carrie* (1900) and *Jennie Gerhardt* (1911), which told of the hard lot of the underpaid working girl in the big cities of the Middle West. Dreiser's books were called immoral because of their realistic style and were suppressed.

It wasn't until 1925 when his *American Tragedy* was published that the importance of Dreiser's novels as authentic documents of American life was recognized. COURTESY LIBRARY OF CONGRESS

Stephen Crane was one of America's first and most brilliant naturalistic novelists, that is, he described life, whether on the battlefield, as in *The Red Badge of Courage,* or the slums of New York, as in *Maggie, a Girl of the Streets,* exactly as it happened without making any moral judgments about his characters. COURTESY PUBLIC LIBRARY, NEWARK, N.J., DICTIONARY OF AMERICAN PORTRAITS

Ambrose Bierce (1842–1914), unlike Stephen Crane, actually fought in the Civil War. Embittered after the war, he joined the San Francisco literary group and is remembered for his sardonic stories of terror, as well as his cynical witticisms collected in *The Devil's Dictionary* (1906). Bierce mysteriously disappeared in Mexico in 1913; his exact fate is unknown. COURTESY CALIFORNIA HISTORICAL SOCIETY, DICTIONARY OF AMERICAN PORTRAITS

W. E. B. DuBois (1868–1963) shown at left, was the most influential black author in the late nineteenth and early twentieth century, as well as a noted historian, scholar and civil rights leader. In his classic book, *The Souls of Black Folk,* published in 1903, DuBois insisted that the black person had little chance for advancement in America unless he fought for change. "The problem of the twentieth century is the color line," DuBois wrote, and to help solve the problem he founded the National Association for the Advancement of Colored People. A small memorial to the black author and leader may be seen on Egremont Road, Great Barrington, Massachusetts, on the site of his childhood home. COURTESY NATIONAL PORTRAIT GALLERY, SMITHSONIAN INSTITUTION, WASHINGTON, D.C.

Not all authors writing at this period were downbeat and cynical. Willa Cather's novels, *O Pioneers* and *My Antonia*, evoked the courage and stamina of the pioneer lives of immigrants in late nineteenth century Nebraska. COURTESY WILLA CATHER PIONEER MEMORIAL AND EDUCATIONAL FOUNDATION

Willa Cather grew up in the above house in Red Cloud, Nebraska. As she herself said, "The ideas for all my novels have come from things that happened around Red Cloud when I was a child." Today, not only is her home open to the public, but conducted tours are available in and around Red Cloud to actual places that appear in Miss Cather's novels. COURTESY WILLA CATHER PIONEER MEMORIAL AND EDUCATIONAL FOUNDATION

Laura Ingalls Wilder (extreme right in photograph) is shown with her sisters, Carrie and Mary, at the time the events of *Little Town on the Prairie* took place. At the time the Ingalls family was living in De Smet, South Dakota. As a child, Laura shared the hardships and joys of pioneer life with the rest of the Ingalls family. Much later, she recalled with remarkable clarity those early days in Wisconsin, Kansas, Minnesota and the Dakotas in her "Little House" books. The series, which began with *Little House in the Big Woods,* was and still is, tremendously popular. COURTESY LAURA INGALLS WILDER MUSEUM AND HOME

Laura Ingalls Wilder's last home with her husband, Almanzo, was at Rocky Ridge Farm, near Mansfield, Missouri. It was in a small room in this home that she wrote her popular "Little House" books. The home is now restored and open to the public. A museum next door includes exhibits of many items mentioned in the "Little House" books, as well as exhibits from the life of Rose Wilder Lane, Laura's noted author-daughter. PHOTO BY AUTHOR

Main Street, Sauk Centre, Minnesota—today. In 1920, author Sinclair Lewis used this Main Street of his home town as the setting for his best-selling and controversial novel, which he called *Main Street*. The novel attacked the narrow-mindedness and hypocrisy of middle-class small-town life. At first, the citizens of Sauk Centre weren't happy about the novel. However, today the birth home of the prize-winning author has been restored, and a Sinclair Lewis Interpretive Center built at Sauk Centre. COURTESY SINCLAIR LEWIS FOUNDATION, INC.

CARL SANDBURG
1878-1967

The town of Galesburg, Illinois, is a large, flourishing community today, but when the poet Carl Sandburg was born there, it was a small farm and railroad town, surrounded by miles of black prairie farmland.

Born into a Swedish immigrant family, Carl Sandburg had a happy childhood even though the Sandburg family was poor. The tiny three-room house in which he was born was crowded with children, who slept on cornhusk mattresses. Sandburg, himself, at the age of eleven had to go to work at various odd jobs to help support the family. Nevertheless, young Carl, a lively, inquisitive boy, was to write years later in his autobiography, *Always the Young Strangers,* that "In those years as a boy in that prairie town, I got my education in scraps and pieces of many kinds, not knowing that they were part of my education."

Part of this early education was becoming familiar with stories about a man Sandburg admired greatly, Abraham Lincoln. Lincoln had visited Galesburg often, and one of his famous debates with Stephen Douglas was held at Knox College in Galesburg. It was this same Knox College that the young Sandburg, while on his milk route, would stop at to eavesdrop on college classes.

In addition to his other odd jobs, Sandburg harvested ice in zero weather, and for a short time became a hobo, riding the rails through the Midwest and West, harvesting wheat in Kansas, washing dishes in Denver. Wherever he wandered, he took his guitar with him, gathering up folk ballads of the country as he went. The spirituals of the black people, the songs of the cowboys, tramps and working men and women, all became part of Sandburg's collection. Later, he gathered these bits and pieces of America's musical heritage into one of his more popular books, *The American Songbag.*

Even more important, in his wanderings he was learning about the ordinary man and woman of America, how they lived and spoke, their dreams and fears. For a short time, Sandburg joined the army as a recruit in the Spanish–American war, but always his real ambition was to become a writer.

He returned to Galesburg, attended college for several years, then drifted to Milwaukee, where he met and married Lilian Steichen, sister of the noted photographer, Edward Steichen.

The young couple moved to Chicago. Sandburg worked for the Chicago *Daily News,* became interested in industrial and social reform and closely associated with other writers in that city in what has become known as the Chicago Literary Renaissance. In 1914 *Poetry* magazine in Chicago published Sandburg's poem, "Chicago." The poem was considered radical for its time because it told of the "unpoetical" seamier side of life in Chicago and used the slangy speech patterns of the man on the street. Also the poem was written in rhymeless, free verse instead of more traditional patterns.

Harriet Monroe, editor of *Poetry* magazine, encouraged Sandburg to keep writing in his controversial new style, which was, in a way, reminiscent of another famous, earlier American poet, Walt Whitman. Other collections of Sandburg's poetry followed: *Cornhuskers* in 1918, *Smoke and Steel* in 1920, *Slabs of the Sunburnt West* in 1922, and perhaps Sandburg's best known and most important collection of poetry, *The People, Yes* in 1936.

Written during the dark days of America's depression years, *The People, Yes,* has been called "one of the great American books," catching the folk speech, humor and dogged determination of the common American man and woman.

In addition to his writing, Sandburg traveled the country with his guitar, giving readings of his poetry and singing the folk songs he loved. While he traveled, he was always in search of material on Abraham Lincoln, his childhood hero. He wanted to write a biography of the President that would catch the true spirit of the man. After many years of research and writing, Sandburg finished a two-volume work of the early life of Lincoln, called *The Prairie Years,* in 1926. Then he wrote four more volumes, *Abraham Lincoln, the War Years,* published in 1939. This monumental biography was awarded the Pulitzer Prize for history and is still considered the outstanding biography of President Lincoln.

Sandburg also wrote a novel, *Remembrance Rock,* in

1948. However, his novel was not a success, and it is for his poetry, biographies, ballads and children's stories, such as the *Rootabaga Stories* (1922), that Sandburg achieved his greatest fame.

Like another Midwest author, Mark Twain, Carl Sandburg was more than a writer. He had great popular appeal and was able to reach a wide audience. As one critic has said, Sandburg wrote "of the people, for the people, and in a sense, by the people." No other poet since Walt Whitman had so recorded the heart, mind and emotions of the American people with his poetry.

The tiny frame house in which Carl Sandburg was born is today, thanks partly to contributions from Galesburg schoolchildren, a shrine in the poet's memory. The house still has the plain wooden floor, low ceilings and modest pieces of furniture that were part of the poet's childhood. Surrounding the town of Galesburg stretches the black loam prairie farmland that inspired much of Sandburg's poetry. One can walk down the streets of Galesburg and recognize houses and streets and places Sandburg described in his biography, *Always the Young Stranger,* later published in a special edition for young people, *Prairie Boy.*

At his request, Sandburg is buried in the grounds behind the modest house under a boulder called Remembrance Rock.

Sandburg's last years were spent at Connemara Farm in North Carolina. Here he wrote many of his best-known books while Mrs. Sandburg ran the farm and raised prize-winning herds of goats. Sandburg liked to work late in the evening in a tiny upstairs room with his typewriter perched on an old orange crate. In the afternoons he would do his correspondence on the front porch of the house, overlooking

the Blue Ridge Mountains. Many evenings he would entertain friends with his guitar, which can still be seen in the
front room, next to a pile of sheet music. The whole house is
exactly as it was when Sandburg lived there, with a casual
clutter in the rooms, Sandburg's sweater draped over his
desk chair, his slippers beside his bed. In 1968 Connemara
became a national historic site, administered by the National
Park Service, and the home and grounds are open to the
public.

Location: CARL SANDBURG BIRTHPLACE, 331 East
Third Street, Galesburg, Illinois. No admission charge.

Location: CARL SANDBURG HOME (CONNEMARA
FARM) is located 5 miles south of Hendersonville, North
Carolina. Turn off U.S. 25 onto Little River Road at the
Flat Rock Playhouse. The farm is also 28 miles south of
Asheville via Interstate 26. No admission charge.

ROBERT FROST
1874-1963

On a cold, windy day in January, 1961, a white-haired man with a rough-hewn, weathered face stepped up to the speaker's podium at the inauguration of President John F. Kennedy. Before the thousands of onlookers, and as part of the inaugural ceremony, Robert Frost read aloud one of his poems, "The Gift Outright." It was the first time that an American poet had ever been so honored. For Robert Frost, however, the unofficial poet laureate of America, it was only one of many honors gathered in his lifetime.

Yet, ironically, by the age of forty, Robert Frost had published only a few scattered pieces of poetry, and after struggling for twenty years to become a poet, considered himself a failure. In desperation, he and his wife with their four children pulled up stakes and moved to England where, as Frost later said, he could "write and be poor without further scandal to the family."

Robert Frost had always been, if not a scandal, then a puzzle to his family and his New England neighbors. A brilliant student, he attended Dartmouth College and Harvard University but dropped out of both schools without graduating. For several years he drifted aimlessly from job to job before marrying his high-school sweetheart when he was twenty-one. To support his new wife, he taught school, but then at age twenty-six, he abruptly gave up teaching and moved his wife and family to a small farm near Derry, New Hampshire.

Unfortunately, he had neither the desire nor talent to become a successful farmer. To the amazement of his neighbors, he milked his cow and did his farm chores late at night, to leave his days free for his one consuming passion in life . . . "shaping poetry."

The farm failed, and his poetry didn't sell. With four children and a wife to support, the poet determined to make one last attempt to have his poetry accepted, if not in America then in England. And it was in England, where the poet moved his family in 1912, that Frost's first book of poetry, *A Boy's Will*, was published. The next year a second collection of dramatic verse with New England themes, called *North of Boston*, was published. This volume contained two of Robert Frost's best known poems, "Mending Wall," and "Death of the Hired Man." With the publication of these two books, the poet was hailed by critics in both England and America as a new, important poetic voice.

In 1915 Frost and his family returned to America. Although the poet's growing fame and popularity was such that he never again had to make his living by farming, the Frost family first lived on a farm in New Hampshire and then on another farm at Ripton, Vermont. Frost's great affection for rural New England life, for rocky farms, old houses, stone fences and the rugged New England people, may be seen in the titles of some of his poems: "Two Tramps in Mud-time," "Stopping by Woods on a Snowy Evening," "Birches," "West-running Brook," and "Apple Picking."

In the years that followed his return from England, Frost split his time between writing poetry, teaching and lecturing at colleges, and giving poetry readings to enthusiastic audiences. Each new volume of poetry he wrote brought him added honors. In 1955 the state of Vermont even named a mountain near Ripton after him. In an era when several excellent poets were writing in America, including Carl Sandburg in Illinois, and Edgar Arlington Robinson in Maine, Robert Frost still managed to win four separate Pulitzer Prizes for his books of poetry—more than any other American author. In addition, like Carl Sandburg, Robert Frost became a literary celebrity as well as a poet.

Carl Sandburg and Robert Frost had much in common. They both came from rural backgrounds, struggled for years to achieve success as poets and popular lecturers, and both continued writing well into old age. But there were differences between the two men, as much difference as there is between the fertile prairie country of Sandburg's Illinois and the rocky, hardscrabble farms of Frost's New England. Sandburg's poetry was influenced by the free verse style of Walt Whitman. Frost followed a more classical tradition. To Robert Frost, free, unstructured verse, which was all the rage of the new poets of Chicago, was "like playing tennis without a net!"

Yet, just as Sandburg caught the dynamic life of rough and booming Chicago and the awe-filled beauty of the prairie, so Frost in his poetry captured in vivid imagery the rural beauty of New England as well as the voice tones of the New England farm people with their dry humor and uncomplaining courage. Robert Frost's poems, however, were much more complicated and subtle than simple descriptions of a place and people. There are many levels of meanings in his poems, a strong sense of drama and a ceaseless probing to make the reader "remember what you didn't know you knew." Frost's poetry, one critic has said, "begins in delight and ends in wisdom."

Like his poetry, Robert Frost was a much more complicated man than he appeared on the surface. His public face was outwardly genial, good-humored and folksy, but he had a private face that was often dark and moody. He suffered several family tragedies but continued writing his poetry until almost the last year of his life. In 1962, a year before his death, he published one of his finest works, *In the Clearing*.

Robert Frost's last years were spent at a farm near Ripton, Vermont (the Herman Noble farm), but he always said "to a large extent the terrain of my poetry is the Derry landscape, the Derry Farm." It was at Derry Farm he struggled to perfect his poetic voice and where he and his wife spent their early married years. The west-running brook, which served as the theme for one of his most important poems, meanders west not far from the Derry Farm.

Today the Robert Frost Foundation has been formed to save the Robert Frost farm at Derry as a living memorial to one of America's greatest poets. The simple white clapboard two-story farmhouse on the farm was built in the 1880s. The farmhouse, typical of the New England of that time, is being restored and furnished as authentically as possible, with the help of Robert Frost's daughter, to reflect the poet and his life at Derry Farm.

Amherst, Massachusetts, also has memories of Frost, for the poet taught and lectured for many years at Amherst College. At the Jones Library of the college there is a room dedicated to him and his works.

Location: ROBERT FROST HOME, RFD 1, Derry, New Hampshire. Derry is off I 93 in southern New Hampshire. The home may presently be seen from the outside but will not be opened to the public until restoration is completed.

EDNA ST. VINCENT MILLAY
1892–1950

In the late 1700s, Washington Square in the heart of Greenwich Village, New York City, was a cemetery for plague
victims. In the early 1800s the square was a drill ground for
the militia, and by 1830 Greenwich Village had become the
home for old, aristocratic New York families. After World
War I, as property values fell, Greenwich Village took in a
new class of citizen. Unknown but often talented authors,
actors and artists, who were "very, very poor and very, very
merry" occupied the garrets and charming red-brick, white-
trimmed homes around the square and west of it. Called
Bohemians because of their casual life styles, no other author
so typified the carefree life of Greenwich Village in the 1920s,
as a copper-haired, green-eyed young poet by the name of
Edna St. Vincent Millay.

Miss Millay arrived in the village in 1917, and although

a struggling young poet, she was not completely unknown. Her poem "Renascence," published in 1912 when she was only twenty years old, had already aroused critical appreciation for its fresh, lyric beauty. Written in Camden, Maine, where she had grown up, "Renascence" was influenced by Miss Millay's love of the sea, the islands and the Maine coast.

The young poet came to the Village to write and act in the Provincetown Playhouse, located in the village. It was her poetry, though, that brought her fame. In 1920, her first collection of poetry, *A Few Figs from a Thistle,* was published, which displayed Miss Millay's special genius for the sonnet form. In 1923, *The Harp-Weaver and Other Poems* won Miss Millay the Pulitzer prize.

The popularity of Miss Millay's poetry, especially with young people, made her a literary celebrity as well as a poet. For many young people of her generation, the beautiful Miss Millay with her liberated lifestyle, her passionate creed of "burning the candle at both ends" stood for rebellious flaming youth in its revolt against Victorian morality.

Miss Millay married in 1923. Later, with her husband, she moved to a farm in Austerlitz, New York, which she named Steepletop after the wildflowers that grew around the house. Her later poetry, more serious, less concerned with grief and passion than with social reform, did not have the intensely popular personal style of her earlier poetry. After her husband's death in 1949, the poet withdrew more and more from social contact and died, alone, at Steepletop, in 1950.

Camden, Maine, where Miss Millay grew up and wrote her earliest poetry, and which always remained a source of inspiration, has placed a plaque at the top of Mt. Battie, about two miles north of Camden, accessible by a paved road. It was the scene from this point that inspired Millay's famous poem, "Renascence." On the plaque can be read the opening lines of the poem . . . "From where I stood was three long mountains and a wood; I turned and looked the other way and saw three islands in the bay . . ."

At Whitehall Inn in Camden, where the young poet read aloud her poetry for the first time, there is a special Edna St. Vincent Millay Room, containing pictures and other items from her life.

Although Greenwich Village in New York City today has become too expensive a place for all except the most successful authors and artists to live, one can still stroll down the crooked back streets of the village and imagine life as it must have been during the Bohemian days of the early 1900s. Miss Millay's first home in the village was at 25 Charlton Street, but her best known home in the village is at 75½ Bedford Street. Called the Millay home, the tiny three-story house, painted pink, is only nine and one-half feet wide! Privately owned, the house is not open to the public.

In 1975 the Millay home, Steepletop, was turned into the Millay Colony for the Arts, whose primary purpose is to provide writers, artists and composers with work space and living quarters. In addition to residential areas for visiting writers and artists, those areas at Steepletop that are personally associated with Edna St. Vincent Millay are in the process of being made accessible, on a limited basis, to the public. Eventually a museum is planned on the grounds to house Millay memorabilia.

Location: WHITEHALL INN (Millay Room), Camden, Maine.

Location: MILLAY HOME, 75½ Bedford Street, Greenwich Village, New York, New York. Not open to the public.

Location: THE MILLAY COLONY FOR THE ARTS, Steepletop, Austerlitz, New York.

MARIANNE MOORE
1887–1972

Writers who lived in Greenwich Village in New York in the 1920s were often accused of leading riotous, unconventional lives. One young poet in the village, however, lived quietly with her mother and worked in a nearby public library. Yet of all the new poets who broke with the old traditional forms of poetry, Marianne Moore's poetry has been called "the most daringly original of any of her day."

Like many other residents of Greenwich Village, Miss Moore was not a native New Yorker. She was born in Kirkwood, Missouri, the granddaughter of a prominent minister. Later the family moved to Pennsylvania, where she went to school and college. During Miss Moore's college days, she occasionally contributed poetry to the campus literary magazine. Most of her college career, though, she spent in art classes and in the biology laboratory. It was her art classes that taught her to see with a painter's eyes, and in the laboratory that she learned to respect precision and economy of statement, both qualities that showed up later in her poetry.

After graduation, she taught at the United States Indian School in Carlisle for several years. One of her favorite students was Jim Thorpe, the young Indian who was to become a world-renowned athlete. The skill and grace of the athlete was a quality that Miss Moore admired. Baseball was a sport she knew well and a subject she was to write about in her poetry.

In 1918 Miss Moore and her mother moved to a basement apartment on St. Luke's Place in Greenwich Village. By then Miss Moore had already achieved a reputation as an important new poet. Her poems had been published in *Poetry* magazine and had caught the attention of poet and critic Ezra Pound as well as the distinguished poet, T. S. Eliot.

Eliot published Marianne Moore's first collection of poetry in England in 1921. Three years later the poems were published in America, under the title *Observations*. The poems included several on life in Greenwich Village and were filled with the sharp wit, brevity and economy of word and image that were to be characteristic of Miss Moore's poetry.

For several years, Miss Moore edited *The Dial*, a New York literary magazine dedicated to introducing new and experimental styles of writing to the reading public. Then in 1929 Miss Moore gave up her post as editor and moved to Brooklyn, where she once again devoted her time to writing her own poetry—as well as becoming a devoted fan of the Brooklyn Dodgers.

During her last years, Miss Moore returned to Green-

279

wich Village, where she was a beloved literary figure, recognized everywhere she went by the cape and tricornered hat she delighted in wearing. By the time of her death, she had received nearly every honor and award given to an American poet, including the Pulitzer Prize for poetry.

Miss Moore's place is unique in the history of American literature. Her collections of poetry—among them *The Arctic Ox* (1964), *O To Be a Dragon* (1959), and *Tell Me, Tell Me* (1967) —are not tied to any one geographic region or place or to a special theme. Miss Moore's interests were so varied that she could take horse races and baseball games, clippings from newspapers, exotic animals, any and all "things" and create a poem. Although she wrote in free verse, it was a tightly disciplined free verse. The length of each line was controlled visually. In the poem, "To a Chameleon," for example, the poem actually looks like a chameleon, the words undulating across the page.

After Miss Moore's death, her living room in her Greenwich Village apartment was removed and reassembled at the Rosenbach Foundation in Philadelphia. All the furnishings, books and literary material accumulated through the years by Miss Moore, her notebooks and diaries, photographs, the Morris chair where she wrote and even a treasured possession, a Yankee warm-up jacket, may now be seen at the Foundation. Miss Moore's famous tricornered hat is also part of the collection.

Location: MARIANNE MOORE LIVING ROOM AND COLLECTION, The Philip H. and A. S. W. Rosenbach Foundation Museum, 2010 De Lancey Place, Philadelphia, Pennsylvania. Admission charge.

POETIC RENAISSANCE OF THE EARLY 1900s

THE EARLY 1900S SAW A POETIC RENAISSANCE IN AMERICA. *Poetry Magazine* IN CHICAGO PUBLISHED MANY NEW IMPORTANT MIDWESTERN POETS, SUCH AS VACHEL LINDSAY, EDGAR LEE MASTERS AND CARL SANDBURG, AS WELL AS NEW ENGLAND POETS, ROBERT FROST AND EDWIN ARLINGTON ROBINSON. GREENWICH VILLAGE, NEW YORK CITY, BECAME THE BOHEMIAN CENTER OF LITERARY LIFE IN AMERICA, WHILE HARLEM, NEW YORK, WITH ITS BLACK AUTHORS, INTRODUCED A LITERARY RENAISSANCE OF ITS OWN DURING THE SAME PERIOD.

It is from this home in Springfield, Illinois, that the poet Vachel Lindsay went out as a modern-day troubadour, bringing his poetry and his "gospel of beauty" to Americans as he tramped across the country. The Lindsay home is open to the public in the summer.
PHOTO BY AUTHOR

"All, all are sleeping, sleeping, sleeping, on the hill." The Spoon River cemetery that Edgar Lee Masters immortalized in his collection of poems/epitaphs, entitled *Spoon River Anthology,* was actually the Oakland Cemetery, Petersburg, Illinois, (shown here) and the Lewistown Cemetery, Illinois. Masters's poems were not flattering to the people of Petersburg, and for many years he was not welcome in his hometown. Today, however, the small house in Petersburg where he was born is open in the summer as a memorial to the poet. PHOTO BY AUTHOR

Carl Sandburg started life in Galesburg, Illinois, in the tiny three-room house shown here. It was in Galesburg also that Sandburg first heard stories of Abraham Lincoln, which later inspired him to write his Pulitzer-Prize-winning biography of Lincoln. Sandburg's home, as well as the small Lincoln museum attached, is open to the public. COURTESY ILLINOIS OFFICE OF TOURISM

Carl Sandburg spent his last years at his home, Connemara, in the Blue Ridge Mountains near Flat Rock, North Carolina. Shown here is the living room of the house with one of Sandburg's guitars. For many years Sandburg traveled the country with his guitar and banjo, collecting and singing folk songs, which he finally published in his *American Songbag*. Connemara is a National Historic Shrine, open to the public. It looks today almost exactly as it did when Sandburg lived there. PHOTO BY AUTHOR

With his typewriter perched on an upturned orange crate, Sandburg did much of his writing in this small, cluttered garret room at Connemara. PHOTO BY AUTHOR

Robert Frost was one of the most popular—as well as critically well-received—poets of his day. Frost used conventional forms of poetry, particularly the dramatic monologue. He called writing free verse "like playing tennis without a net!" COURTESY AMHERST COLLEGE, AMHERST, MASS.

Derry Farm in New Hampshire was the home for five years of Robert Frost, and the inspiration for some of his best poems. The state of New Hampshire has acquired Derry Farm, and the home and grounds are being restored as a memorial to Robert Frost. COURTESY STATE OF NEW HAMPSHIRE DIVISION OF PARKS AND RECREATION

The wistful young lady above is Edna St. Vincent Millay, who more than any other poet in Greenwich Village became the symbol of rebellious "flaming youth" in the 1920s. Although Miss Millay wrote fresh, lyrical poetry of her native Maine, it was her intensely personal poetry of passion and grief, and her free, uninhibited life style, that made her the idol of the youth of her day—and shocked and dismayed their elders.

This tiny nine-foot-wide house at 75½ Bedford Street in Greenwich Village was Miss Millay's home. Today, the house is privately owned. However, walking through the colorful, meandering streets of Greenwich Village—MacDougal, Bleecker, St. Luke's, Grove, Gay and Christopher Streets—gives the feel of Village life as it might have been for authors and artists during the legendary Bohemian days of the 1920s. PHOTO BY AUTHOR

Another distinguished Greenwich Village poet was Marianne Moore, shown in her famous tricorn hat. The elegant Miss Moore's life style was more conservative than Edna St. Vincent Millay's, but her poetry was much more original and radical in style and technique. Miss Moore's study-living room in her Greenwich Village apartment has been transferred intact to the Rosenbach Foundation in Philadelphia. COURTESY OF THE PHILIP H. AND A. S. W. ROSENBACH FOUNDATION, PHILADELPHIA

The best-known poets to come out of the Harlem Renaissance were Countee Cullen (1903–1946), (above left) and Langston Hughes (1902–   ) (above right). Cullen's books of poetry, such as *Color,* in 1925, were written in traditional lyrical style and in most cases were non-racial in tone.

Langston Hughes published his first poem "The Negro Speaks of Rivers" when he was nineteen. Unlike Cullen, Hughes in his writing tried "to explain and illuminate the Negro condition in America." Hughes experimented with all forms of poetry and also wrote songs, novels, plays, history and biography. His most popular series of short stories called the "Simple" stories exposed with shrewd humor the weakness of racist arguments.

Other well-known authors of this period who wrote especially on the black people's situation are Jean Toomer, Arna Bontemps, Helen Johnson and Gwendolyn Brooks. COURTESY NATIONAL PORTRAIT GALLERY, SMITHSONIAN INSTITUTION

James Weldon Johnson (1871–1938) was not only a writer of poems, short stories and novels, but also a lawyer, civil rights leader and a diplomat. He was also a successful song writer. His popular "Lift Every Voice and Sing," for which his brother wrote the music, became the national anthem for black people. Two of Johnson's best-known works are his novel, *Autobiography of an Ex-colored Man* (1927), and his book of black folk poetry, *God's Trombones,* published the same year. COURTESY NATIONAL PORTRAIT GALLERY, SMITHSONIAN INSTITUTION

THOMAS WOLFE
1900-1938

Five minutes from the city square of Asheville, North Carolina, sprawls an old-fashioned, two-story white frame house. Once a boarding house catering to traveling salesmen, this home today is one of the most important literary sites in America. For this rambling, turn-of-the-century house with its wide veranda and bay windows was the home of author Thomas Wolfe, as well as the Dixieland boarding house forever immortalized in Wolfe's remarkable first novel, *Look Homeward, Angel.*

The years Thomas Wolfe lived at the boarding house, which was owned and run by his mother, in fact the whole "weather of his youth" spent in the city of Asheville was to shade and color all of Wolfe's writings.

Mrs. Wolfe, a frugal, energetic woman, bought the

house in 1906 and turned it into a boarding house, which she called the Old Kentucky Home. She brought with her to live at the boarding house her son Tom and his older brother Ben. Her stonecutter husband refused to move to the boarding house and remained at the previous residence on Woofin Street with the remaining Wolfe children.

Young Thomas Wolfe detested living in the boarding house, the shuttling of his brothers and sisters between the two houses, the never-ending quarreling between his parents. Yet he was to remember later everything about the Old Kentucky Home, "the way it felt, the way it smelled, even the strange smells in the old pantry." He would recall the constant stream of boarders who came and went, often taking over his bedroom, so there was never any one place in the house he could call his own. Most particularly, he remembered the death of his beloved brother Ben in one of the upstairs bedrooms, a memory that would scar Thomas Wolfe emotionally for life.

Wolfe left Asheville in 1916 to attend first the University of North Carolina and then Harvard. These college experiences, too, he used later in his novels. He hoped to become a dramatist, but his plays received no encouragement in New York. So instead he began to teach and started writing his first novel.

Wolfe's writing, like the man, himself, reflected his insatiable appetite to experience all aspects of life, a passionate, lyrical outpouring with little discipline or structure. The colossal manuscript that resulted from this torrent of words was turned down by twelve publishers before being accepted by Maxwell Perkins, an editor at a New York publishing house. Perkins worked patiently with Wolfe in cutting through the great mass of words; and in 1929, *Look Home-*

ward, Angel was published.

The novel was the story of a young man, Eugene Gant, and his boyhood in a southern town. Although the critical reaction to the book was mixed, there was no lack of criticism of the book from the citizens of Asheville. The novel, which was largely autobiographical, only thinly disguised real people, places and incidents in Asheville, and it infuriated the townspeople. Even members of Wolfe's own family appeared in the book in a not very flattering fashion. Thomas Wolfe was denounced as a traitor and immoral, and "for months the town seethed with a fury of resentment."

The author, himself, was surprised and dismayed at the hostile reception his book received in his hometown. Nevertheless, he continued to write a second book about Eugene Gant. This time he took Eugene through his college years at the University of North Carolina at Chapel Hill, called Pulpit Hill in the book. Once again working with the editorial assistance of Maxwell Perkins, *Of Time and the River* was published in 1935.

Wolfe's second book received excellent reviews, but the author was annoyed because some of the reviewers hinted that Wolfe could not write a book without editor Maxwell Perkins. Wolfe went to Europe to write and came back with thousands of manuscript pages, over a million words, which he turned over to a new editor and a new publisher. He had hoped to work himself at pruning the manuscript down to a manageable size, when tragically and suddenly, he died at the age of thirty-eight.

After his death, two posthumous novels were published from the mass of manuscript pages Wolfe left behind: *The Web and the Rock* (1939) and *You Can't Go Home Again* (1940). Although the main character in these two novels is named George Webber, the books are really a continuation of the story of Eugene Gant. In fact, to more easily understand parts of *Of Time and the River,* one should first read *The Web and the Rock.*

Wolfe's last two books reflect his growing maturity as a writer. His earlier books, however, with their exuberant, lyrical prose, the masterful dialogue, and the unforgettably drawn Gant family contain some of the best writing ever done by an American author. Wolfe's imagination was boundless and ranged through all experience. He wanted to absorb and recreate all America through his writing, but what comes through most clearly is his passionate attachment to the South, his bitter homesickness whenever he was far from the "hills of home." Whatever the qualities that make the novels of Thomas Wolfe so popular, they are discovered with delight by each new generation of young people.

By 1937 the resentment against Thomas Wolfe in Asheville had diminished. He was not only able to make a triumphant return to his hometown, but after his death, the Wolfe home was refurbished by the city of Asheville and the State of North Carolina. With the help of Thomas Wolfe's family, the house began to look much as it had during the days of the Old Kentucky Home boarding house.

One can wander through the drafty, high-ceilinged rooms and remember incidents and scenes from *Look Homeward, Angel:* the veranda where the boarders rocked interminably; the creaking swing where young Eugene and Laura sat, holding hands; the parlor with the piano where Helen sang for the boarders; the dining room where young Tom had to wait to eat until the boarders were finished. Perhaps the most poignant room is the plainly furnished front bedroom on the second floor where Ben Wolfe died, one of the most powerfully recreated scenes in *Look Home-ward, Angel.*

Location: THE THOMAS WOLFE MEMORIAL, 48 Spruce Street, Asheville, North Carolina. Small admission charge.

WILLIAM FAULKNER
1897–1962

In the hilly section of north Mississippi is a town and county that on the map are called Oxford and Lafayette County. However, to readers familiar with William Faulkner's novels, this area of Mississippi will always be Yoknapatawpha County, the legendary home of the Sartoris and the Snopes families.

It was at Oxford, Mississippi, that the author William Faulkner lived almost his whole life, the middle and last years in a gracious, white-columned mansion he named Rowan Oak. When Faulkner lived at Rowan Oak, the house was supposedly haunted by a young southern girl who had committed suicide there during the Civil War. If Rowan Oak is haunted today, however, it is by the genius of one of America's greatest authors. For it was in a small first-floor office of the house that William Faulkner created, with his typewriter, a complete, mythical southern world of his own as a setting for his novels and short stories. It was a world of Gothic horrors, mindless violence and grotesque humor, peopled by southern aristocrats, poor white sharecroppers, ex-slaves and Indians.

William Faulkner, like another southern author, Thomas Wolfe, was born in the South. But unlike Wolfe, Faulkner was descended from a once-wealthy, powerful southern family ruined by the Civil War and reduced to genteel poverty. Despite the fact that Oxford is the home of the University of Mississippi, Faulkner's formal education was brief. Most of his education was gained through reading widely and closely observing the life and people of Oxford.

Faulkner left Oxford several times as a young man to live briefly in New York and New Orleans. He also served for a short time in the Royal Canadian Air Force during World War I. However, unlike other authors of his generation disillusioned by the war, he did not go off to Europe to live. He returned to Oxford.

Another author, Sherwood Anderson, encouraged Faulkner to become a writer and write about "that little patch up there in Mississippi where you started from." After writing two unsuccessful novels, Faulkner in his third novel, *Sartoris,* did turn to writing about the town of Oxford and the Mississippi he knew so well. In his novel he renamed Oxford, Jefferson, and used the town as a setting for the proud but defeated Sartoris family, which closely resembled Faulkner's own.

Sartoris was the first of a series of books Faulkner wrote about the imaginary town of Jefferson and Yoknapatawpha County. The novels were a continuing story of the proud but decaying South as represented by the Sartoris family, as well as other once-wealthy families, and the grasping, opportunist "poor white" Snopes family that gradually takes control of the town and the land.

Although Faulkner's books were well-received critically, he needed more money than they brought him. He deliberately sat down to "invent the most horrific tale" he could imagine, hoping it would be a best-seller. But the book, *Sanctuary*, was rejected by publishers as being too violent. Discouraged, Faulkner took a job at night shoveling coal, and, using a wheelbarrow at his desk, wrote *As I Lay Dying* in 1930. He then rewrote *Sanctuary*, which was published a year later. Both novels with their primitive and evil characters, their stories of psychological violence and degeneration, brought Faulkner critical acclaim and financial success as well.

He was now able to devote all his time to writing as well as tending his farm at Rowan Oak, enjoying the outdoor life of a country squire, hunting, horseback riding and fishing. He used his knowledge of hunting in one of his best-known stories, *The Bear,* the symbolic story of a young man's coming of age on a bear hunt.

Within the next years he also continued the story of the various families in Jefferson with *Light in August* (1932), *O Absolom* (1936) and *The Unvanquished* (1938). The story of the Snopes family was continued in a more humorous vein in a separate series of novels. He also wrote several books of short stories with a Mississippi setting, one of the most popular being "A Rose for Emily." The story can be read for its symbolism of the old and new South, as well as its atmosphere of Gothic horror.

So real was the world that Faulkner created in his own mind, that he drew for one of the books a map of imaginary

Yoknapatawpha County, complete in every detail.

Although success came late in Faulkner's life, his writings received some twenty prizes and awards, including the Nobel and the Pulitzer Prize for literature. Despite his fame, he never strayed far from Oxford, and it was at his beloved home, Rowan Oak, that he died in July of 1962.

Of all the twentieth century novelists, William Faulkner was the most boldly experimental in style. His long flowing sentences require careful reading to be understood. Although Faulkner has been criticized for emphasizing violence, degeneration and horror in his books, he is a powerful storyteller. He brings to his stories the cruelties and indignities suffered by man, but he also stresses the dignity and nobility of man, the "human heart in conflict" with itself.

Rowan Oak, where William Faulkner spent most of his mature life, is the most famous home in Oxford and is visited by people from all over the world. Originally built in 1840, the house was bought by Faulkner in 1930. He added a room behind the library, which became his study. Spartanly furnished, the room has been left as it was when Faulkner died. There is Faulkner's old typewriter on a scratched wooden table, and such simple details as a bottle of horse liniment and an ashtray made from an artillery shell casing. On one wall of the room may be seen an outline for one of his last novels, *A Fable,* written in his close, vertical handwriting. Rowan Oak is maintained by the University of Mississippi as a memorial to Faulkner.

Rowan Oak is the sort of home the Sartoris family might have lived in, in quiet luxury, before the Civil War. Driving around Lafayette County, however, one can still occasionally see the broken-down ruins of plantation homes, as well as the shacks of black and white sharecroppers, typifying the

Snopes family. Oxford, itself, has been modernized since its courthouse and courthouse square figured so prominently in several of Faulkner's novels. But farmers still gather around the square on weekends, "sat and talked and drowsed" as Faulkner described the square in *Sartoris*.

In the nearby University of Mississippi Library there is a special Faulkner room, which contains Faulkner memorabilia, including several scrapbooks filled with clippings, photographs and letters of Faulkner. Special permission is needed from the library to visit this room.

Location: ROWAN OAK is adjacent to the University of Mississippi campus, Oxford, Mississippi. The house is accessible directly from the four lane bypass linking the university to Interstate 55, or from University Avenue, leading east to Oxford. Open only during the times that the university is in session. No admission charge.

MARJORIE KINNAN RAWLINGS
1896–1953

The Ocala National Forest of Central Florida is a region of
scrub, pine wood and mossy oaks, as well as hundreds of
clear lakes, streams and springs. This subtropical wilderness
was the setting for the popular novel, *The Yearling,* written
by Marjorie Kinnan Rawlings.

Mrs. Rawlings came to Florida as a young married
woman. She had graduated from the University of Wisconsin, worked as a journalist for several years and tried, without
much success, to become a published writer. In 1928 she
gave up journalism, decided to give full time to her writing,
and bought seventy acres of orange groves and a house at
Cross Creek, near Hawthorn, Florida. The first time she saw
the isolated, tumbledown farmhouse at the edge of a jungle
of "piney-woods," she felt instantly at home.

Shortly after purchasing the home, Mrs. Rawlings and

her husband separated, and she soon discovered that trying to build a productive orange grove by herself, while writing on the side, was no easy task. She was harassed by "poison ivy, mosquitoes, roaming livestock, drunken or crazy farm-hands and cooks, poisonous snakes and neighborhood feuds" to name only some of the hardships she faced during her first years at Cross Creek.

Nevertheless, the longer she lived at Cross Creek, the more she became fascinated by the people of the backwoods, the "Florida crackers," with their unique way of speaking and living. She explored the region on foot and by boat and became close friends with her neighbors who lived so closely with nature that they were almost a part of the soil. Her new friends told her stories of the old days and the fast vanishing way of life of the Florida backwoodsman and woman. It was these stories, and the Cross Creek setting, that Mrs. Rawlings began to use in her short stories and novels.

Mrs. Rawlings' first novel, *South Moon Under* (1933), had a Florida setting, and so did her second novel, *Golden Apples* (1935). They were well received, partly because of the unusual background. It was another book, *The Yearling,* published in 1938, however, that brought Mrs. Rawlings her first national recognition. *The Yearling,* combines the Cross Creek backwoods setting with a young boy character, Jody Baxter, who has become almost as well-known as Mark Twain's Huckleberry Finn. *The Yearling,* on the surface, is the story of young Jody's love for his pet fawn, Flag, but actually it is the universal story of a young boy's coming of age.

A popular success from the day it was published and still considered a minor classic, *The Yearling* received the Pulitzer Prize for fiction in 1939, as one of the great regional works of American literature.

Mrs. Rawlings used the Florida scrub country and its people in several more books, including a humorous and lively autobiographical account of her life at Cross Creek. In her last years the author divided her time between living and writing at St. Augustine and Cross Creek, but when she died in 1953, Marjorie Kinnan Rawlings was buried in the Cross Creek country she knew and loved so well.

The author's home at Cross Creek, near the Ocala National Forest, is today a state historical site. The acreage surrounding the house is a sanctuary for wildlife. A typical old cracker farmhouse when Mrs. Rawlings first bought it, the house, with its porches separating the kitchen and dining area from the bedroom, has had very little modernizing. On the front porch the large wooden table made from a palm log, where Mrs. Rawlings did much of her writing, may still be seen.

Many of the scenes from *The Yearling* took place in nearby Ocala National Forest, with its hidden springs and deep pine woods. It was at a spring deep in these pine woods that the young boy, Jody, made his "flutter mill" of palm fronds, and it was through these woods that he roamed with his pet fawn, Flag.

Location: MARJORIE KINNAN RAWLINGS STATE MUSEUM, Route 1, Box 295, Hawthorn, Florida. The home is located 21 miles through the woods south of Gainesville, Florida on SR 325. Small admission charge.

SOUTHERN WRITERS AFTER WORLD WAR I

AFTER WORLD WAR I, SOME OF THE FINEST WRITERS IN AMER-
ICA CAME FROM THE SOUTHERN STATES. IN ADDITION TO
THOMAS WOLFE FROM NORTH CAROLINA AND WILLIAM FAULK-
NER FROM MISSISSIPPI, THERE WAS ELLEN GLASGOW (1874–
1945) FROM VIRGINIA, KATHERINE ANNE PORTER (1890–   )
FROM TEXAS, MARJORIE KINNAN RAWLINGS FROM FLORIDA,
AND MANY MORE. . . .

Thomas Wolfe lived only thirty-eight years, but in his short life he became one of America's major novelists—and Asheville, North Carolina's most famous son. Wolfe's desire to experience all of life was reflected in his massive, sprawling novels. COURTESY DEPARTMENT OF CULTURAL RESOURCES, RALEIGH, NORTH CAROLINA

The Old Kentucky Home boarding house, run by Thomas Wolfe's mother, became the setting for Wolfe's first and most memorable novel, *Look Homeward, Angel*. The rambling Victorian home, completely furnished as it was when Thomas Wolfe lived there, may be visited in Asheville, North Carolina. PHOTO BY AUTHOR

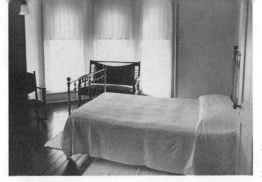

This bedroom in the Old Kentucky Home boarding house is where Thomas Wolfe's beloved brother Ben died and was the setting for one of the most powerfully written scenes in *Look Homeward, Angel*. PHOTO BY AUTHOR

The dining room of the Old Kentucky Home boarding house was also used as a setting in Wolfe's novel. Many of the boarders who gathered here to eat were used as characters in *Look Homeward, Angel*. The Wolfe family ate in a small pantry by the kitchen. COURTESY DEPT OF CULTURAL RESOURCES, RALEIGH, NORTH CAROLINA

Rowan Oak (shown below) was author William Faulkner's home in Oxford, Mississippi. Of all the novelists who wrote after World War I, Faulkner was the most boldly experimental. Although in his books Faulkner explored the violence and moral perversion of his imaginary world of Yoknapatawpha County, in his own hometown of Oxford, Faulkner lived the quiet life of a country squire. Today, the Faulkner home is maintained exactly as Faulkner left it by the University of Mississippi and is open to the public. COURTESY UNIVERSITY OF MISSISSIPPI

Faulkner wrote his novels and created a whole imaginary southern world in the office-study shown here, using an old Underwood portable typewriter on a small table. On the wall of his study (below right) he wrote the outline of one of his last novels, *A Fable,* which is divided by days of the week. PHOTO BY AUTHOR

WEDNESDAY   THURSDAY

One of the spring-fed creeks in the Ocala National Forest, Florida, that young Jody Baxter in *The Yearling* might have visited with his pet fawn, Flag. Marjorie Kinnan Rawlings used the Big Scrub and pine-wood country of Central Florida as the setting for her prize-winning novel. Mrs. Rawlings' home at Cross Creek, near Hawthorn, Florida, is open to the public. COURTESY OCALA NATIONAL FOREST

PEARL BUCK
1892–1973

An ancient Chinese desk sits in the place of honor in an
early American farmhouse in Bucks County, Pennsylvania.
It was at this desk, while she was living in Nanking, China,
that the author Pearl Buck wrote her Pulitzer-Prize-winning novel, *The Good Earth*.

Although Pearl Buck is best known for her novels of
Chinese life, the author was actually born in a small town in
West Virginia. Four months after her birth, her parents returned to their missionary work in Chinkiang, China. The
young Pearl learned to speak Chinese before she spoke
English. As she, herself, said, she grew up "mentally bifocal,"
feeling herself as much Chinese as American. She was sent
back to the United States for her college years, but after college she returned to China, where she taught school and

married an agricultural missionary.

Interested in writing even as a young girl, Pearl Buck began writing in earnest after her marriage. The manuscript for her first novel was lost when Communist revolutionary soldiers invaded Nanking and her home was looted. Undaunted she wrote a second novel, *East Wind, West Wind,* which was published in 1930. However, it was her third novel, *The Good Earth,* published the next year, that brought Mrs. Buck the Pulitzer Prize in 1931. This novel, which told of the Wangs, a peasant family in northern China, remained on the best-seller list for two years, was made into a movie, and was translated into more than thirty languages.

In 1934, with the break-up of her first marriage, Mrs. Buck returned to the United States. She and her second husband purchased an old home in Pennsylvania, which Mrs. Buck said reminded her of the homes she had known in China because of its enormous beams and thick walls and aged garden.

Mrs. Buck brought with her from China the desk at which she had written her early novels, along with its straight-backed chair "for discipline." At her Green Hills Farm home, however, she wrote at a more modern desk in a study built onto the farmhouse. Although in the years that followed, she wrote novels and stories with an American background, her most popular books were those with an Oriental setting, such as *Dragon Seed* (1942) and *Pavilion of Women* (1946).

In 1938 Mrs. Buck won the Nobel Prize for literature, the only American woman to do so. The prize was awarded for the moving biography of Mrs. Buck's missionary mother, *The Exile,* as well as for her novels, which, the Nobel Committee wrote, "were outstanding for their rich and genuine epic portrayals of Chinese peasant life."

Mrs. Buck once said that she was not "truly happy unless I am writing" and claimed that she wrote in the Chinese tradition, with the primary purpose to entertain the reader. But her novels are more than entertainments. All her life Mrs. Buck was interested in improving the understanding between the Chinese and Western peoples. Her books are bridges that reach from the East to the West, presenting an alien culture in an interesting and understandable fashion.

Mrs. Buck's birthplace, the Stulting home in West Virginia, is a large, white-columned house built by Mrs. Buck's grandfather in 1847. She lived briefly at the family home when she was nine and at times during her college years. She later remembered herself as a young girl eating grapes from the arbor that reached the second floor veranda of the house. Some of the original furniture and assorted memorabilia that relate to Pearl Buck may be seen in the house, which has been decorated in the style of the year of Mrs. Buck's birth, 1892. Eventually a cultural center will be built next to the farm to house Mrs. Buck's manuscripts.

The Green Hills Farm in Bucks County, Pennsylvania, where Mrs. Buck lived and wrote for so many years, is decorated in a wonderful combination of Oriental and Early American furnishings. After World War II, Pearl Buck founded at her home a successful center for the care and adoption of American-born children of Asian ancestry, called Welcome House. She and her husband had already adopted nine children of their own, and the children often played in the big barn near the house.

Location: PEARL S. BUCK BIRTHPLACE is located north of Hillsboro, West Virginia on U.S. Rt. 219. Hillsboro is about 35 miles north of Lewisburg, West Virginia. Admission charge.

Location: GREEN HILLS FARM, 520 Dublin Road, Perkasie, Pennsylvania. Take Rt 313 west from Doylestown. Farm is 1 mile from Dublin, Pennsylvania. Reservations for tours needed. Admission charge.

ERNEST HEMINGWAY
1899-1961

The port of Key West, Florida in the prohibition days of the 1920s was a haven for those who brought illegal liquor into the United States from Cuba. Ernest Hemingway, who lived in Key West in the 1930s, used the town and the prohibition era as a setting for his novel, *To Have and Have Not*. Published in 1937, the book was not one of Hemingway's most successful novels, but it did have many of the Hemingway trademarks—death, violence and a disillusioned hero.

In some ways, Ernest Hemingway resembled the hard-living, disillusioned heroes in his novels. As a young boy he spent his summers in the woods of northern Michigan near Horton Bay, where his father, an ardent sportsman, introduced his son to the world of hunting and fishing. It was a world that was to make a deep impression on Hemingway's life and writing.

After graduating from high school, Hemingway worked briefly as a newspaper reporter. Then, when America entered World War I, he volunteered as an ambulance driver in Italy and soon transferred to the Italian Infantry. Just before his nineteenth birthday, he was wounded and invalided home. He resumed his journalist career, married, and determined to become an author.

The years after World War I, however, were a time of disenchantment for many young Americans like Hemingway. They saw World War I as a needless slaughter. Many veterans were left with physical and mental scars that would haunt them the rest of their lives.

Discontented with his life in the United States, Ernest Hemingway and his wife moved to Paris, as did many other young expatriate writers of his generation. It was in Paris that Hemingway met Gertrude Stein, whose home on the Left Bank was a gathering place for young artists and writers of the so-called "lost generation." It has been said that Gertrude Stein single-handedly moved American literature from the nineteenth to the twentieth century. Whether this is true or not, she certainly had a profound influence on young American authors like F. Scott Fitzgerald, Sherwood Anderson—and Ernest Hemingway.

Hemingway's first book, *In Our Time,* was written during his early years in Paris and was published in New York in 1925. A collection of sketches and stories about a young man, named Nick Adams, the stories were based on Hemingway's idyllic summer vacations in Michigan and his grim war experiences. Even in this early work Hemingway's lasting fascination with brutality and death can be seen. The book also used Hemingway's unique sparse, clipped style.

In Our Time was moderately successful, but it was his

first real novel, *The Sun Also Rises,* published in 1926, that turned him into an overnight celebrity. This novel—about pleasure-seeking, war-disillusioned young men and women living in Paris—was again based on episodes in Hemingway's own life. Two years later, Hemingway wrote *A Farewell to Arms,* a tragic story of romance and death against a background of World War I. These two novels placed Hemingway in the forefront of American writers where he was to remain the rest of his life.

Continuing his fascination with "the hunter, the hunted and death," Hemingway went on the first of many big game hunting trips in Africa. He also began to study the violent but controlled world of the Spanish bullfighting ring. These interests showed up in his books, *The Green Hills of Africa* (1935) and *Death in the Afternoon* (1939).

In 1930 Hemingway, with his second wife, purchased a Spanish Colonial home in Key West, Florida, where he could indulge in his love of deep sea fishing whenever his writing was not going well. Although Hemingway wrote several novels at Key West, including *To Have and Have Not,* it was when he returned to the setting of a world at war that he felt most at home. What some critics consider his finest novel, *For Whom the Bell Tolls* (1940), is set during the Spanish Civil War and tells the story of a love found and lost against a background of violent death.

World War II kept Hemingway busy as a war correspondent. After the war he wandered restlessly around the world, finally settling in a home in Cuba. Hemingway, like earlier authors Mark Twain and Jack London, had become a personality, as well as an author. He was as well known for the convivial, hard-fighting, machismo image of "Papa Hemingway" he projected as for his books.

Hemingway's writings after the war were not as well-received by the critics as his earlier works had been. There were even those who said Hemingway was finished as a writer. Then in 1952 he wrote *The Old Man and the Sea.* This short, masterful novel of an old Cuban fisherman trying to bring to shore a giant marlin and being defeated by sharks, may be read simply as an adventure story. On another level, though, the novel skillfully reflects one of Hemingway's favorite themes, the unconquerable spirit of man.

During his last years, Hemingway lived in Ketchum, Idaho. He had been awarded the Pulitzer Prize for literature, as well as the Nobel Prize for literature. But after *The Old Man and the Sea,* Hemingway, who had once said, "you could only write what you truly felt" was never again able to recapture the depth of feeling and simplicity of his earlier books. Physical illness caused a depression, and on the morning of July 21, 1961, Hemingway courted death for the last time, dying from a self-inflicted gunshot wound.

In addition to his novels, Hemingway was also a distinguished short-story writer. Three of his best short stories —"The Short, Happy Life of Frances Macomber," "The Killers" and "The Undefeated"—all contain the typical Hemingway overly masculine hero, (Hemingway's women were never as realistically drawn), as well as Hemingway's preoccupation with death and violence. But it is Hemingway's famous understated style of writing, the by-now familiar clipped dialogue and terse descriptions, the sentences "stripped clean for action" that revolutionized American literature. Since Hemingway, a whole generation of young writers has tried and failed to imitate the master.

Ernest Hemingway's home in Key West is today a National Historic Landmark. The house contains furnishings and mementos from Spain, Africa, France and Cuba, as well as other parts of the world. It was at this home that Hemingway wrote some of his most important novels and short stories. He would rise early, walk via a catwalk to his study in the loft of his poolhouse, and spend the morning working, usually standing at his desk. A unique reminder of the late author may still be seen around the house: descendants of the nearly fifty cats who lived at the house with Hemingway. Tours of the Hemingway home are conducted by friends of the author who still live in Key West.

Location: ERNEST HEMINGWAY HOME AND MUSEUM, 907 Whitehead Street, Key West, Florida. Small admission charge.

JOHN STEINBECK
1902-1968

Several authors are so closely associated through their writings with certain geographical areas of the United States that it is difficult to separate them from their settings. One such author is John Steinbeck. To the many readers of Steinbeck's books, the Salinas Valley of California and the writer are practically synonymous.

As a boy growing up in the town of Salinas, young John Steinbeck roamed the marshes of the Salinas River and the chaparral-covered hillsides of the valley, "learning to love the countryside from the ground up." As a young man, although he read a great deal and attended Stanford University briefly, his real education was gained from the people of the Salinas Valley.

He grew to know and understand the migrant farmworkers when he worked as a fruit picker in the valley orchards, the cowboys when he hired out as a ranch hand, the California–Mexicans when he worked beside them in a cannery in Monterey. And from all these various men and women, Steinbeck gained background material that he used later in his novels and short stories.

Steinbeck took the temporary odd jobs as fruit picker, ranch hand and cannery worker so that he would have time to follow his one ambition in life: to become a writer. Nothing else interested him. In 1925 he went to New York to pursue, without success, a writing career, and finally returned to the Salinas Valley to live and write.

In 1929 his first novel, *Cup of Gold,* was published, but it attracted little attention. His next two novels did little better. His fourth novel, *Tortilla Flat,* published in 1935, was set in Monterey and the Monterey peninsula. The novel is a good-natured tragic-comic takeoff of King Arthur's Knights of the Round Table. Only in Steinbeck's books, the knights are easy-going, fun-loving Mexicans, the "dropouts" from society of their generation.

Tortilla Flat, although not very popular with the Monterey Chamber of Commerce, was a success with the reading public. Steinbeck returned to the Monterey area as settings for two later novels, *Cannery Row* (1945) and *Sweet Thursday* (1954).

It was the publication in 1937 of the poignant short novel, *Of Mice and Men,* however, that assured Steinbeck's financial and literary future. Set on a ranch near Soledad, California, and written almost entirely in dialogue, the book was so successful that it was dramatized on both the stage and in movies. With the success of *Of Mice and Men,* Steinbeck no longer had to take odd jobs to support his writing.

In the same year that *Of Mice and Men* was published,

Steinbeck wrote another short novel, *The Red Pony,* which also in its own way became a minor classic. This sensitive story of Jody, a young ranch boy, is set in the foothills of the Santa Lucias. Steinbeck said he wanted to "recreate a child's world . . . of colors more clear than they are to an adult . . . I want to put down the way 'afternoon felt.' "

Then in 1939 Steinbeck wrote his most controversial novel, *The Grapes of Wrath.* Steinbeck had always been interested in the problems of social justice, the exploitation of the weak by the strong. His earlier "protest" novel, *In Dubious Battle* (1936), had explored the losing battle of striking migrant fruit pickers against large landowners. In *The Grapes of Wrath,* Steinbeck tells the story of the Joad family, dispossessed by the drought and the depression of the 1930s from their Oklahoma farm. Like many other dispossessed "Okies," the Joad family went West in a patched-up jalopy, hoping to find a new and better life in California. Instead they found only hatred and exploitation, finally joining the fruit pickers of San Joaquin Valley in a violent, disastrous strike against the giant farm-canning-railroad interests.

The Grapes of Wrath stirred up as much controversy in the United States as Harriet Beecher Stowe's protest novel against slavery, *Uncle Tom's Cabin.* And in its own way, *The Grapes of Wrath* was just as influential in bringing about needed social change. Although the book was banned from some libraries and schools and denounced as "obscene sensationalism" and propaganda, nevertheless it became a best-seller. As one critic said, the book was "burned and banned, borrowed, smuggled, but above all, bought." In 1940 *The Grapes of Wrath* brought John Steinbeck the Pulitzer Prize for literature.

World War II brought an end to the Great Depression. During the war, Steinbeck acted as a war correspondent; but after the war, he returned to writing novels. Two of his best known from this period are *The Pearl,* in 1947, and *East of Eden,* in 1952. The latter book, which Steinbeck originally titled "Salinas Valley," is based in part upon the history of Steinbeck's own family.

In addition to novels, John Steinbeck wrote collections of short stories; among them, *The Long Valley* (1938), also set in the Salinas Valley. Steinbeck delighted in experimenting with all sorts of writing. He wrote dramas, non-fiction and had a lifelong interest in marine biology. In 1962 he received the Nobel Prize for literature for his "unbiased instinct for what is genuinely American be it good or bad."

A superb storyteller, Steinbeck's characters are usually simple, primitive types, but he has a sure flair for vivid and realistic descriptions, "the sound, scents, and tastes of things."

Always a private person, Steinbeck never sought publicity. In his last years, he settled quietly in New York. At his death, his ashes were returned to the Salinas Valley.

Although Steinbeck's early books were not always appreciated in the Salinas Valley, today, the gabled, Victorian-style house in Salinas where he was born is open to the public as a restaurant, with Steinbeck memorabilia on display. A carefully detailed map and brochure showing the locales of the author's novels and important short stories may be secured from the Salinas Chamber of Commerce, Salinas, California.

The Cannery Row area of Monterey became one of the most celebrated streets in the world after Steinbeck's novel, *Cannery Row,* was published. Today the canneries are closed and many of the landmarks of the book have disappeared or are so changed they are no longer recognizable. But the street is still there, along with a statue of the author at one end.

The Salinas Public Library was renamed in honor of the author and also has a life-size statue of John Steinbeck on the grounds. In the library there is a rich collection of Steinbeck mementos, which soon they hope to have on display. They also have extensive recordings on tape of Steinbeck and local residents speaking about Steinbeck and his writings, especially in relation to the history of Salinas County.

Location: THE STEINBECK HOME, 132 Central Avenue, Salinas, California. (Now a restaurant, with tours available upon request.)

Location: JOHN STEINBECK LIBRARY, 110 West San Luis Street, Salinas, California.

Location: CANNERY ROW. Bronze bust of John Steinbeck at Cannery Row and Prescott Streets, Monterey, California.

Location: THE SALINAS VALLEY, "Steinbeck Country" is eighty-five miles long and roughly parallels the California coast. The Valley lies almost thirty miles in from the coast, running from Salinas to King City, between the Gabilan and the Santa Lucia Mountains. Highway 101 bisects the valley.

LATE 1920s, 1930s AND 1940's

IN THE LATE 1920S AND EARLY 1930S, THERE WAS AN ARTIFI-
CIAL ECONOMIC BOOM IN AMERICA, FOLLOWED BY THE STOCK
MARKET CRASH AND THE GREAT DEPRESSION. WRITERS, INFLU-
ENCED BY THE DOWNBEAT MOOD OF THE COUNTRY, ONCE AGAIN
BEGAN TO TURN A CRITICAL EYE UPON AMERICAN SOCIETY.

Ernest Hemingway shown with the eight-hundred-pound swordfish
he caught in connection with the filming of his prize-winning
novel, *The Old Man and the Sea*. Hemingway was a member of the
so-called "lost generation" in Paris after World War I. In his
early novels, Hemingway caught the cynical world of war-disillusioned young men and women. COURTESY BETTMANN ARCHIVES

Ernest Hemingway had many homes in his lifetime. The one above at Key West, Florida, is where he wrote *To Have and Have Not*. The Key West home is now a museum containing mementos from Hemingway's life and travels. COURTESY ERNEST HEMINGWAY HOME AND MUSEUM

Black authors, too, cast a jaundiced eye at America between World War I and World War II. Richard Wright (1908–1960) in his *Uncle Tom's Children* (1938) and his autobiography, *Black Boy* (1945), explored the cruelties and indignities suffered by black men and women in a white world. Wright's books placed him in the front rank of writers during this period. PHOTO BY HART PRESTON

One of the best novels about the depression years was written by California author, John Steinbeck. His *Grapes of Wrath,* which tells of the migration west of the dispossessed "Okies," not only aroused the conscience of America to the plight of the farmers, but established Steinbeck as one of America's most important authors. PORTRAIT BY JOHN ROBY, SALINAS CHAMBER OF COMMERCE

The Salinas Valley in Central California is known as "Steinbeck Country." The green-gold fields and softly rolling foothills of the valley served as the setting for many of Steinbeck's novels and stories, including *The Long Valley* and *The Red Pony.* His home in Salinas is now a restaurant and museum. COURTESY SALINAS CHAMBER OF COMMERCE

Poetry, too, was influenced by the disillusionment of post-World-War-I America. The stone tower (Hawk Tower) was built with his own hands by poet Robinson Jeffers (1887–1962) near the rocky coast of Carmel, California. Revolted by the inhumanity of mankind, Jeffers retreated from the world to this tower and wrote his powerful narrative poems. Many of his poems, such as *Roan Stallion* (1925) and *The Women at Point Sur* (1927), used the Big Sur country of California as a setting. Jeffers' poetry was often experimental in form. Tor House, the stone home next to Hawk Tower where Jeffers lived, is located at 26304 Ocean View Avenue, Carmel, California. Open to visitors by appointment only. PHOTO BY C. J. PETER BENNETT

GEOGRAPHICAL INDEX

GEOGRAPHICAL INDEX

GEOGRAPHICAL INDEX

Sarah Orne Jewett Home, South
  Berwick
Tory House, South Berwick
Whitehall Inn, Millay Room,
  Camden

MARYLAND

Edgar Allan Poe House and
  Museum, Baltimore

MASSACHUSETTS

Alcott School of Philosophy,
  Concord
Arrowhead, Herman Melville
  Home, Pittsfield
Antiquarian Museum, Concord
Courthouse Hill, Lenox
Edward Bellamy Home,
  Chicopee
Emily Dickinson Home, Amherst
First Church of Christ,
  Congregational,
  Northampton
Fruitlands, Harvard
Henry Wadsworth Longfellow
  Home, Cambridge
Herman Melville Memorial
  Room, Berkshire
  Athenaeum, Pittsfield
House of Seven Gables, Salem
John Alden Home, Duxbury
James Greenleaf Whittier Home,
  Amesbury
James Greenleaf Whittier Home,
  Haverhill
Museum of Afro-American
  History, Boston
Nathaniel Hawthorne's
  Birthplace, Salem

Nathaniel Hawthorne Home,
  Berkshire Music Center,
  Tanglewood, Lenox
New England Authors Exhibit,
  Boston
North Bridge, Concord
Old Custom House, Salem
Old Manse, Concord
Orchard House, Concord
Pilgrim Hall Museum, Plymouth
Plymouth Plantation, Plymouth
Robert Frost Room, Amherst
  Library, Amherst College,
  Amherst
Seamen's Bethel, New Bedford
Sleepy Hollow Cemetery,
  Concord
Thoreau Lyceum, Concord
Walden Pond, Concord
Wayside House, Concord
Wayside Inn, South Sudbury
Whaling Museum, Nantucket
Whaling Museum, New Bedford
William Cullen Bryant Home,
  Cummington
Witch Museum, Salem

MICHIGAN

Noah Webster Home, Greenfield
  Village, Dearborn

MINNESOTA

Minnehaha Park, Minneapolis
Sinclair Lewis Home, Sauk
  Centre
Sinclair Lewis Interpretive
  Center, Sauk Centre
Walnut Grove (Laura Ingalls
  Wilder plaque)

GEOGRAPHICAL INDEX

GEOGRAPHICAL INDEX

AUTHOR-TITLE INDEX

SUBJECT INDEX